The Stuff of Legend

Book 1: The Dark

Story by
Mike Raicht & Brian Smith

Illustrated by
Charles Paul Wilson III

Design & Color by
Jon Conkling & Michael DeVito

VILLARD TRADE PAPERBACKS • NEW YORK

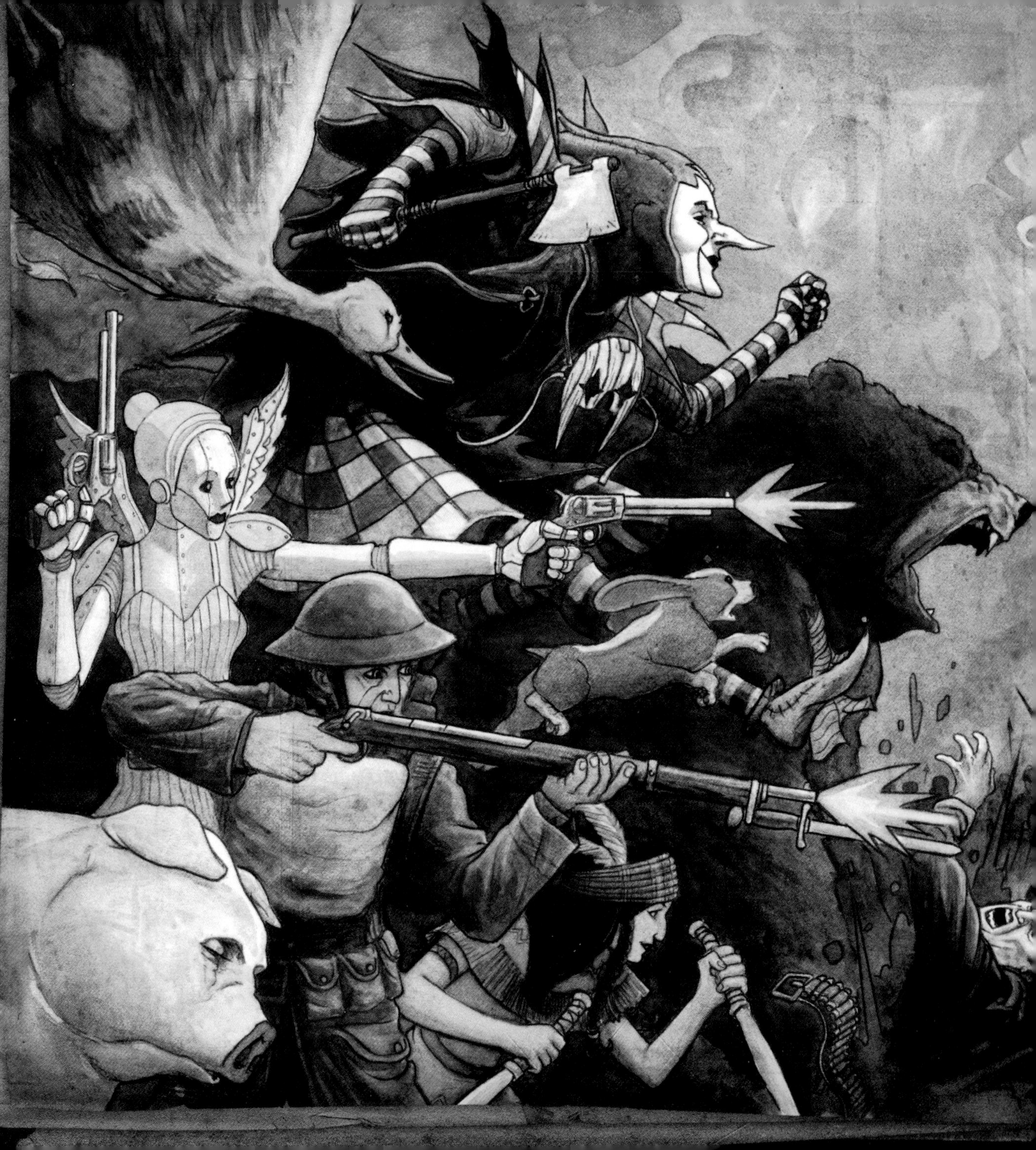

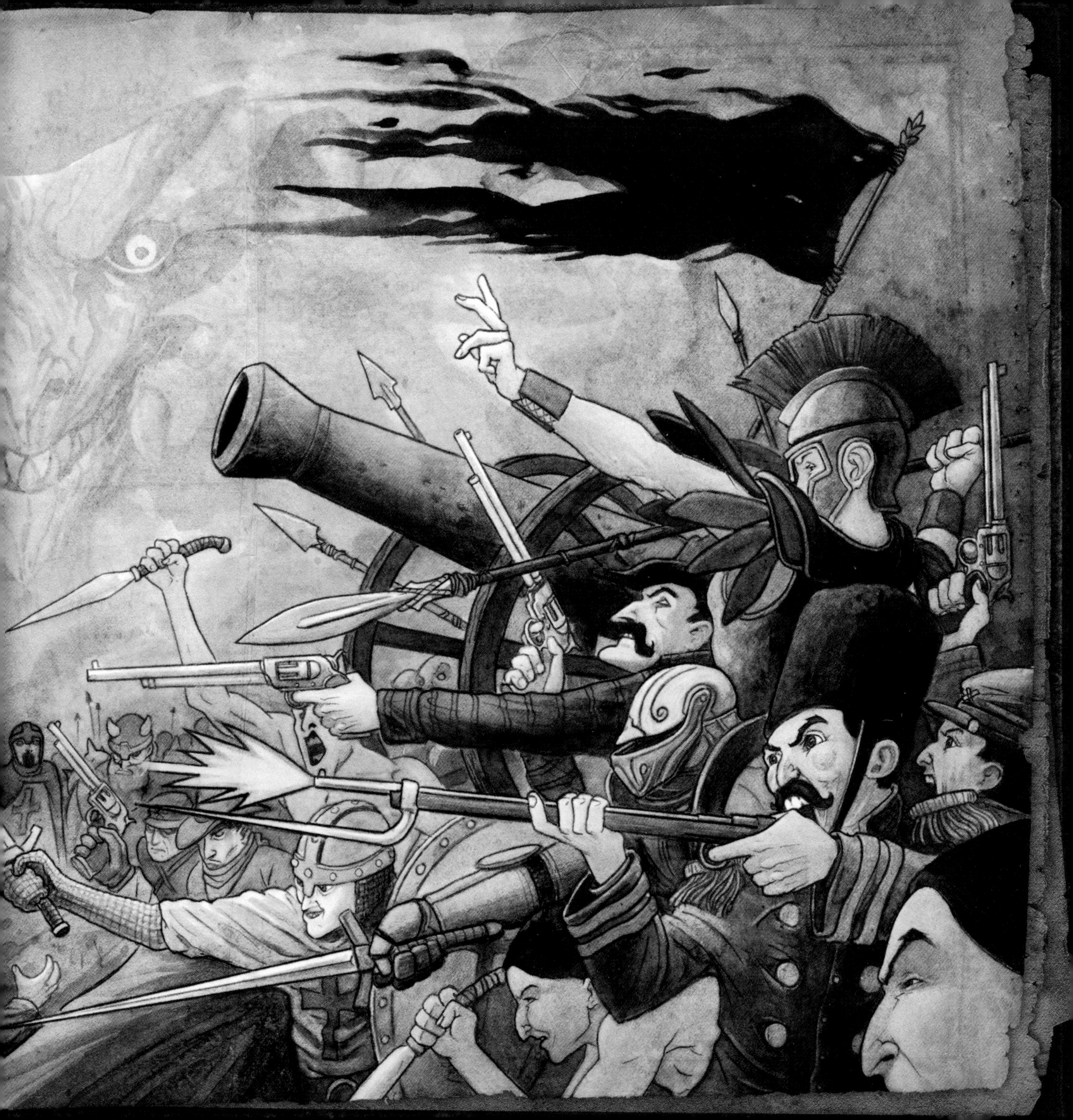

2010 Villard Books Trade Paperback Edition

Published in the United States of America by Villard Books, an imprint of The Random House Publishing Group, a division of Random House, Inc., New York.

Villard and the "V" Circled Design are registered trademarks of Random House, Inc.

The chapters in this book first appeared in the comic book *The Stuff of Legend,* © and TM 2009 by Mike Raicht, Brian Smith, and Th3rd World Studios and published by Th3rd World Studios.

ISBN 978-0-345-52100-2

Printed in China on acid-free paper

9 8 7 6 5 4 3 2 1

PUBLISHERS
Michael DeVito
Jon Conkling

WWW.TH3RDWORLD.COM

The Stuff of Legend ™

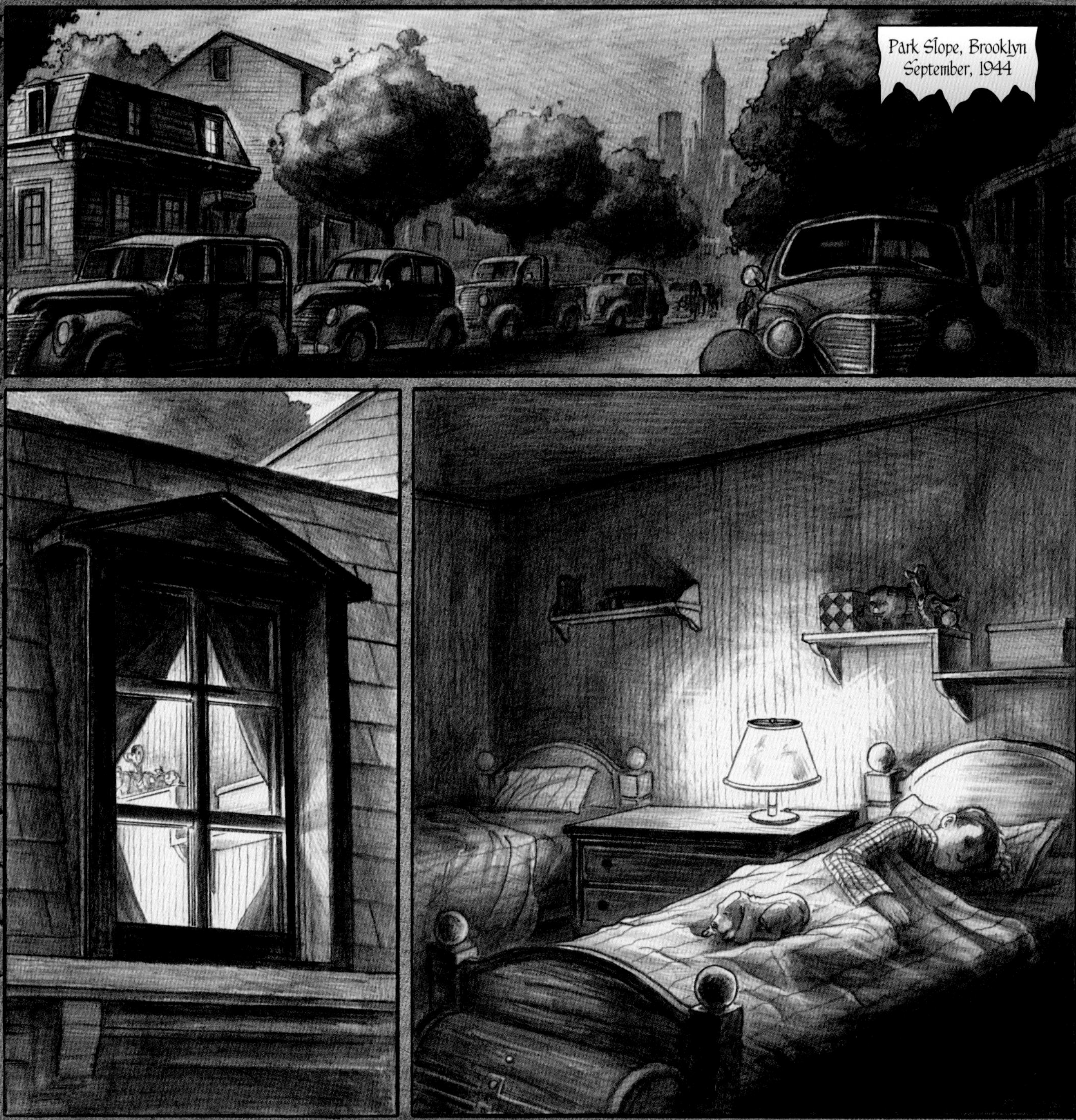
Park Slope, Brooklyn
September, 1944

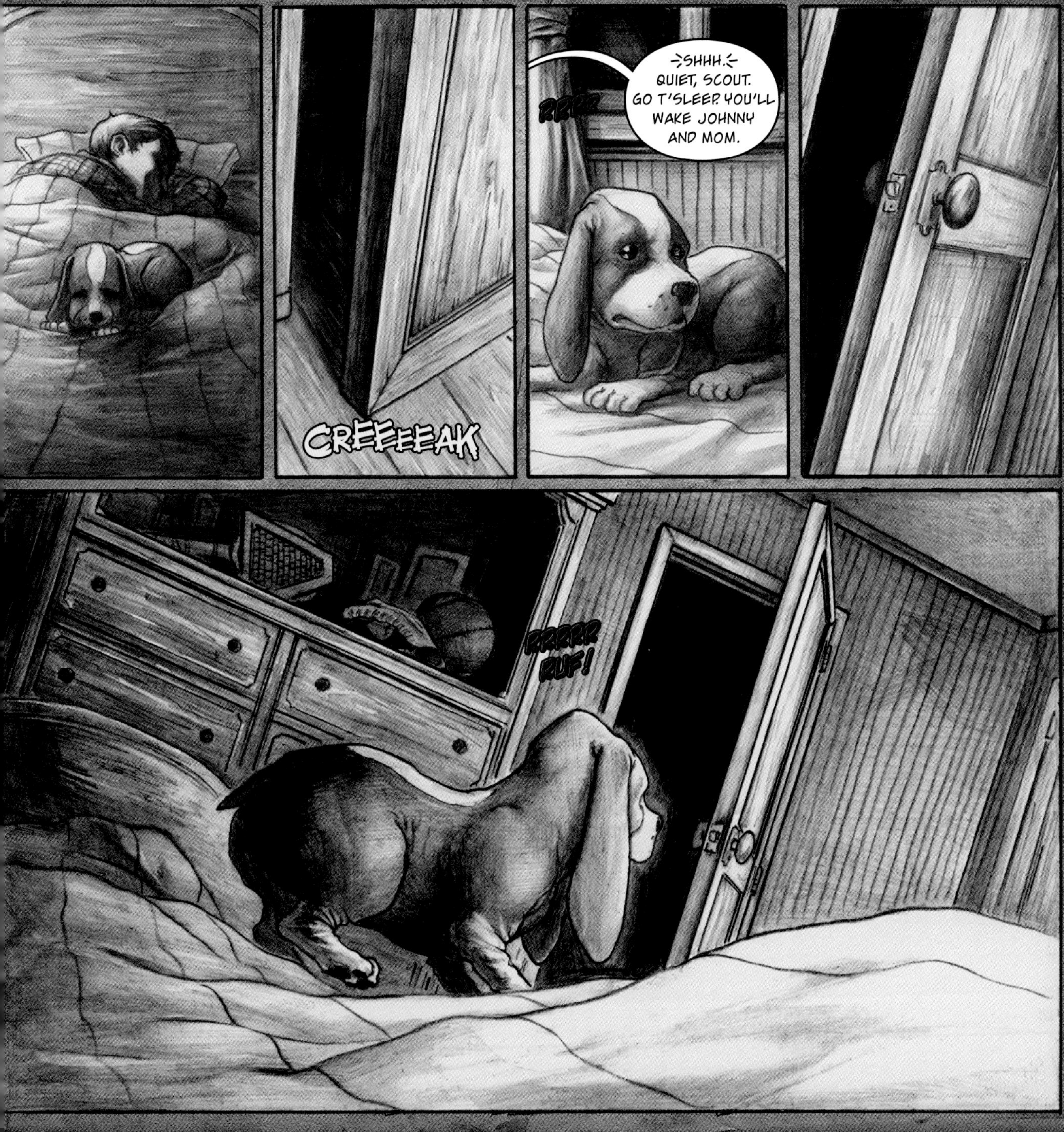

CREEEEEAK
RRRR
SHHH.
QUIET, SCOUT. GO T'SLEEP. YOU'LL WAKE JOHNNY AND MOM.
RRRRR RUF!

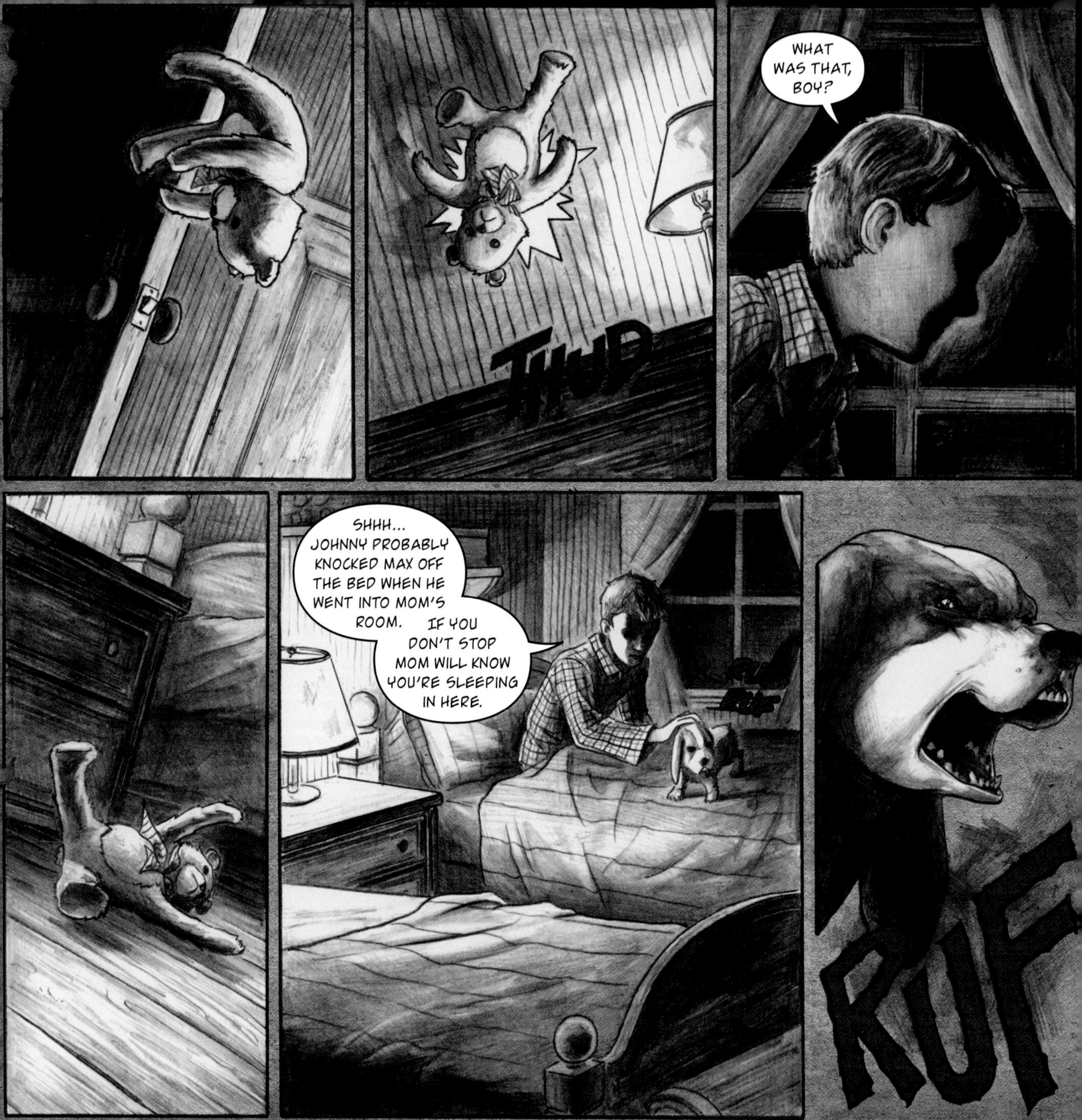
THUD
WHAT WAS THAT, BOY?
SHHH... JOHNNY PROBABLY KNOCKED MAX OFF THE BED WHEN HE WENT INTO MOM'S ROOM.
IF YOU DON'T STOP MOM WILL KNOW YOU'RE SLEEPING IN HERE.
RUF

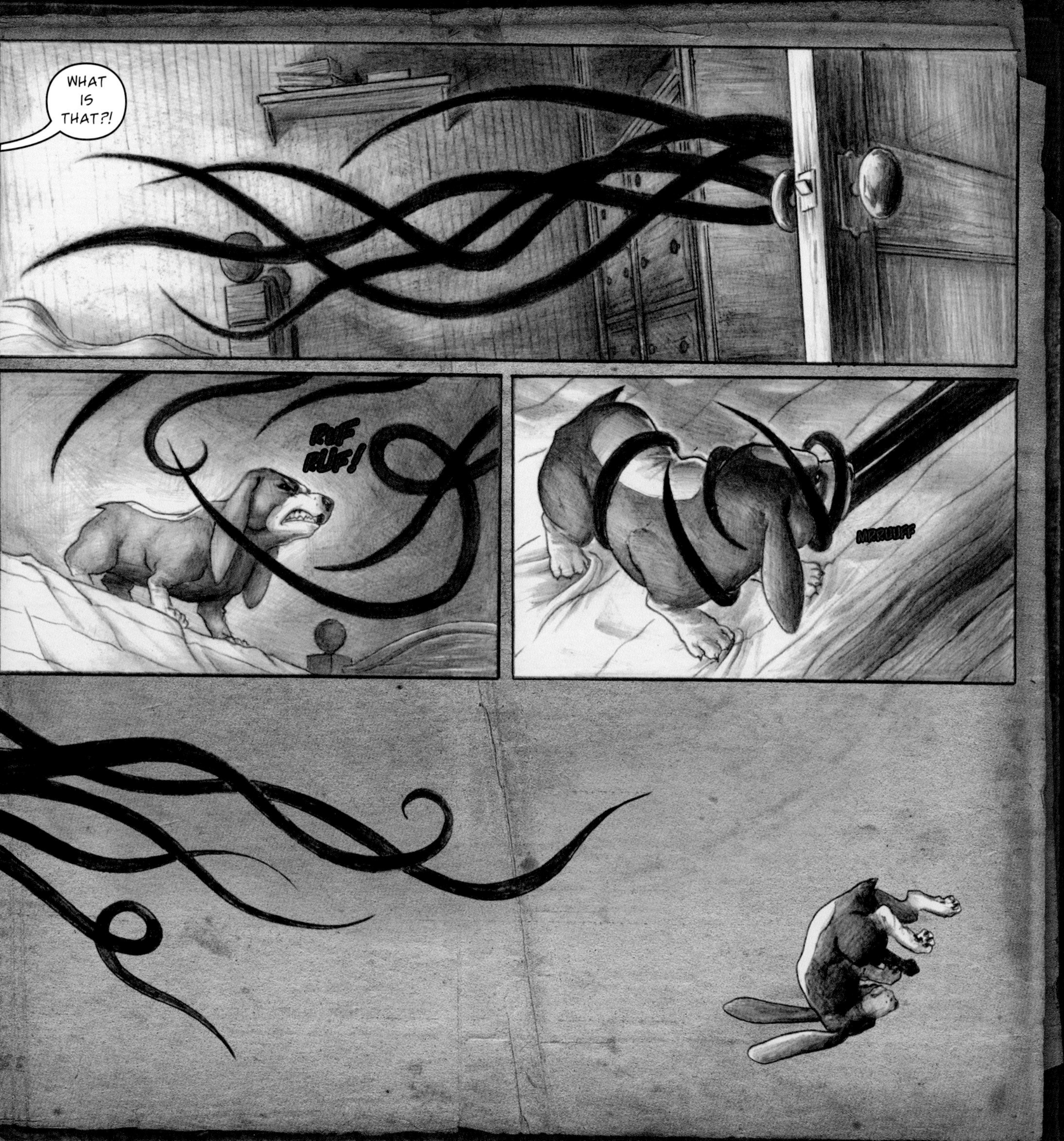
WHAT IS THAT?!
RUF RUF!
MRRUUFF

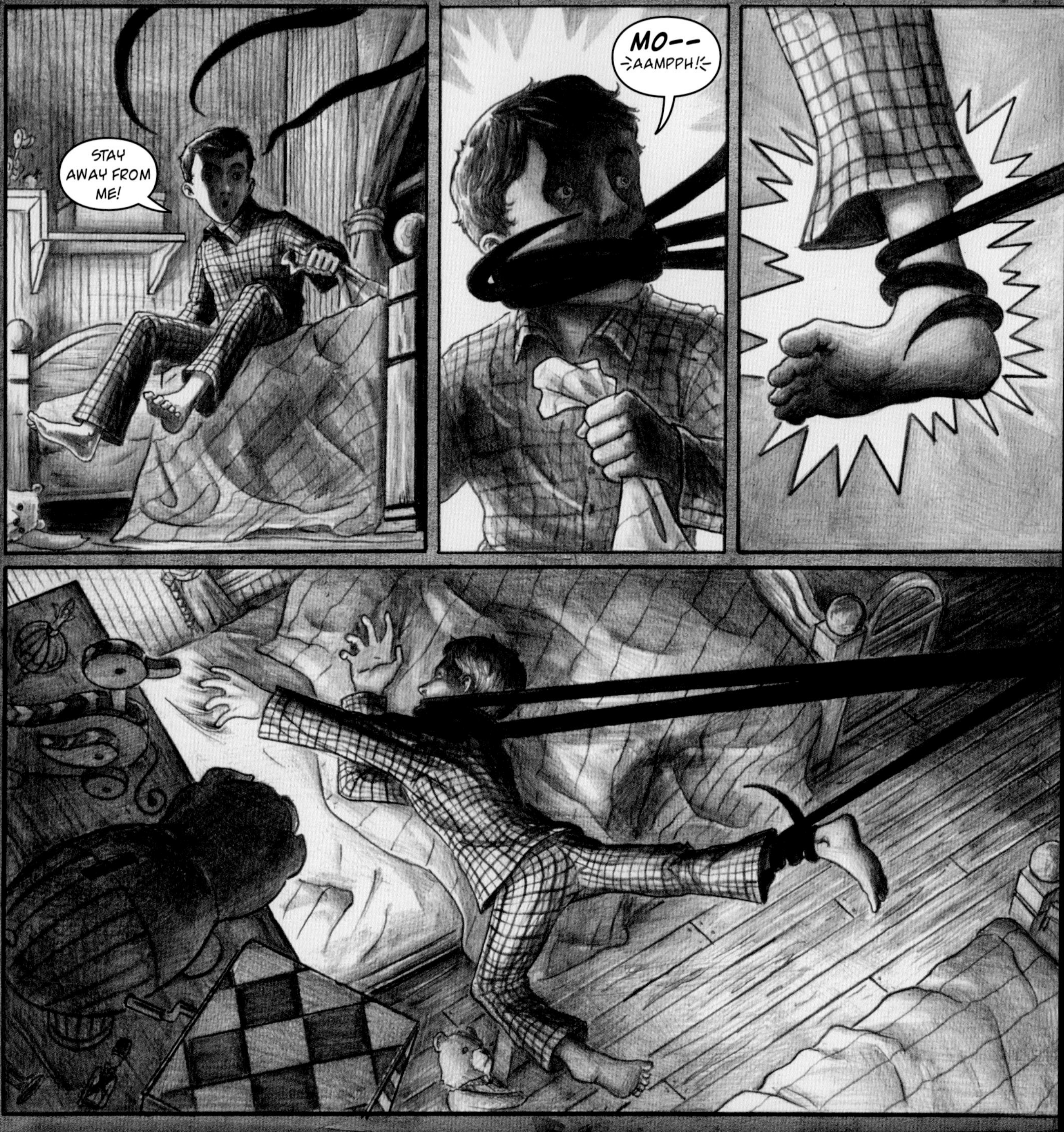
STAY AWAY FROM ME!
MO-- -AAMPPH!-

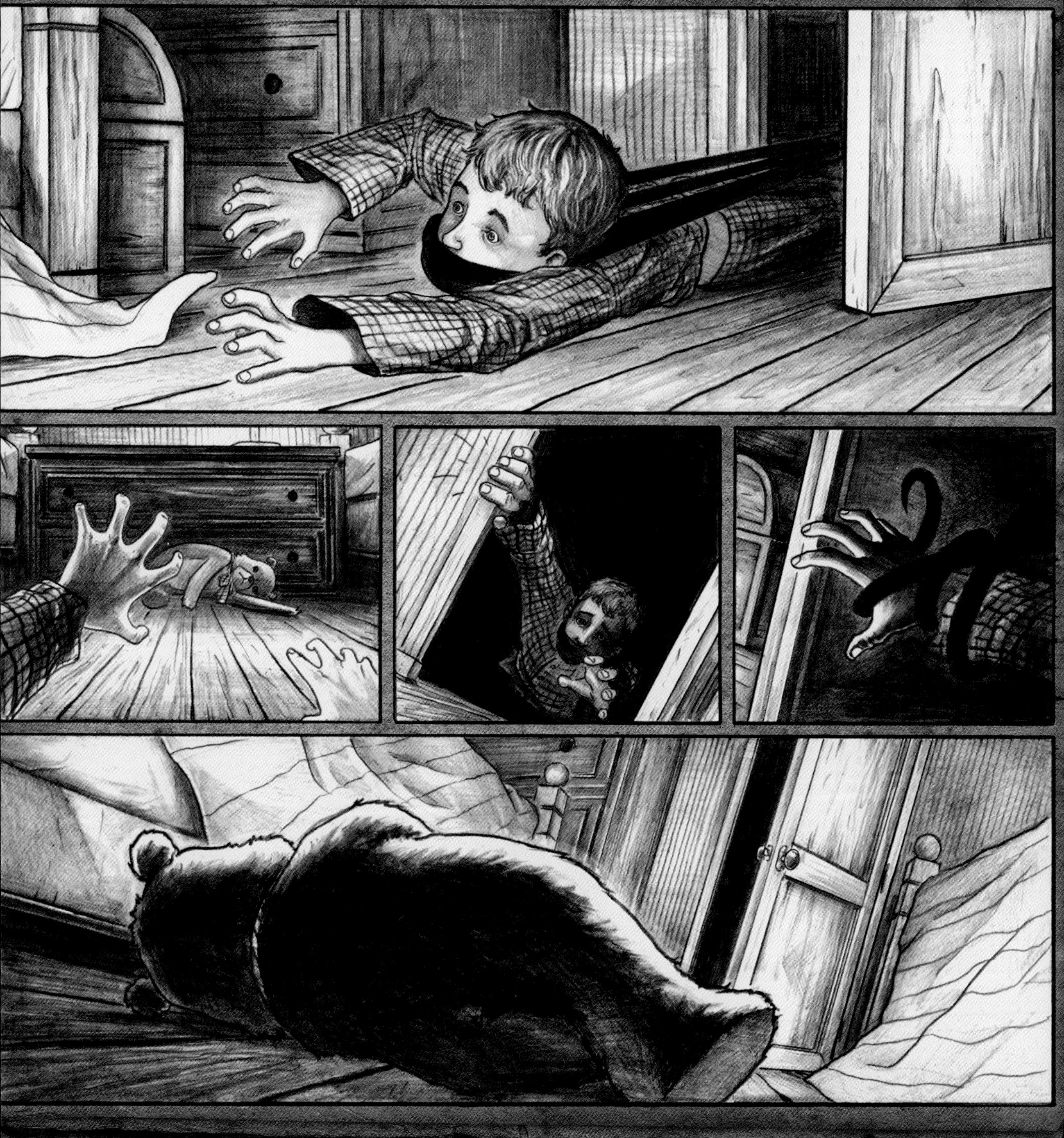

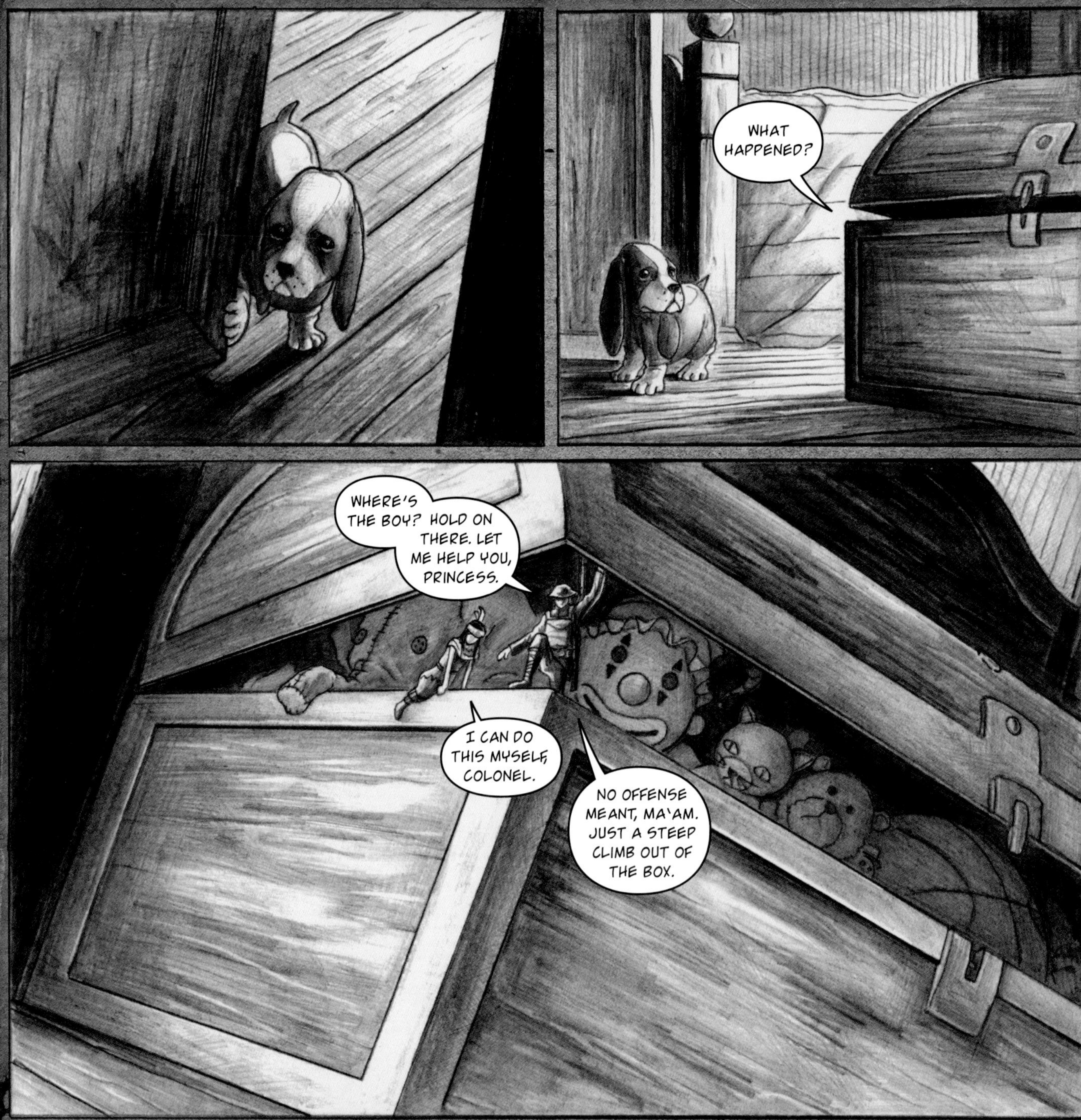
WHAT HAPPENED?
WHERE'S THE BOY? HOLD ON THERE. LET ME HELP YOU, PRINCESS.
I CAN DO THIS MYSELF, COLONEL.
NO OFFENSE MEANT, MA'AM. JUST A STEEP CLIMB OUT OF THE BOX.

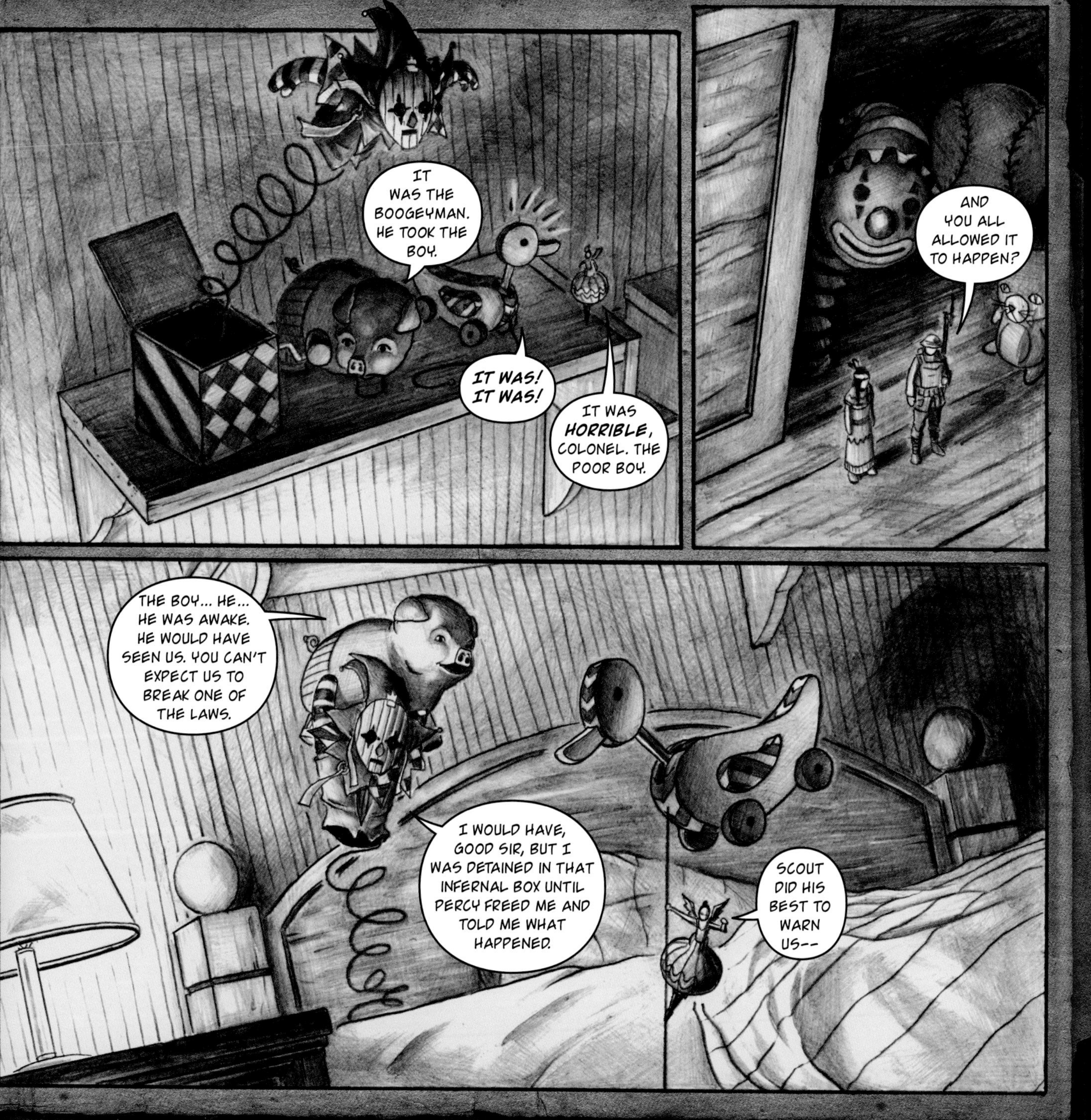
IT WAS THE BOOGEYMAN. HE TOOK THE BOY.
IT WAS! IT WAS!
IT WAS HORRIBLE, COLONEL. THE POOR BOY.
AND YOU ALL ALLOWED IT TO HAPPEN?
THE BOY... HE... HE WAS AWAKE. HE WOULD HAVE SEEN US. YOU CAN'T EXPECT US TO BREAK ONE OF THE LAWS.
I WOULD HAVE, GOOD SIR, BUT I WAS DETAINED IN THAT INFERNAL BOX UNTIL PERCY FREED ME AND TOLD ME WHAT HAPPENED.
SCOUT DID HIS BEST TO WARN US--

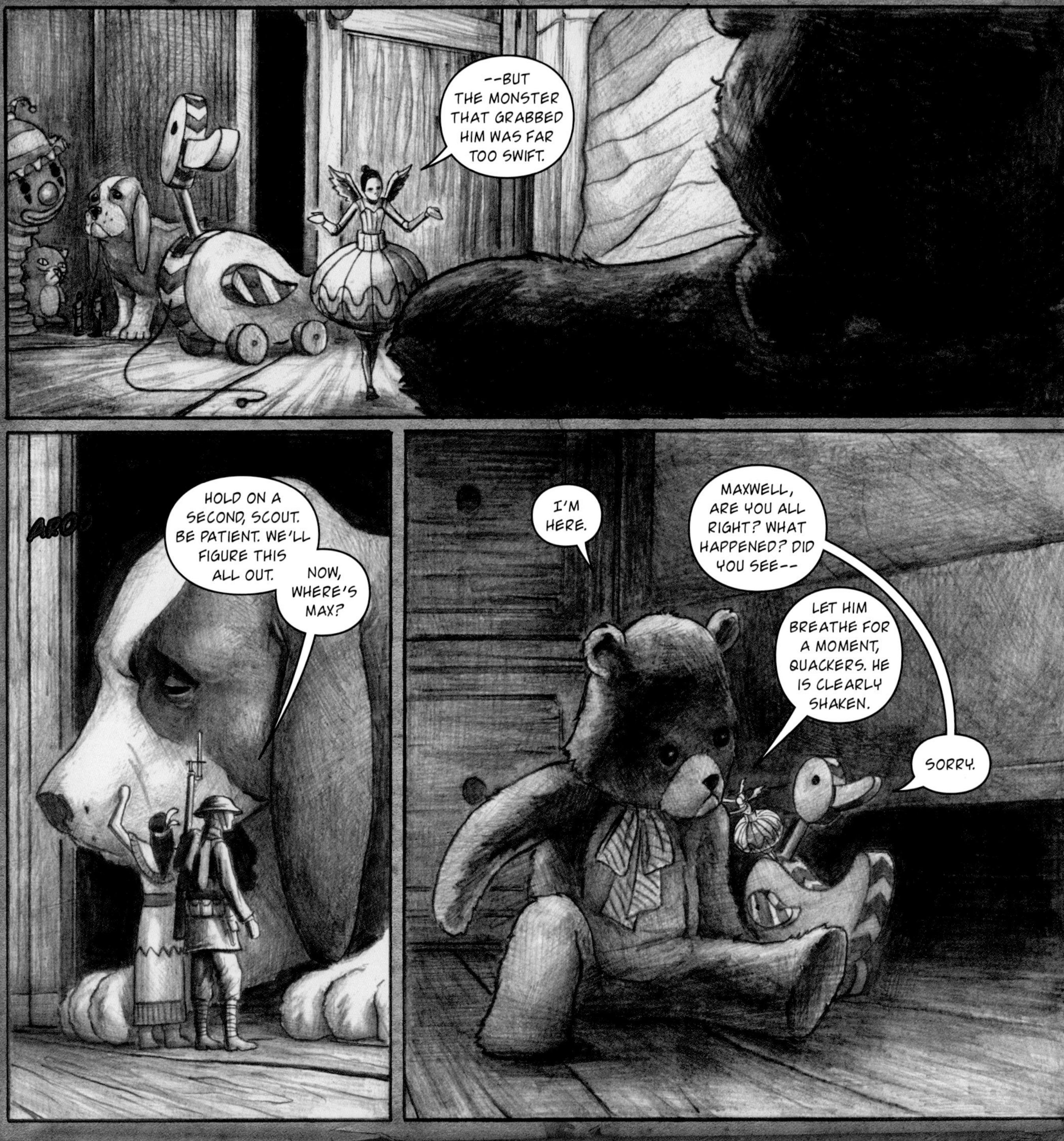
--BUT THE MONSTER THAT GRABBED HIM WAS FAR TOO SWIFT.
AROO
HOLD ON A SECOND, SCOUT. BE PATIENT. WE'LL FIGURE THIS ALL OUT.
NOW, WHERE'S MAX?
I'M HERE.
MAXWELL, ARE YOU ALL RIGHT? WHAT HAPPENED? DID YOU SEE--
LET HIM BREATHE FOR A MOMENT, QUACKERS. HE IS CLEARLY SHAKEN.
SORRY.

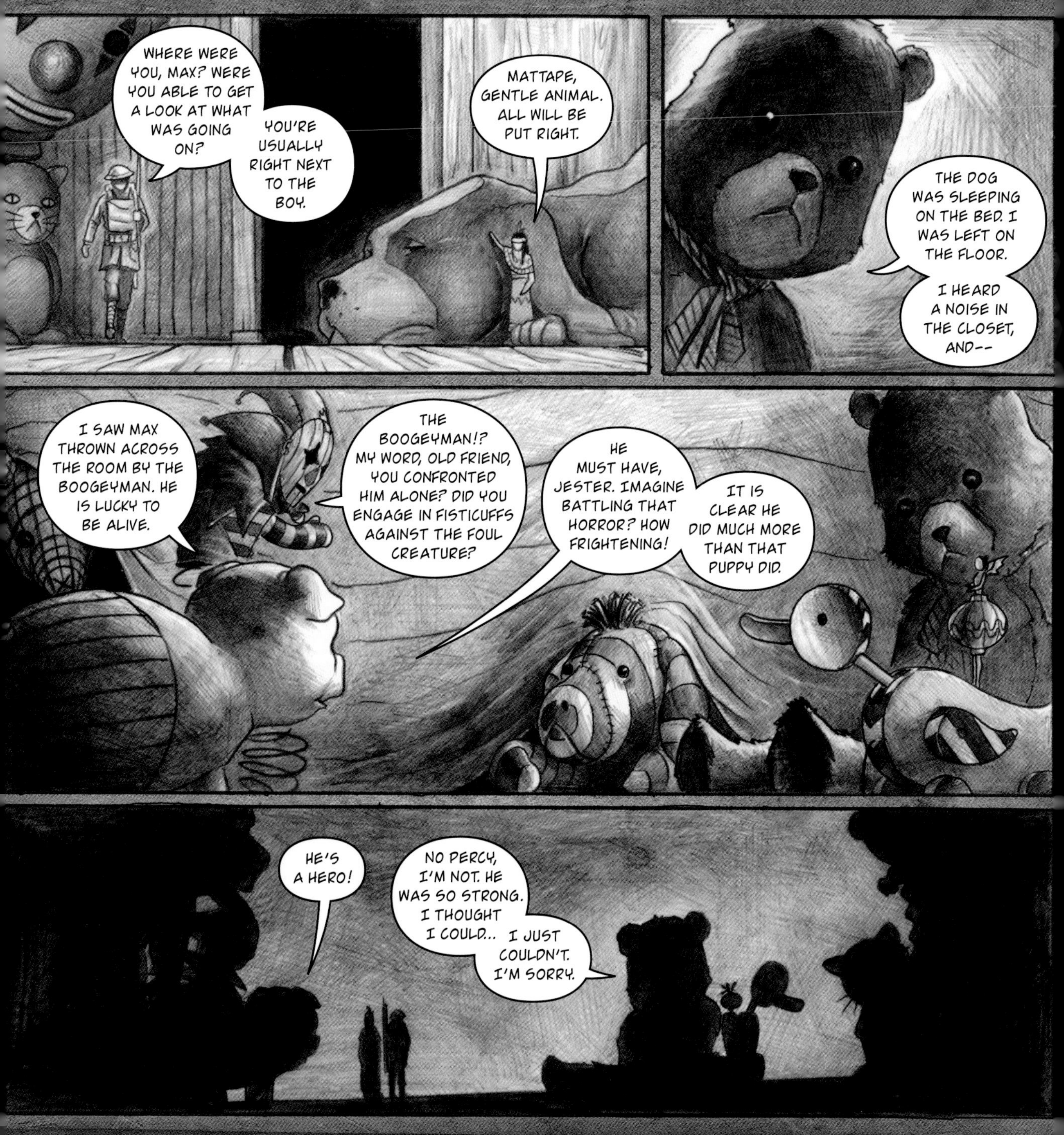
WHERE WERE YOU, MAX? WERE YOU ABLE TO GET A LOOK AT WHAT WAS GOING ON?
YOU'RE USUALLY RIGHT NEXT TO THE BOY.
MATTAPE, GENTLE ANIMAL. ALL WILL BE PUT RIGHT.
THE DOG WAS SLEEPING ON THE BED. I WAS LEFT ON THE FLOOR.
I HEARD A NOISE IN THE CLOSET, AND--
I SAW MAX THROWN ACROSS THE ROOM BY THE BOOGEYMAN. HE IS LUCKY TO BE ALIVE.
THE BOOGEYMAN!? MY WORD, OLD FRIEND, YOU CONFRONTED HIM ALONE? DID YOU ENGAGE IN FISTICUFFS AGAINST THE FOUL CREATURE?
HE MUST HAVE, JESTER. IMAGINE BATTLING THAT HORROR? HOW FRIGHTENING!
IT IS CLEAR HE DID MUCH MORE THAN THAT PUPPY DID.
HE'S A HERO!
NO PERCY, I'M NOT. HE WAS SO STRONG. I THOUGHT I COULD...
I JUST COULDN'T. I'M SORRY.

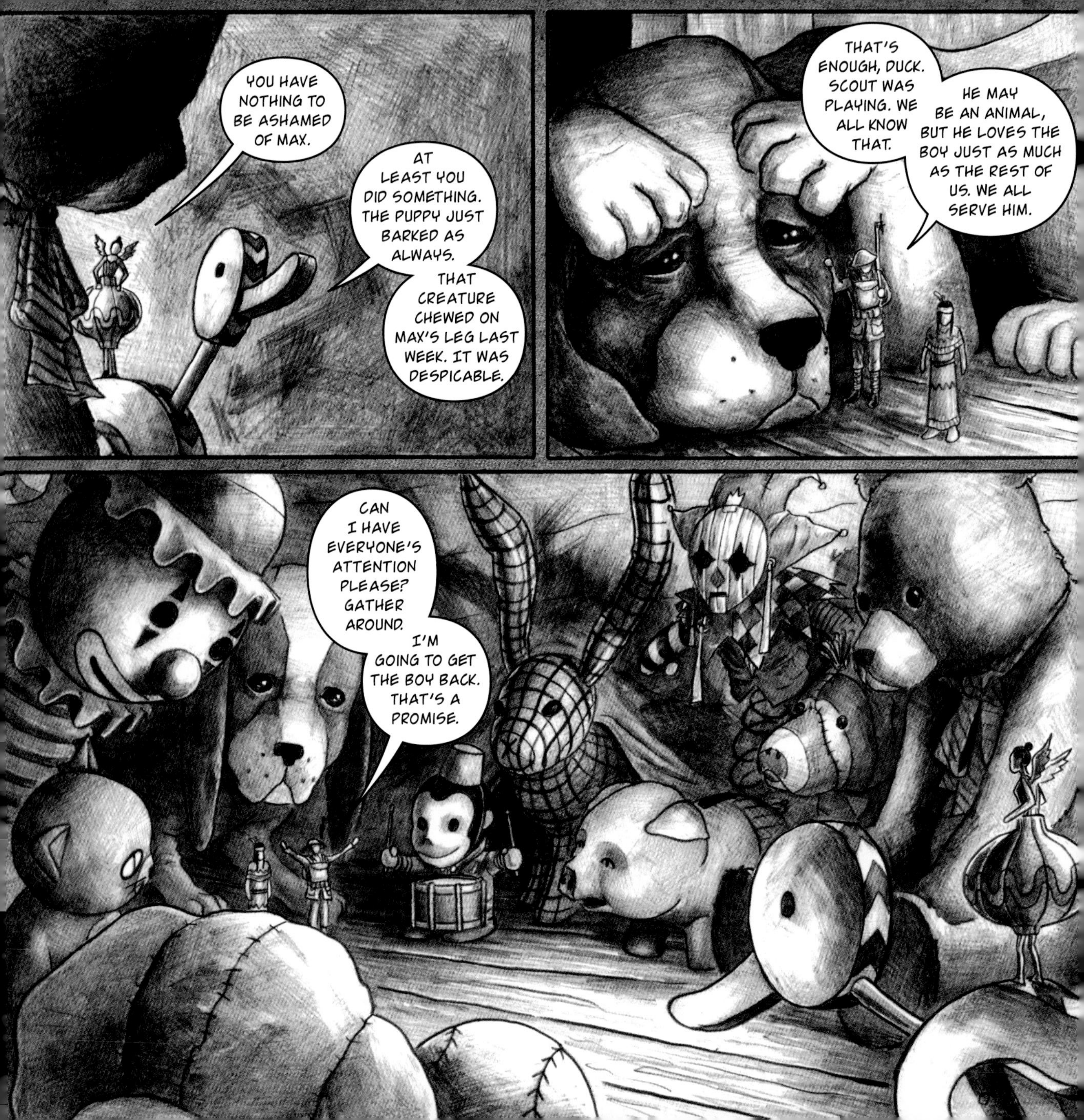
YOU HAVE NOTHING TO BE ASHAMED OF MAX.
AT LEAST YOU DID SOMETHING. THE PUPPY JUST BARKED AS ALWAYS.
THAT CREATURE CHEWED ON MAX'S LEG LAST WEEK. IT WAS DESPICABLE.
THAT'S ENOUGH, DUCK. SCOUT WAS PLAYING. WE ALL KNOW THAT.
HE MAY BE AN ANIMAL, BUT HE LOVES THE BOY JUST AS MUCH AS THE REST OF US. WE ALL SERVE HIM.
CAN I HAVE EVERYONE'S ATTENTION PLEASE? GATHER AROUND.
I'M GOING TO GET THE BOY BACK. THAT'S A PROMISE.

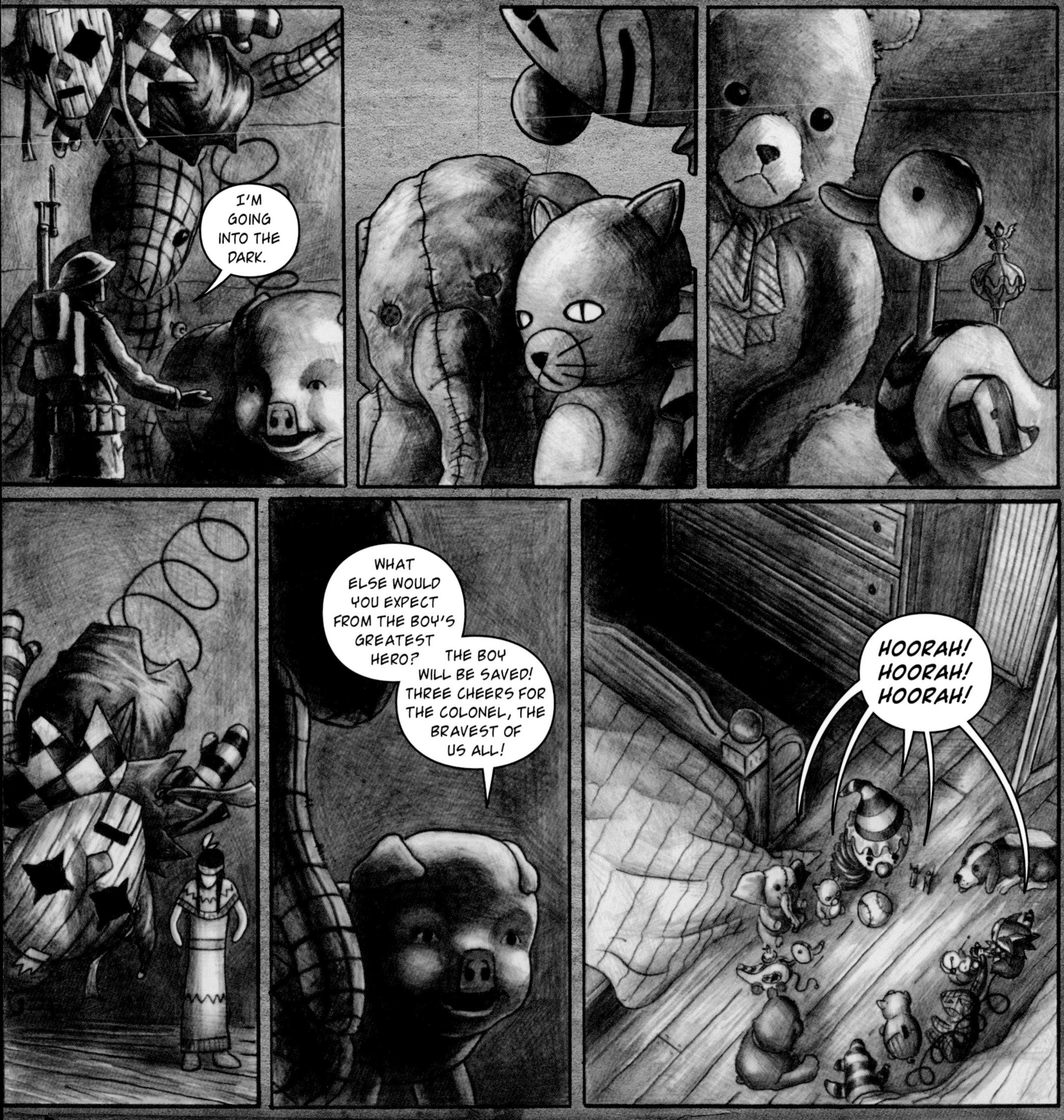
I'M GOING INTO THE DARK.
WHAT ELSE WOULD YOU EXPECT FROM THE BOY'S GREATEST HERO?
THE BOY WILL BE SAVED! THREE CHEERS FOR THE COLONEL, THE BRAVEST OF US ALL!
HOORAH! HOORAH! HOORAH!

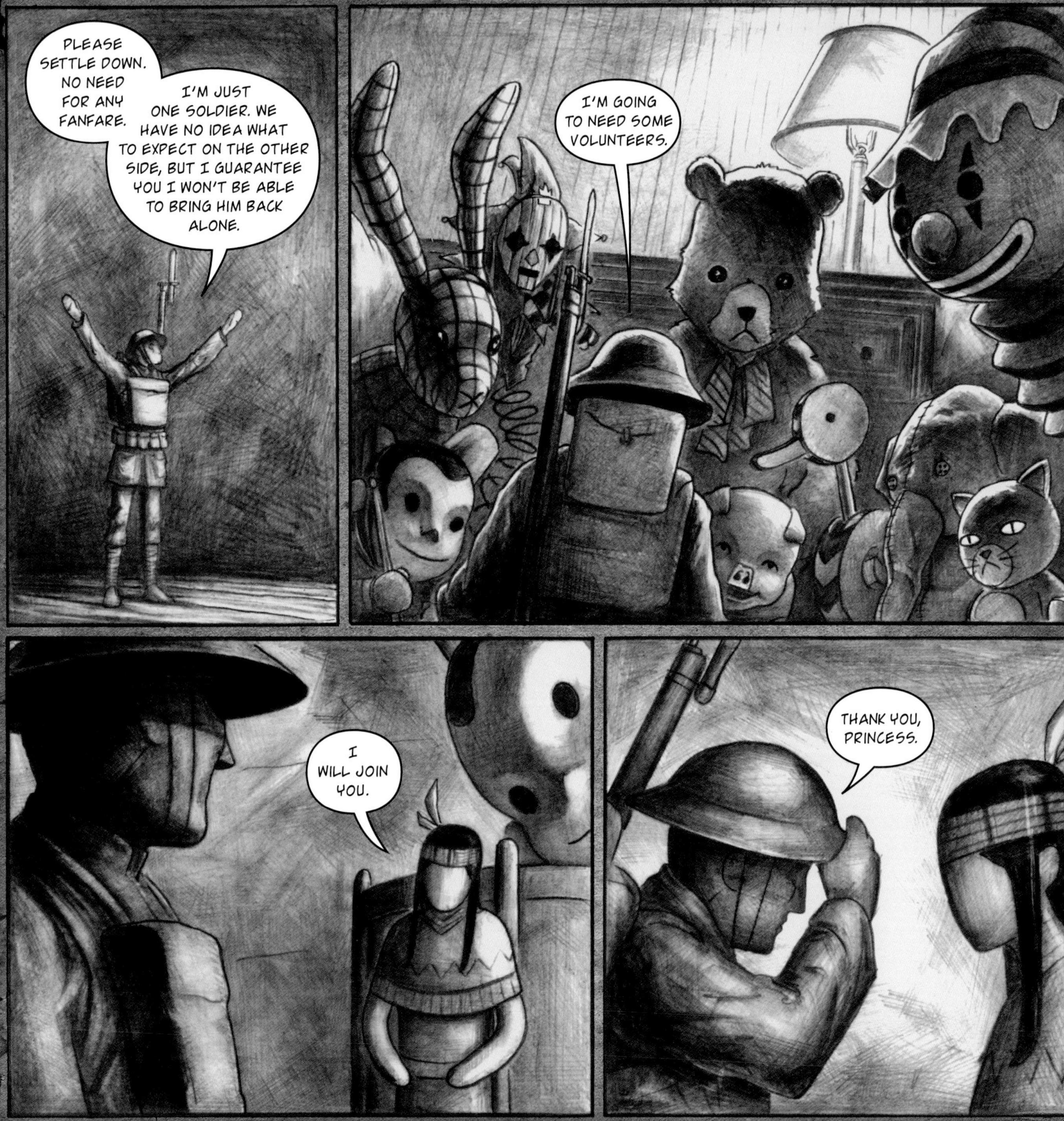
PLEASE SETTLE DOWN. NO NEED FOR ANY FANFARE.
I'M JUST ONE SOLDIER. WE HAVE NO IDEA WHAT TO EXPECT ON THE OTHER SIDE, BUT I GUARANTEE YOU I WON'T BE ABLE TO BRING HIM BACK ALONE.
I'M GOING TO NEED SOME VOLUNTEERS.
I WILL JOIN YOU.
THANK YOU, PRINCESS.

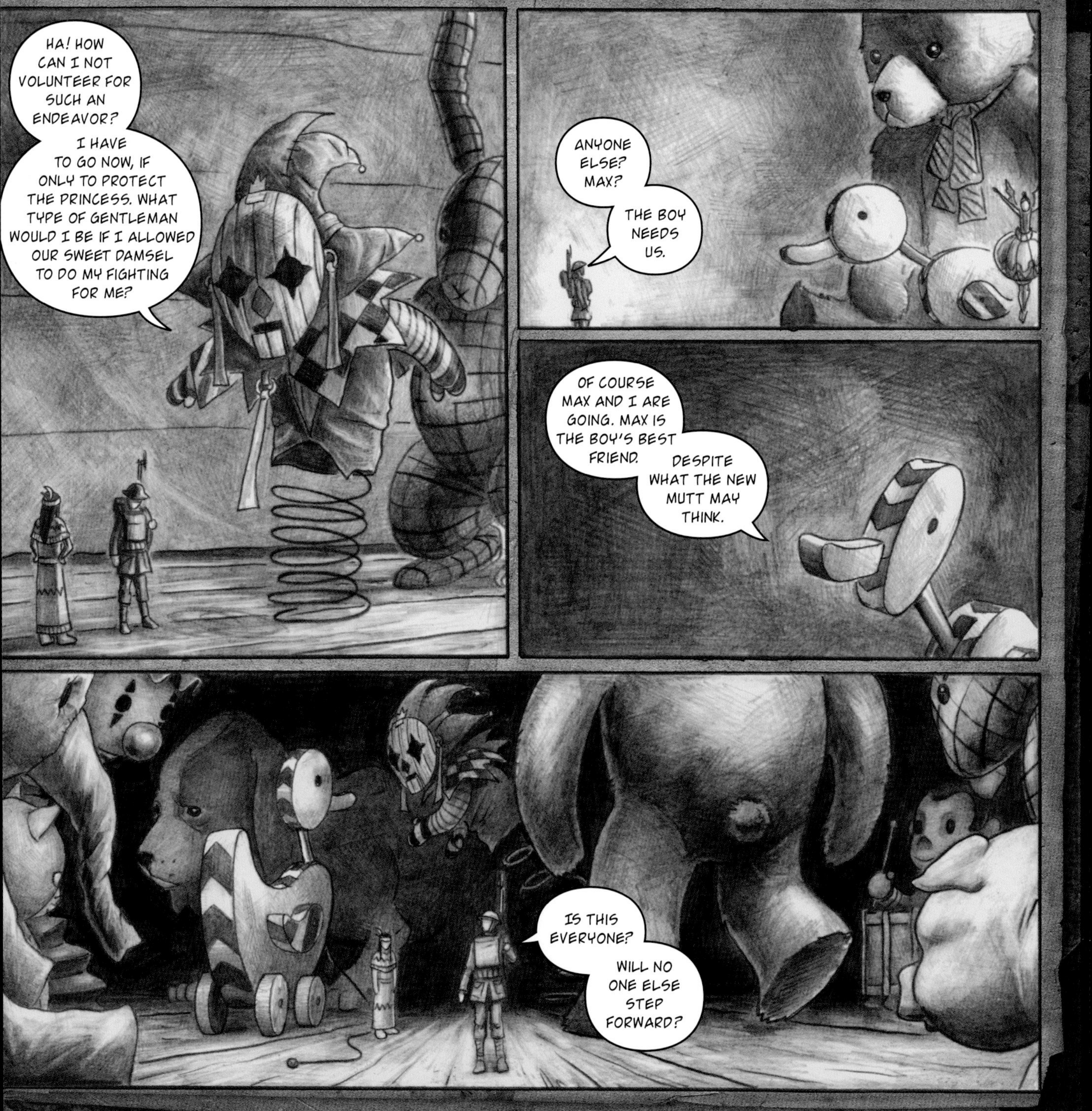
HA! HOW CAN I NOT VOLUNTEER FOR SUCH AN ENDEAVOR?
I HAVE TO GO NOW, IF ONLY TO PROTECT THE PRINCESS. WHAT TYPE OF GENTLEMAN WOULD I BE IF I ALLOWED OUR SWEET DAMSEL TO DO MY FIGHTING FOR ME?
ANYONE ELSE? MAX?
THE BOY NEEDS US.
OF COURSE MAX AND I ARE GOING. MAX IS THE BOY'S BEST FRIEND.
DESPITE WHAT THE NEW MUTT MAY THINK.
IS THIS EVERYONE?
WILL NO ONE ELSE STEP FORWARD?

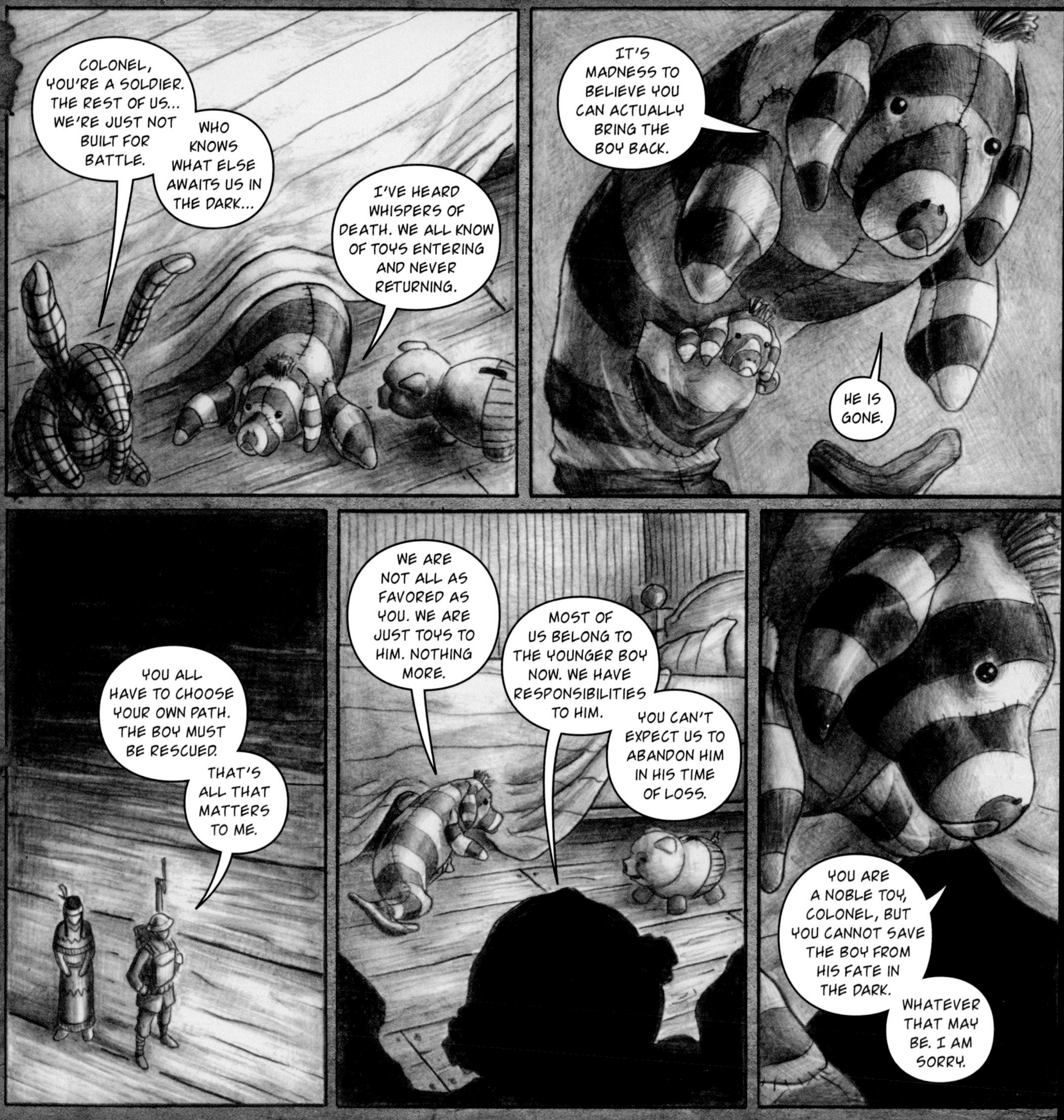
COLONEL, YOU'RE A SOLDIER. THE REST OF US... WE'RE JUST NOT BUILT FOR BATTLE.
WHO KNOWS WHAT ELSE AWAITS US IN THE DARK...
I'VE HEARD WHISPERS OF DEATH. WE ALL KNOW OF TOYS ENTERING AND NEVER RETURNING.
IT'S MADNESS TO BELIEVE YOU CAN ACTUALLY BRING THE BOY BACK.
HE IS GONE.
YOU ALL HAVE TO CHOOSE YOUR OWN PATH. THE BOY MUST BE RESCUED.
THAT'S ALL THAT MATTERS TO ME.
WE ARE NOT ALL AS FAVORED AS YOU. WE ARE JUST TOYS TO HIM. NOTHING MORE.
MOST OF US BELONG TO THE YOUNGER BOY NOW. WE HAVE RESPONSIBILITIES TO HIM.
YOU CAN'T EXPECT US TO ABANDON HIM IN HIS TIME OF LOSS.
YOU ARE A NOBLE TOY, COLONEL, BUT YOU CANNOT SAVE THE BOY FROM HIS FATE IN THE DARK.
WHATEVER THAT MAY BE. I AM SORRY.

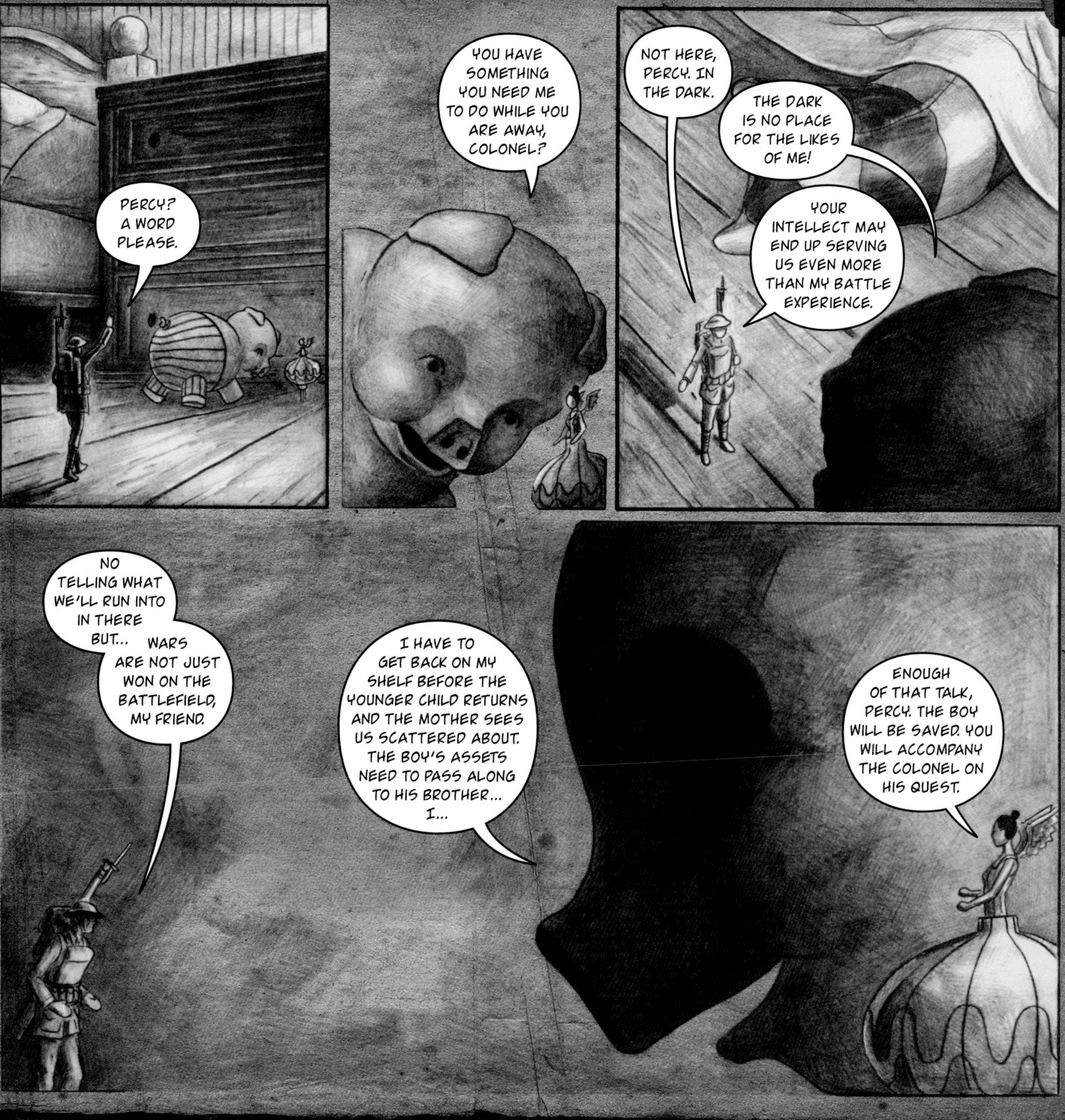
PERCY? A WORD PLEASE.
YOU HAVE SOMETHING YOU NEED ME TO DO WHILE YOU ARE AWAY, COLONEL?
NOT HERE, PERCY. IN THE DARK.
THE DARK IS NO PLACE FOR THE LIKES OF ME!
YOUR INTELLECT MAY END UP SERVING US EVEN MORE THAN MY BATTLE EXPERIENCE.
NO TELLING WHAT WE'LL RUN INTO IN THERE BUT...
WARS ARE NOT JUST WON ON THE BATTLEFIELD, MY FRIEND.
I HAVE TO GET BACK ON MY SHELF BEFORE THE YOUNGER CHILD RETURNS AND THE MOTHER SEES US SCATTERED ABOUT. THE BOY'S ASSETS NEED TO PASS ALONG TO HIS BROTHER... I...
ENOUGH OF THAT TALK, PERCY. THE BOY WILL BE SAVED. YOU WILL ACCOMPANY THE COLONEL ON HIS QUEST.

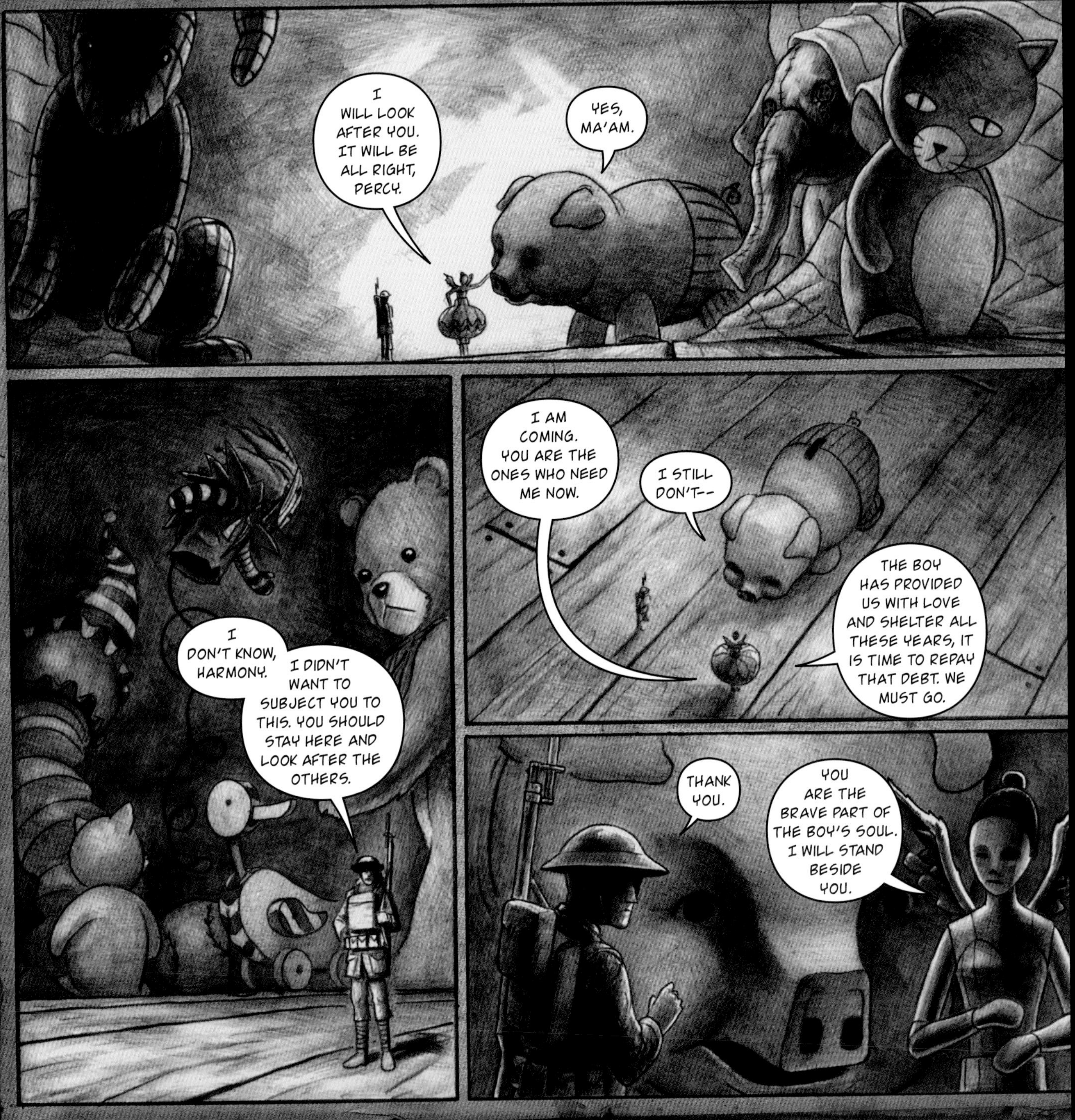

I WILL LOOK AFTER YOU. IT WILL BE ALL RIGHT, PERCY.
YES, MA'AM.
I DON'T KNOW, HARMONY.
I DIDN'T WANT TO SUBJECT YOU TO THIS. YOU SHOULD STAY HERE AND LOOK AFTER THE OTHERS.
I AM COMING. YOU ARE THE ONES WHO NEED ME NOW.
I STILL DON'T--
THE BOY HAS PROVIDED US WITH LOVE AND SHELTER ALL THESE YEARS, IT IS TIME TO REPAY THAT DEBT. WE MUST GO.
THANK YOU.
YOU ARE THE BRAVE PART OF THE BOY'S SOUL. I WILL STAND BESIDE YOU.

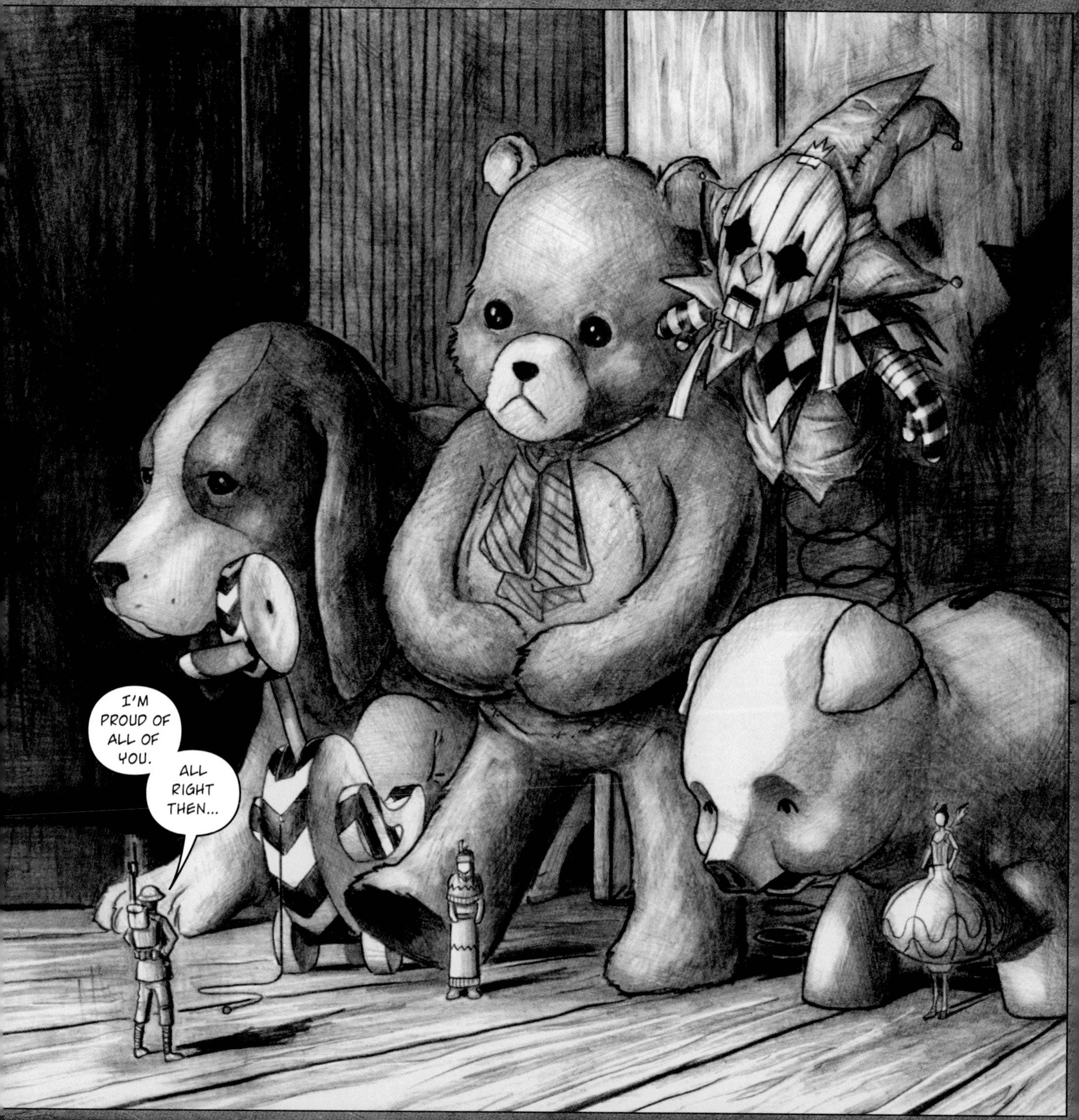
I'M PROUD OF ALL OF YOU.
ALL RIGHT THEN...

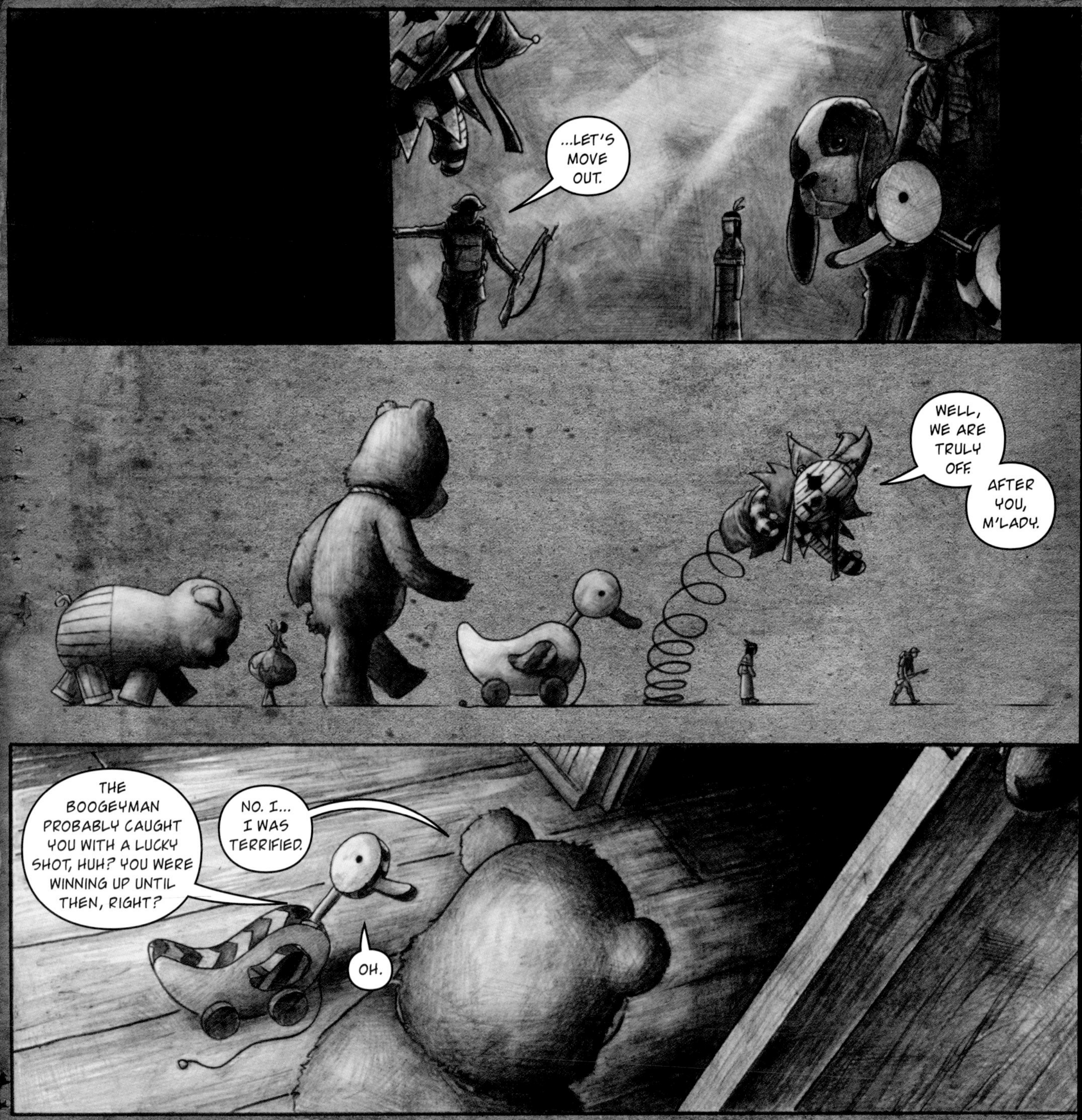
...LET'S MOVE OUT.
WELL, WE ARE TRULY OFF.
AFTER YOU, M'LADY.
THE BOOGEYMAN PROBABLY CAUGHT YOU WITH A LUCKY SHOT, HUH? YOU WERE WINNING UP UNTIL THEN, RIGHT?
NO. I... I WAS TERRIFIED.
OH.

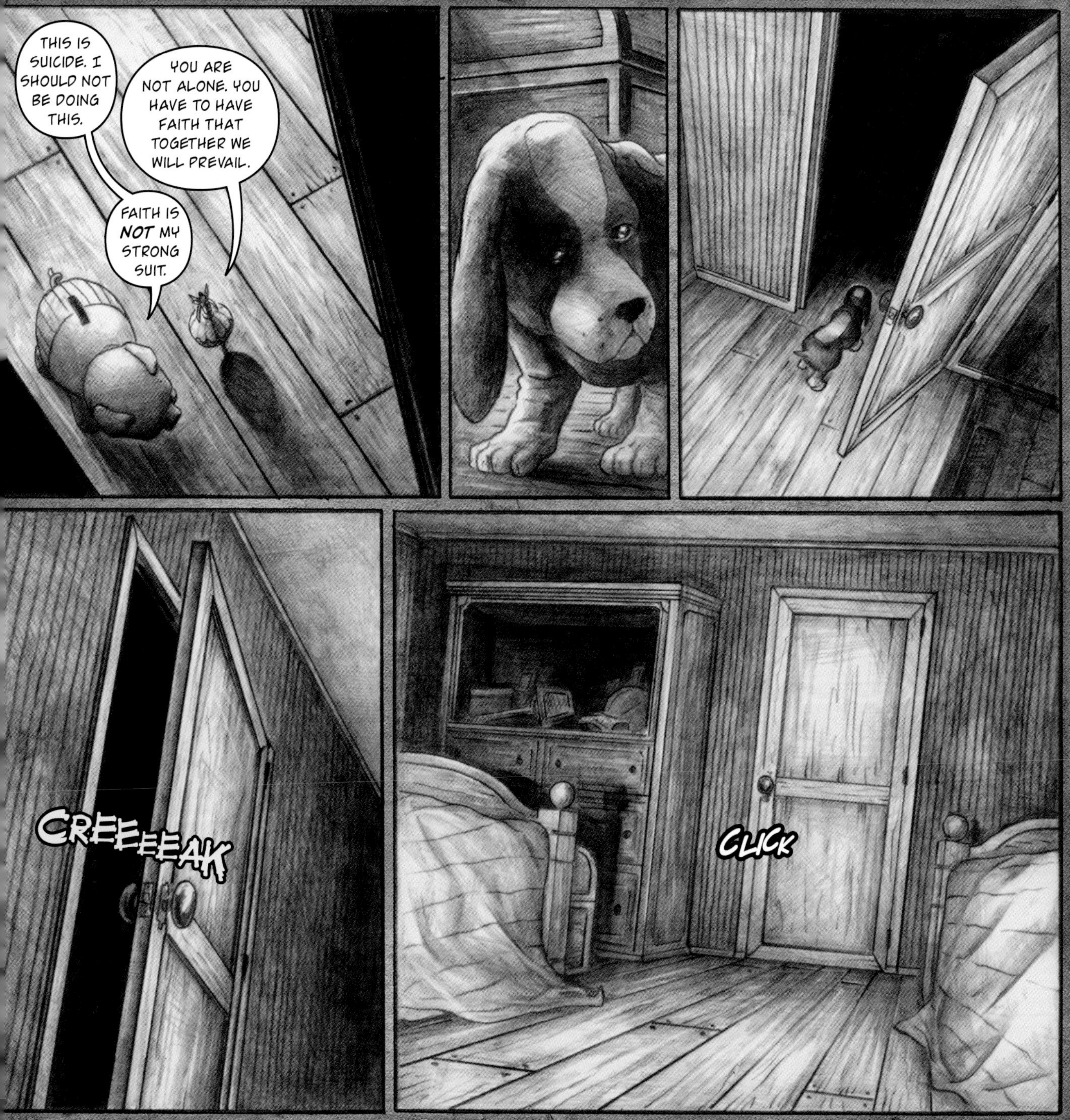
THIS IS SUICIDE. I SHOULD NOT BE DOING THIS.
YOU ARE NOT ALONE. YOU HAVE TO HAVE FAITH THAT TOGETHER WE WILL PREVAIL.
FAITH IS *NOT* MY STRONG SUIT.
CREEEEEAK
CLICK

Chapter 1:
The Battle of Brooklyn Creek

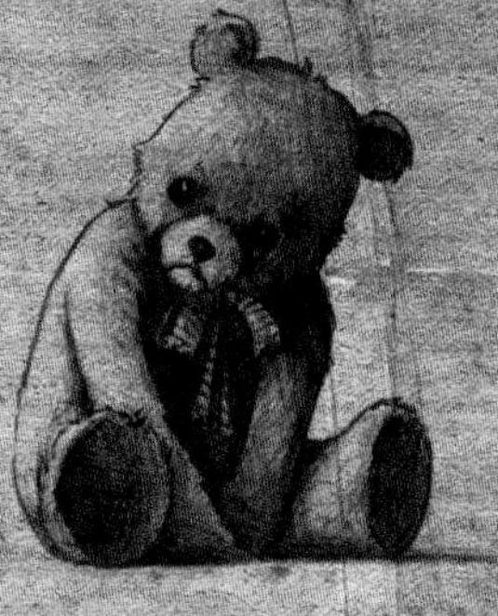

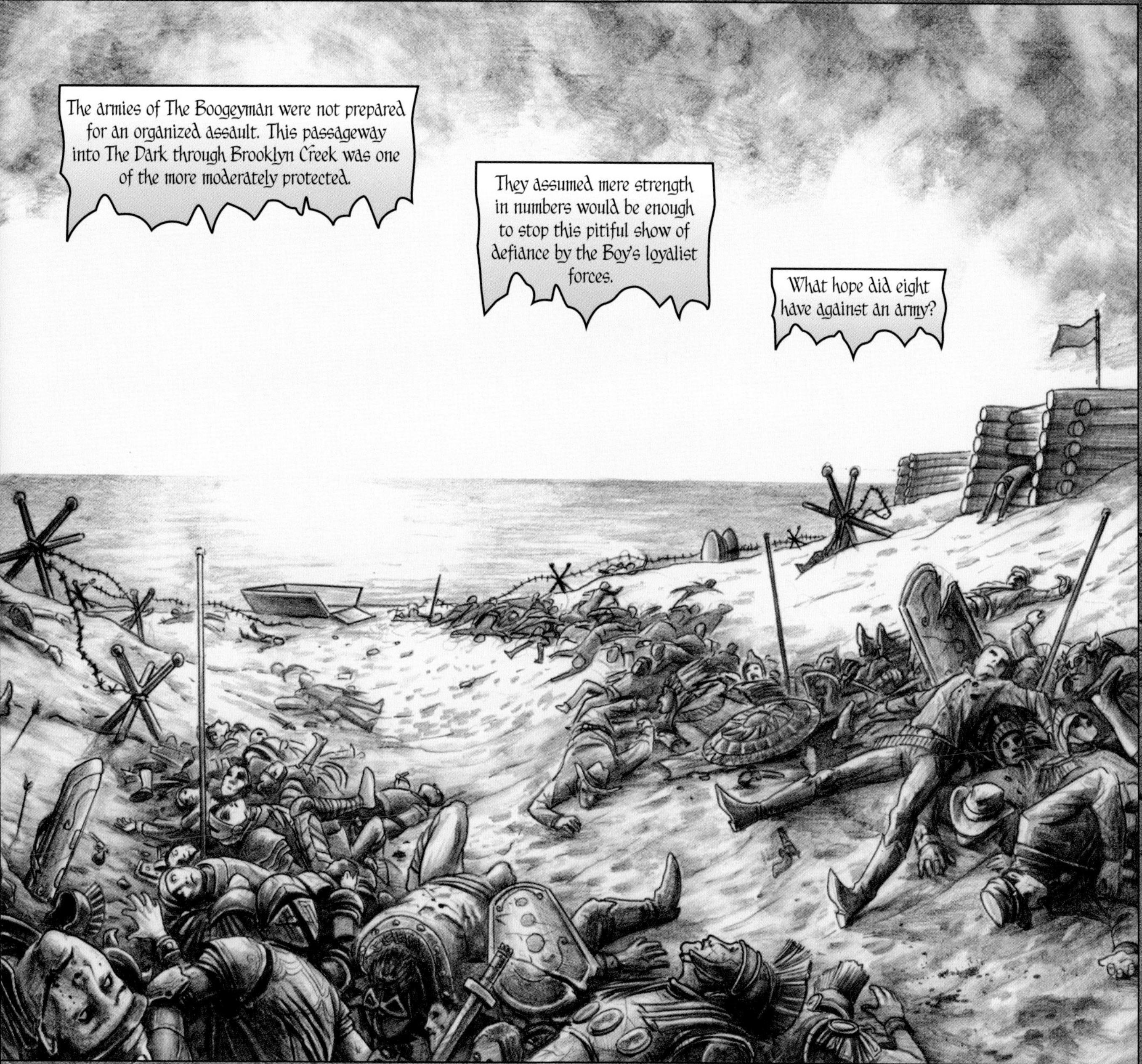
The armies of The Boogeyman were not prepared for an organized assault. This passageway into The Dark through Brooklyn Creek was one of the more moderately protected.
They assumed mere strength in numbers would be enough to stop this pitiful show of defiance by the Boy's loyalist forces.
What hope did eight have against an army?

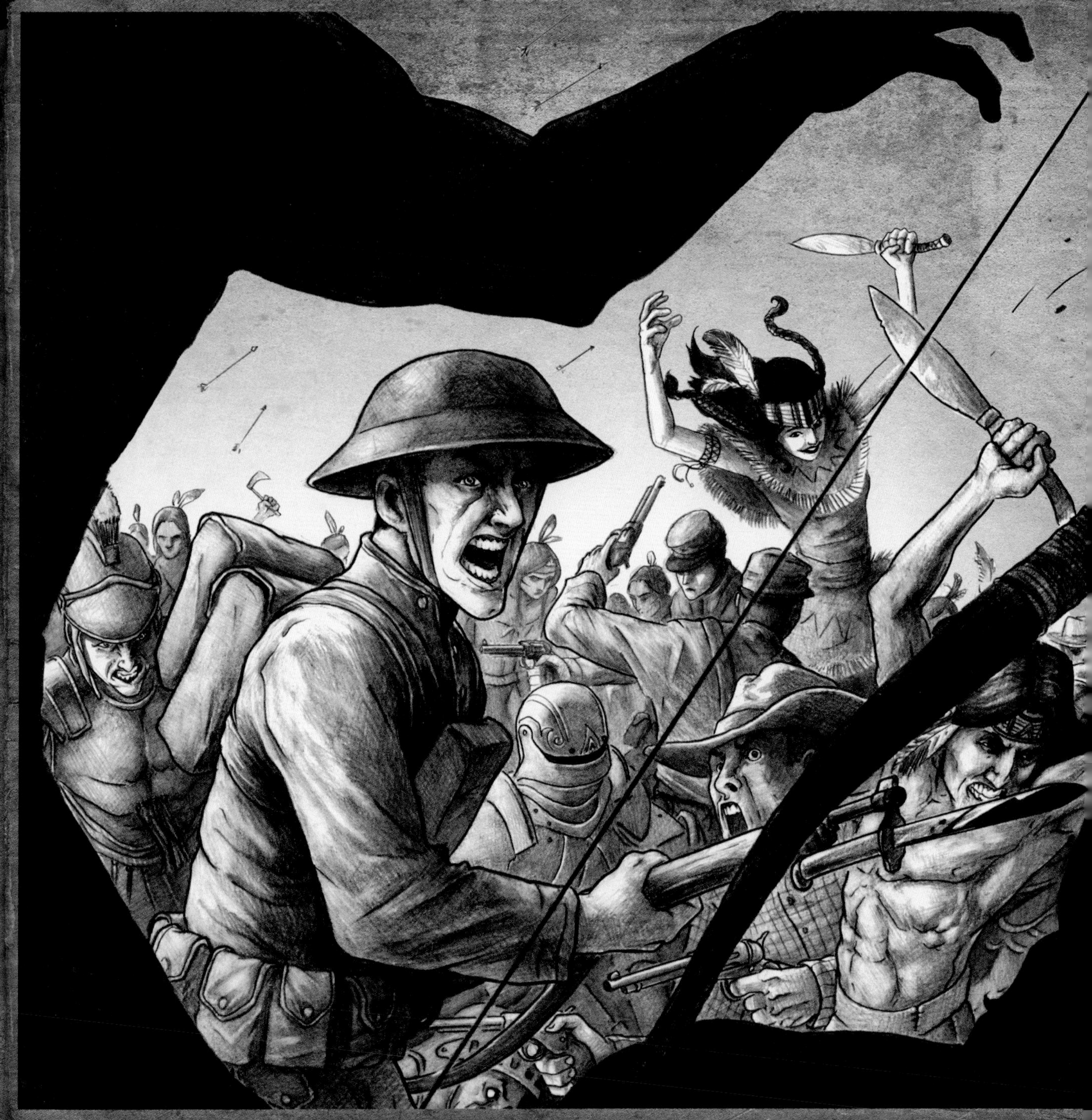

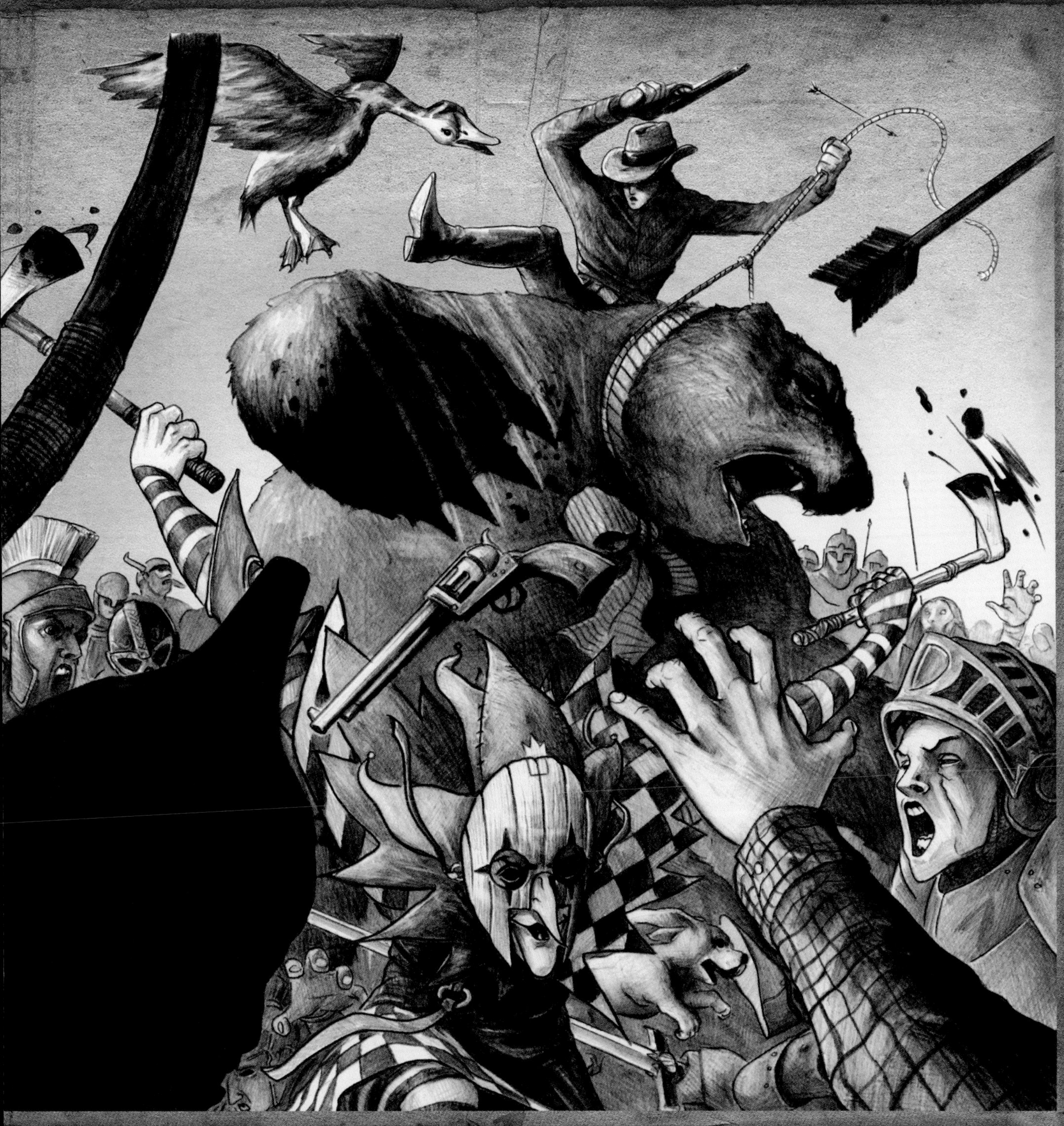

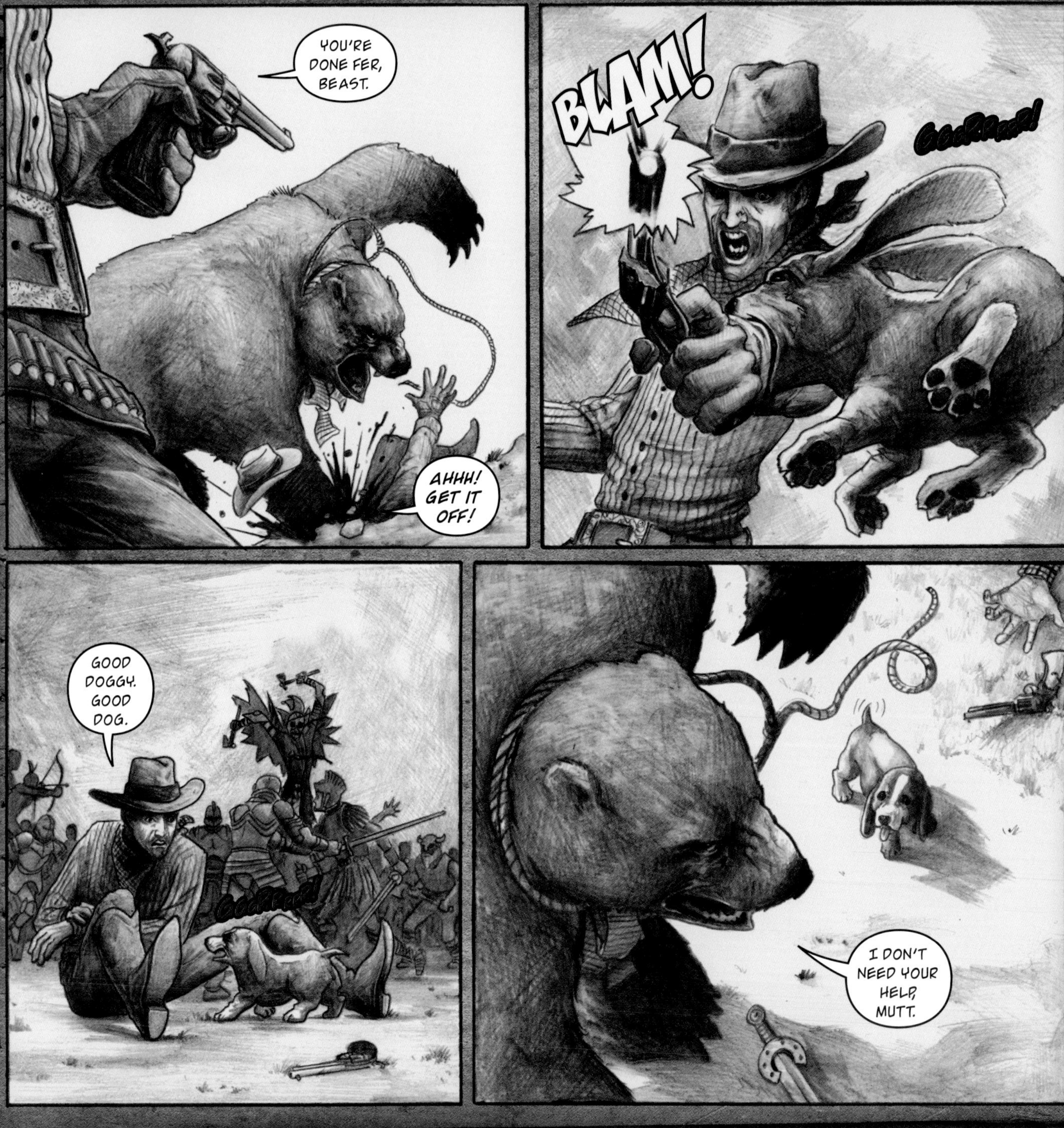
YOU'RE DONE FER, BEAST.
AHHH! GET IT OFF!
BLAM!
GGGRRRRR!
GOOD DOGGY. GOOD DOG.
I DON'T NEED YOUR HELP, MUTT.

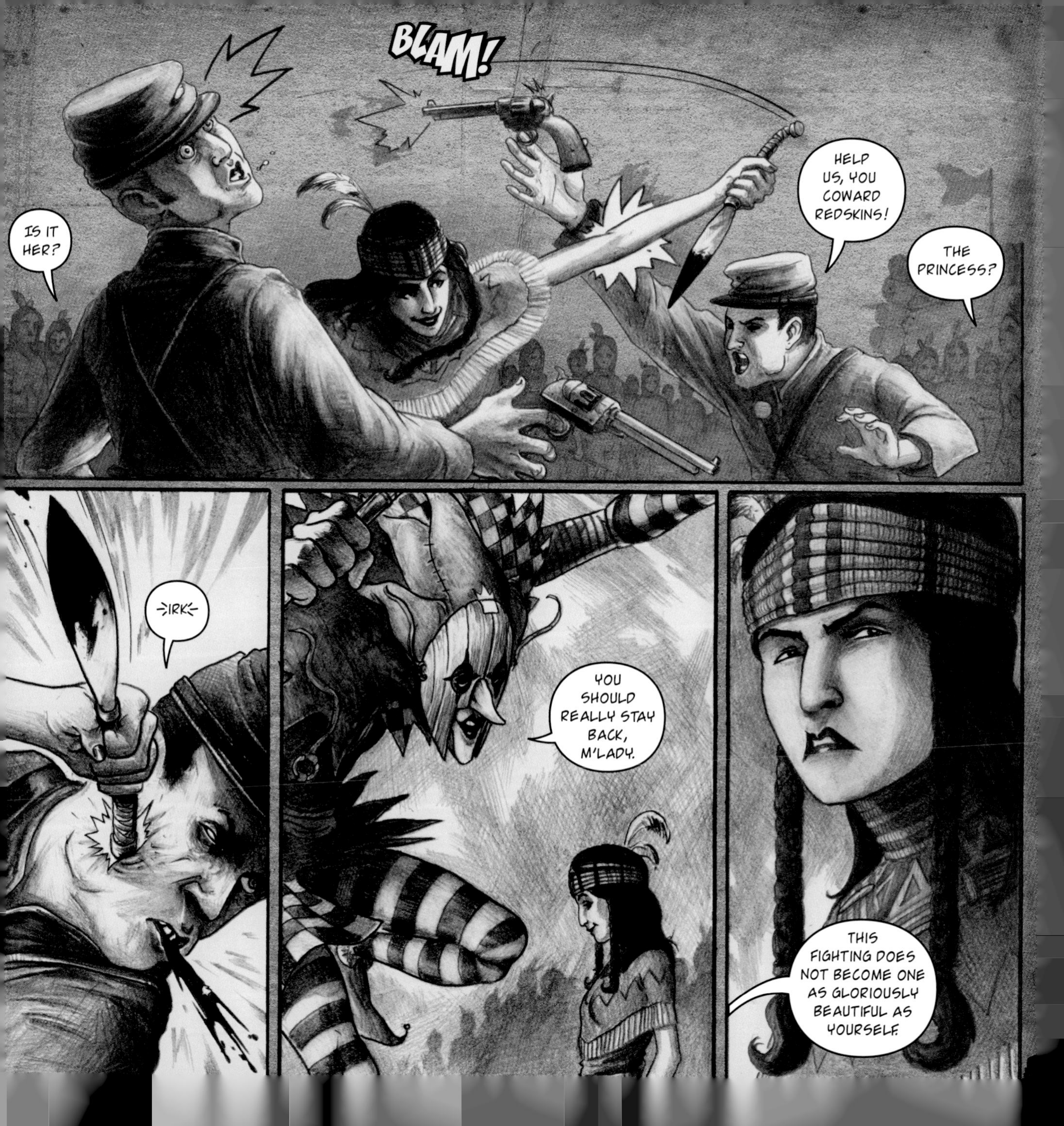
BLAM!
IS IT HER?
HELP US, YOU COWARD REDSKINS!
THE PRINCESS?
IRK
YOU SHOULD REALLY STAY BACK, M'LADY.
THIS FIGHTING DOES NOT BECOME ONE AS GLORIOUSLY BEAUTIFUL AS YOURSELF.

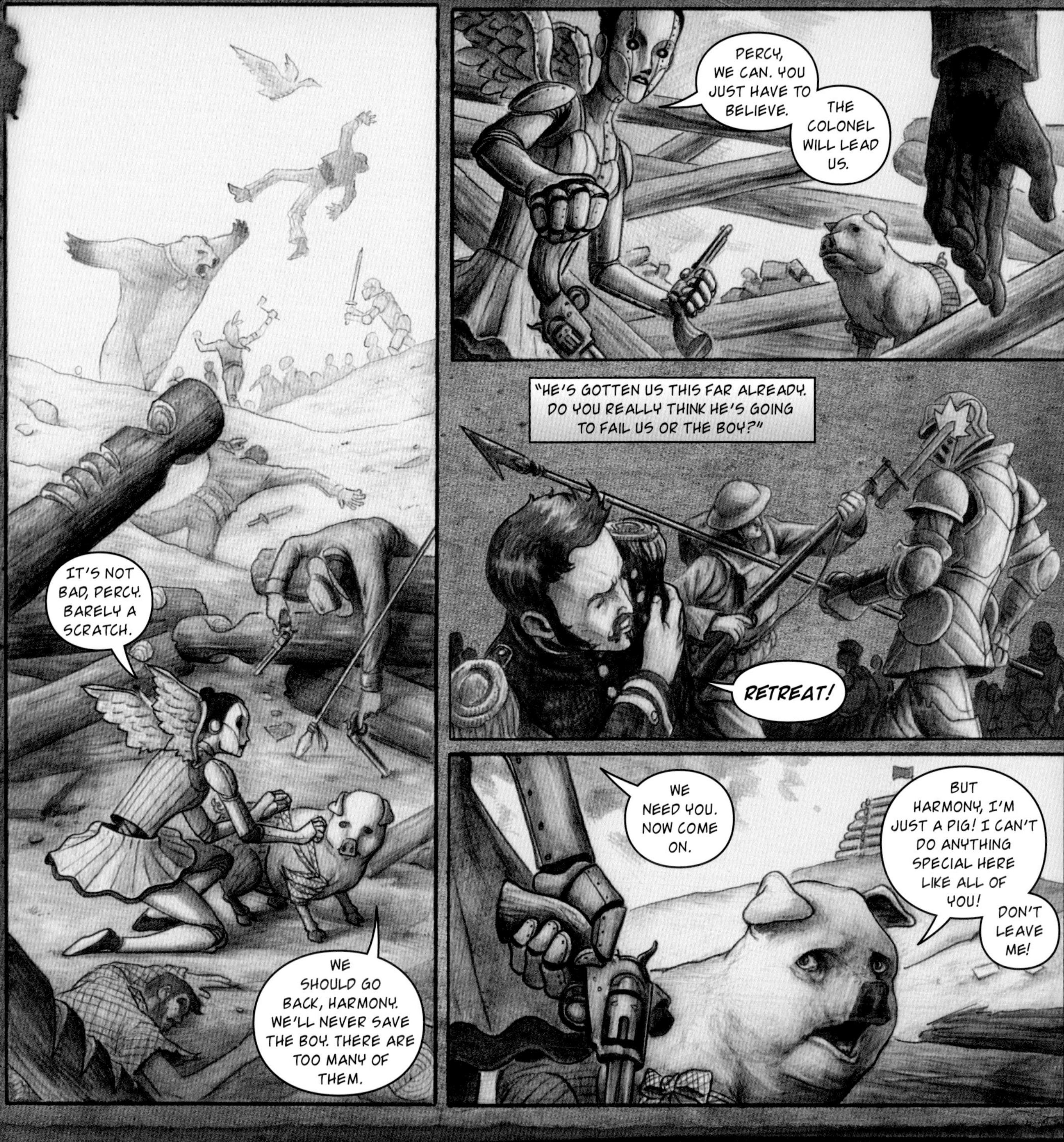

IT'S NOT BAD, PERCY. BARELY A SCRATCH.
WE SHOULD GO BACK, HARMONY. WE'LL NEVER SAVE THE BOY. THERE ARE TOO MANY OF THEM.
PERCY, WE CAN. YOU JUST HAVE TO BELIEVE.
THE COLONEL WILL LEAD US.
"HE'S GOTTEN US THIS FAR ALREADY. DO YOU REALLY THINK HE'S GOING TO FAIL US OR THE BOY?"
RETREAT!
WE NEED YOU. NOW COME ON.
BUT HARMONY, I'M JUST A PIG! I CAN'T DO ANYTHING SPECIAL HERE LIKE ALL OF YOU!
DON'T LEAVE ME!

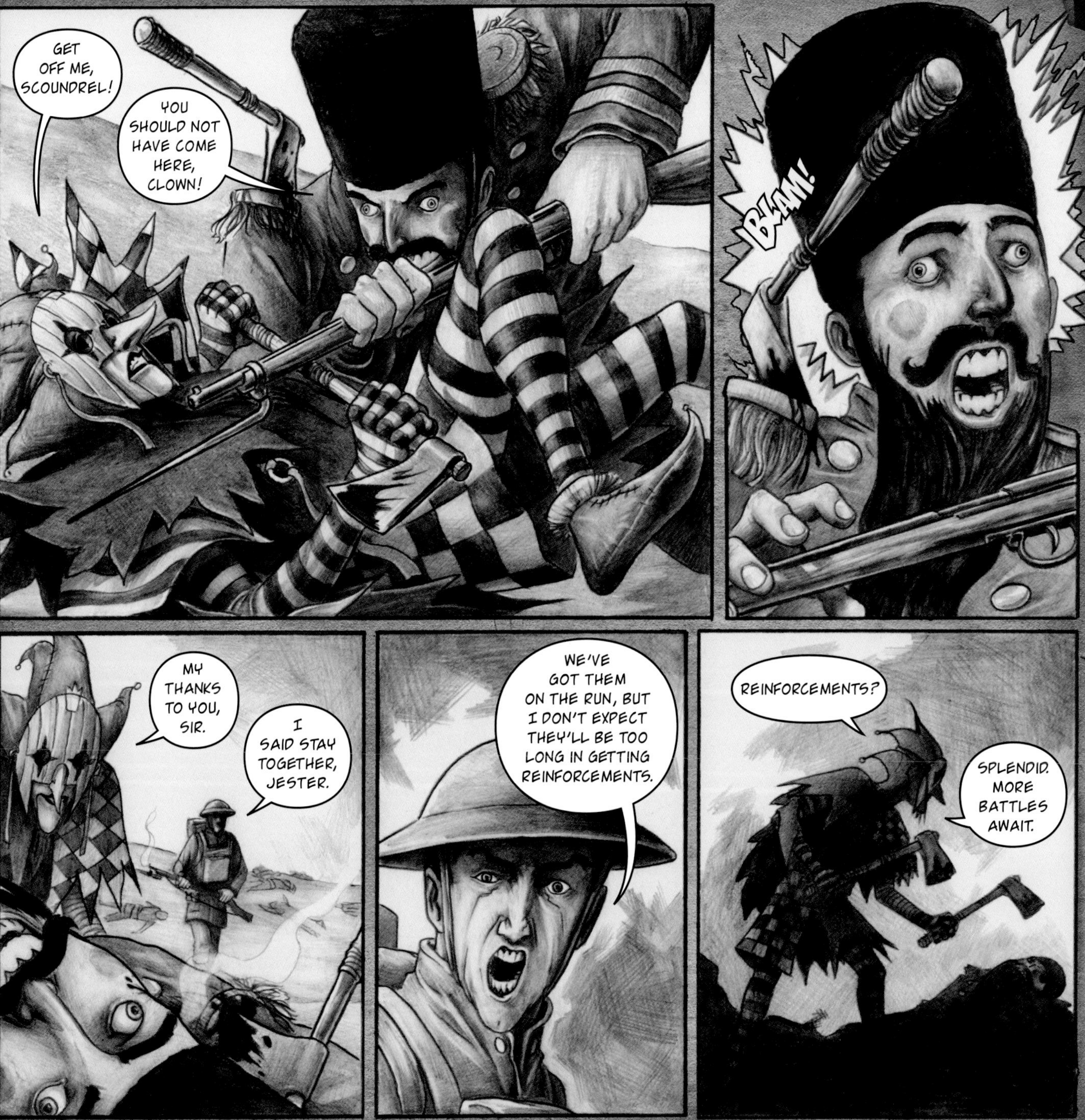
GET OFF ME, SCOUNDREL!
YOU SHOULD NOT HAVE COME HERE, CLOWN!
BLAM!
MY THANKS TO YOU, SIR.
I SAID STAY TOGETHER, JESTER.
WE'VE GOT THEM ON THE RUN, BUT I DON'T EXPECT THEY'LL BE TOO LONG IN GETTING REINFORCEMENTS.
REINFORCEMENTS?
SPLENDID. MORE BATTLES AWAIT.

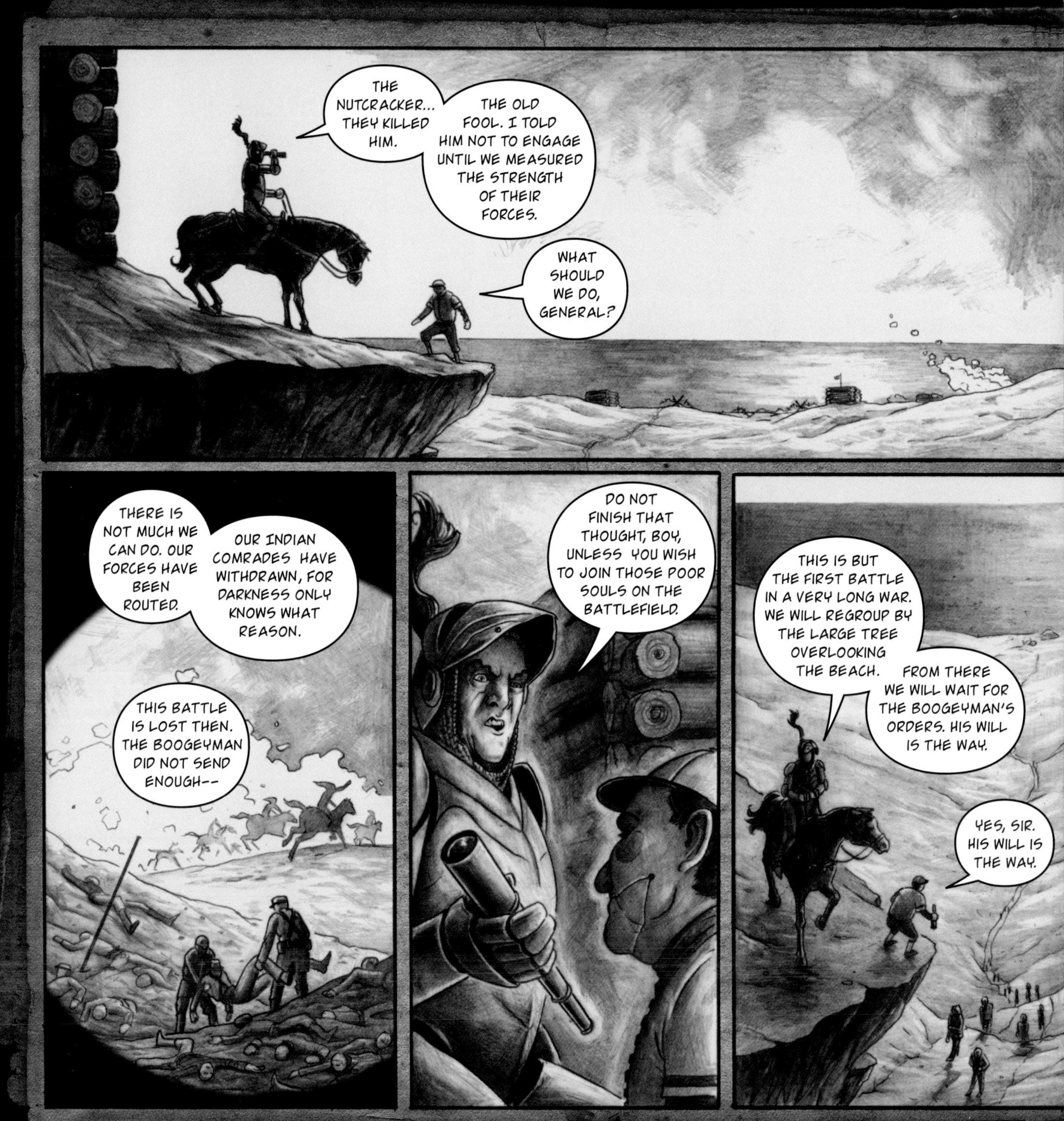
THE NUTCRACKER... THEY KILLED HIM.
THE OLD FOOL. I TOLD HIM NOT TO ENGAGE UNTIL WE MEASURED THE STRENGTH OF THEIR FORCES.
WHAT SHOULD WE DO, GENERAL?
THERE IS NOT MUCH WE CAN DO. OUR FORCES HAVE BEEN ROUTED.
OUR INDIAN COMRADES HAVE WITHDRAWN, FOR DARKNESS ONLY KNOWS WHAT REASON.
THIS BATTLE IS LOST THEN. THE BOOGEYMAN DID NOT SEND ENOUGH--
DO NOT FINISH THAT THOUGHT, BOY, UNLESS YOU WISH TO JOIN THOSE POOR SOULS ON THE BATTLEFIELD.
THIS IS BUT THE FIRST BATTLE IN A VERY LONG WAR. WE WILL REGROUP BY THE LARGE TREE OVERLOOKING THE BEACH.
FROM THERE WE WILL WAIT FOR THE BOOGEYMAN'S ORDERS. HIS WILL IS THE WAY.
YES, SIR. HIS WILL IS THE WAY.

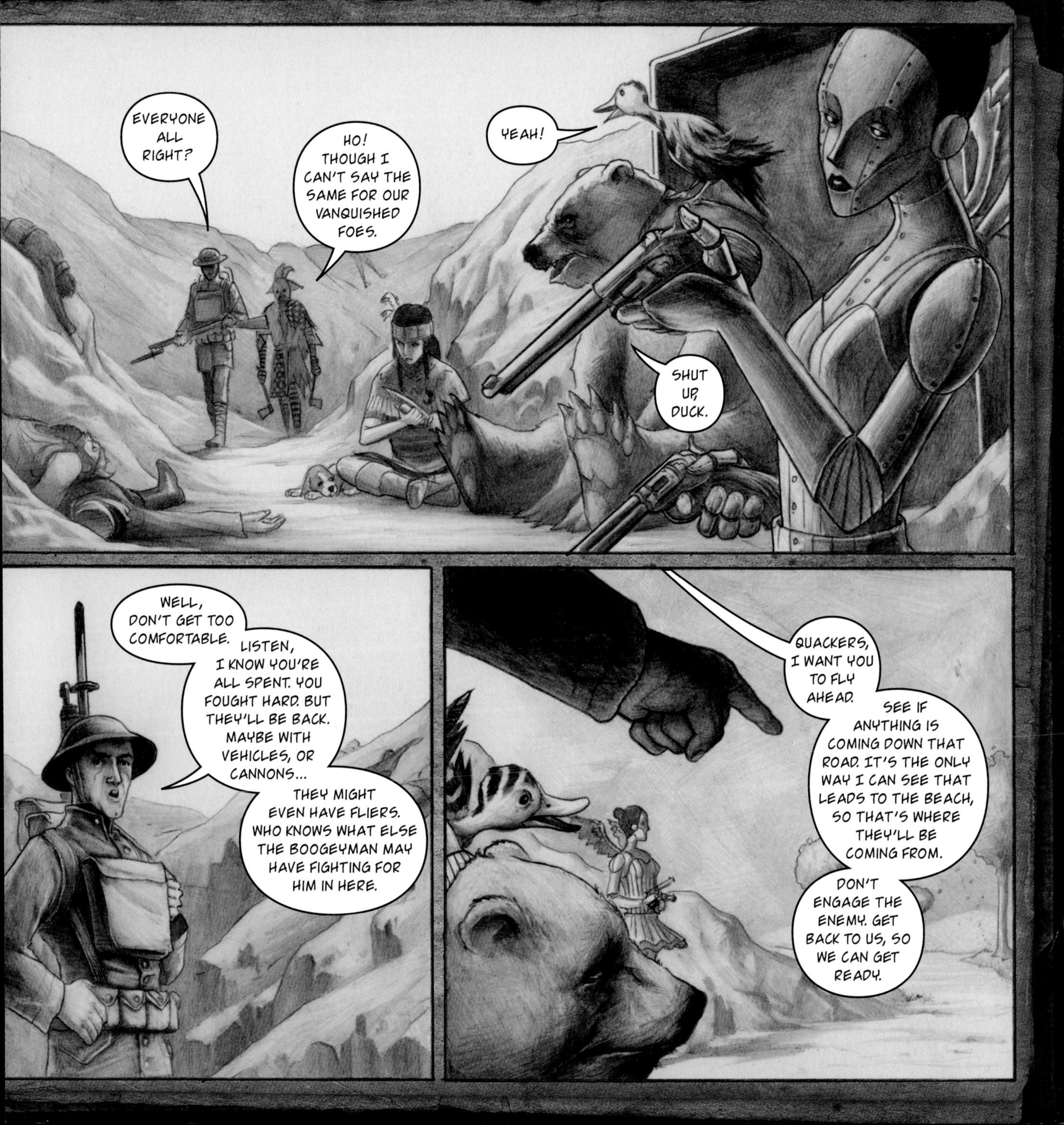
EVERYONE ALL RIGHT?
HO! THOUGH I CAN'T SAY THE SAME FOR OUR VANQUISHED FOES.
YEAH!
SHUT UP, DUCK.
WELL, DON'T GET TOO COMFORTABLE.
LISTEN, I KNOW YOU'RE ALL SPENT. YOU FOUGHT HARD. BUT THEY'LL BE BACK. MAYBE WITH VEHICLES, OR CANNONS...
THEY MIGHT EVEN HAVE FLIERS. WHO KNOWS WHAT ELSE THE BOOGEYMAN MAY HAVE FIGHTING FOR HIM IN HERE.
QUACKERS, I WANT YOU TO FLY AHEAD.
SEE IF ANYTHING IS COMING DOWN THAT ROAD. IT'S THE ONLY WAY I CAN SEE THAT LEADS TO THE BEACH, SO THAT'S WHERE THEY'LL BE COMING FROM.
DON'T ENGAGE THE ENEMY. GET BACK TO US, SO WE CAN GET READY.

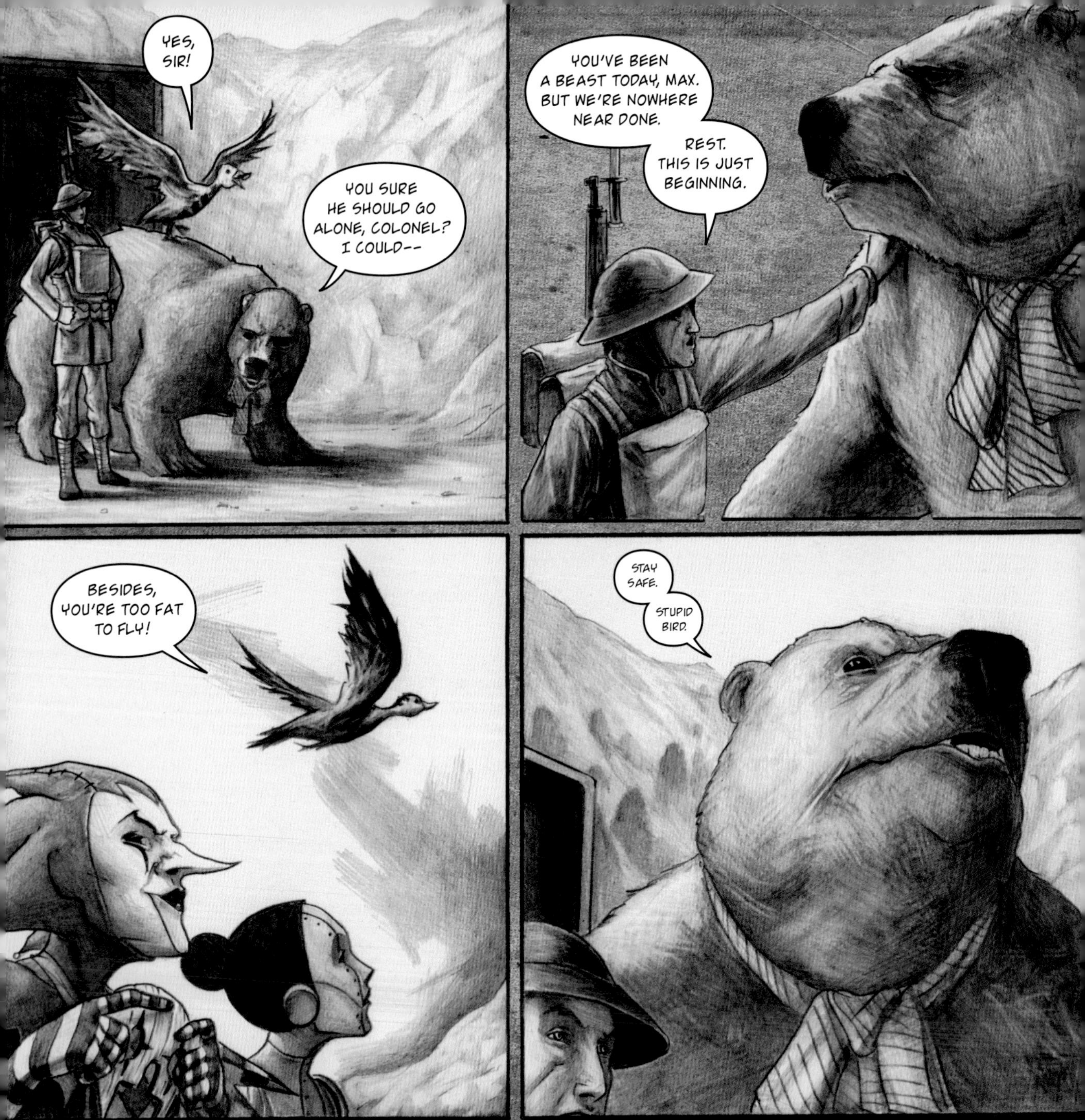
YES, SIR!
YOU SURE HE SHOULD GO ALONE, COLONEL? I COULD--
YOU'VE BEEN A BEAST TODAY, MAX. BUT WE'RE NOWHERE NEAR DONE.
REST. THIS IS JUST BEGINNING.
BESIDES, YOU'RE TOO FAT TO FLY!
STAY SAFE.
STUPID BIRD.

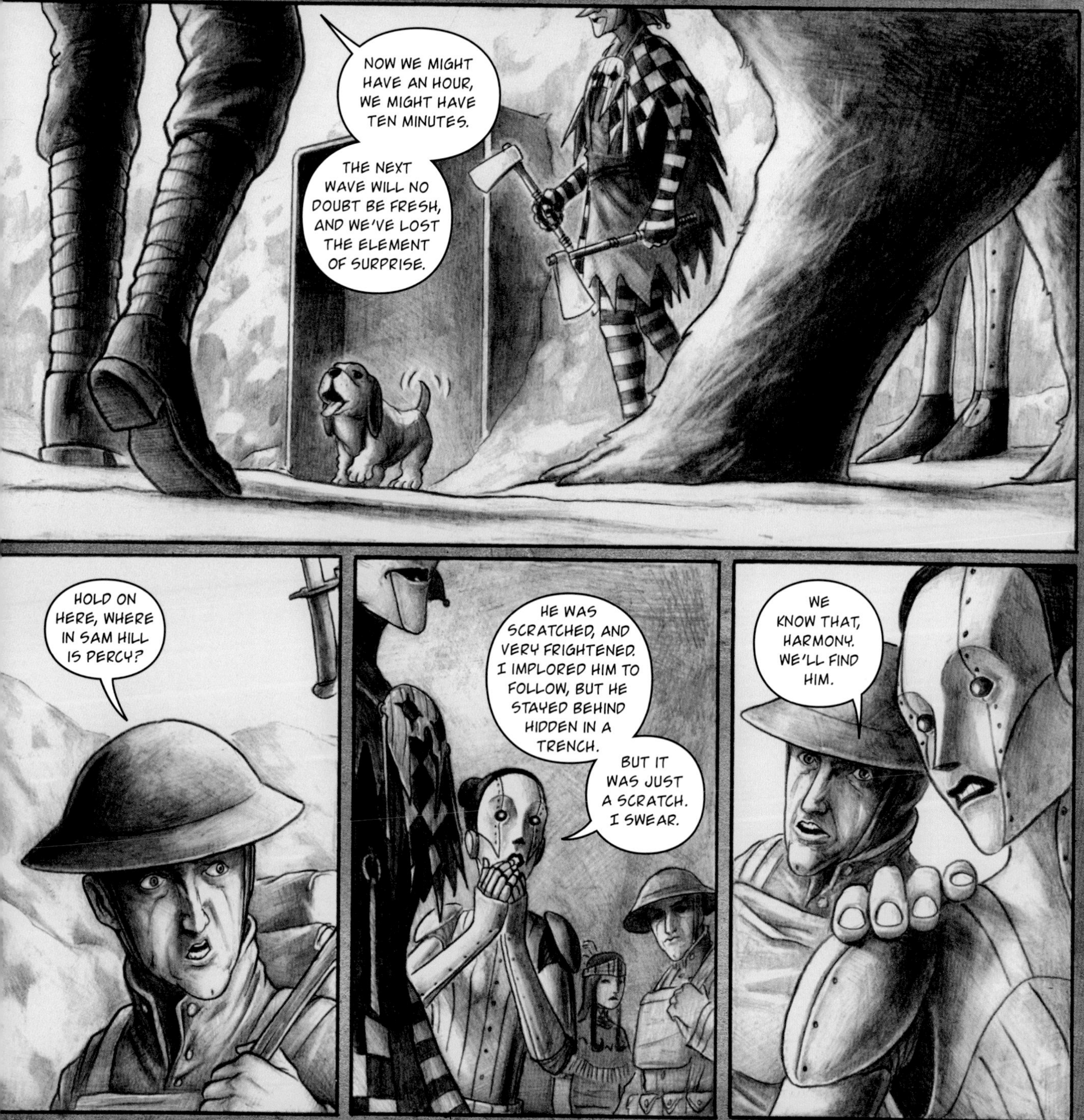
NOW WE MIGHT HAVE AN HOUR, WE MIGHT HAVE TEN MINUTES.
THE NEXT WAVE WILL NO DOUBT BE FRESH, AND WE'VE LOST THE ELEMENT OF SURPRISE.
HOLD ON HERE, WHERE IN SAM HILL IS PERCY?
HE WAS SCRATCHED, AND VERY FRIGHTENED. I IMPLORED HIM TO FOLLOW, BUT HE STAYED BEHIND HIDDEN IN A TRENCH.
BUT IT WAS JUST A SCRATCH. I SWEAR.
WE KNOW THAT, HARMONY. WE'LL FIND HIM.

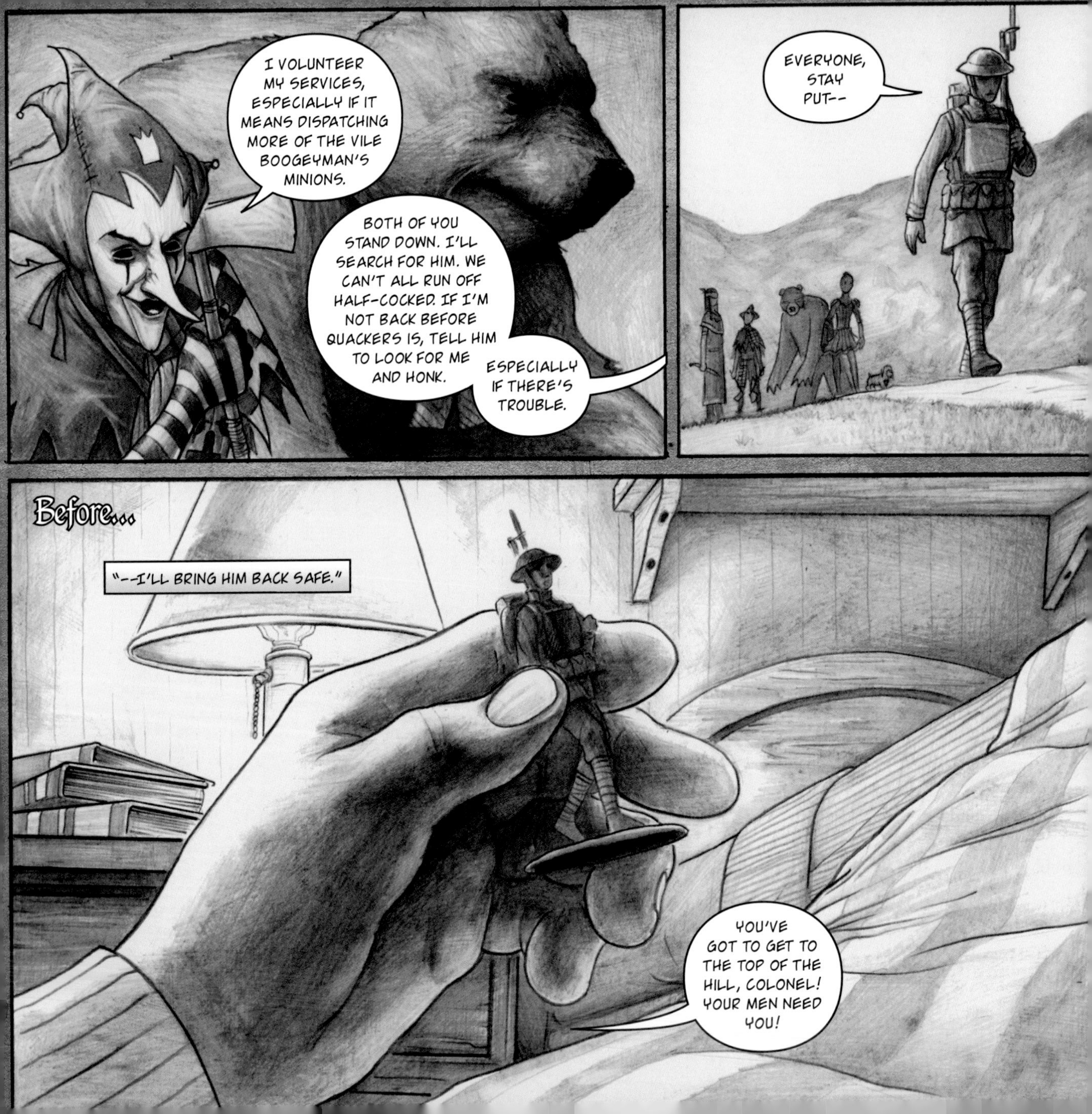
I VOLUNTEER MY SERVICES, ESPECIALLY IF IT MEANS DISPATCHING MORE OF THE VILE BOOGEYMAN'S MINIONS.
BOTH OF YOU STAND DOWN. I'LL SEARCH FOR HIM. WE CAN'T ALL RUN OFF HALF-COCKED. IF I'M NOT BACK BEFORE QUACKERS IS, TELL HIM TO LOOK FOR ME AND HONK.
ESPECIALLY IF THERE'S TROUBLE.
EVERYONE, STAY PUT--
Before...
"--I'LL BRING HIM BACK SAFE."
YOU'VE GOT TO GET TO THE TOP OF THE HILL, COLONEL! YOUR MEN NEED YOU!

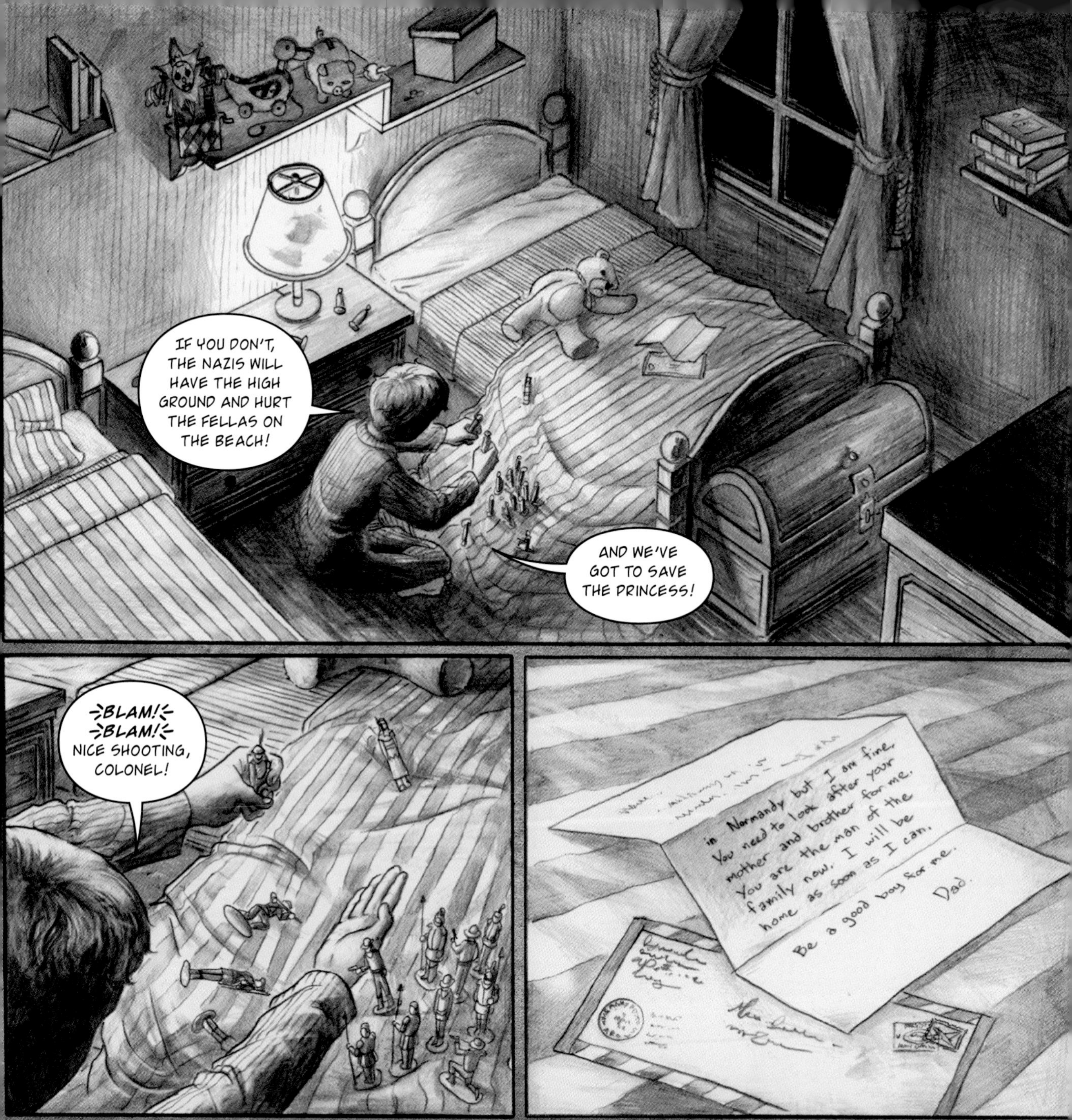
IF YOU DON'T, THE NAZIS WILL HAVE THE HIGH GROUND AND HURT THE FELLAS ON THE BEACH!
AND WE'VE GOT TO SAVE THE PRINCESS!
BLAM! BLAM! NICE SHOOTING, COLONEL!
in Normandy but I am fine. You need to look after your mother and brother for me. You are the man of the family now. I will be home as soon as I can.
Be a good boy for me.
Dad.

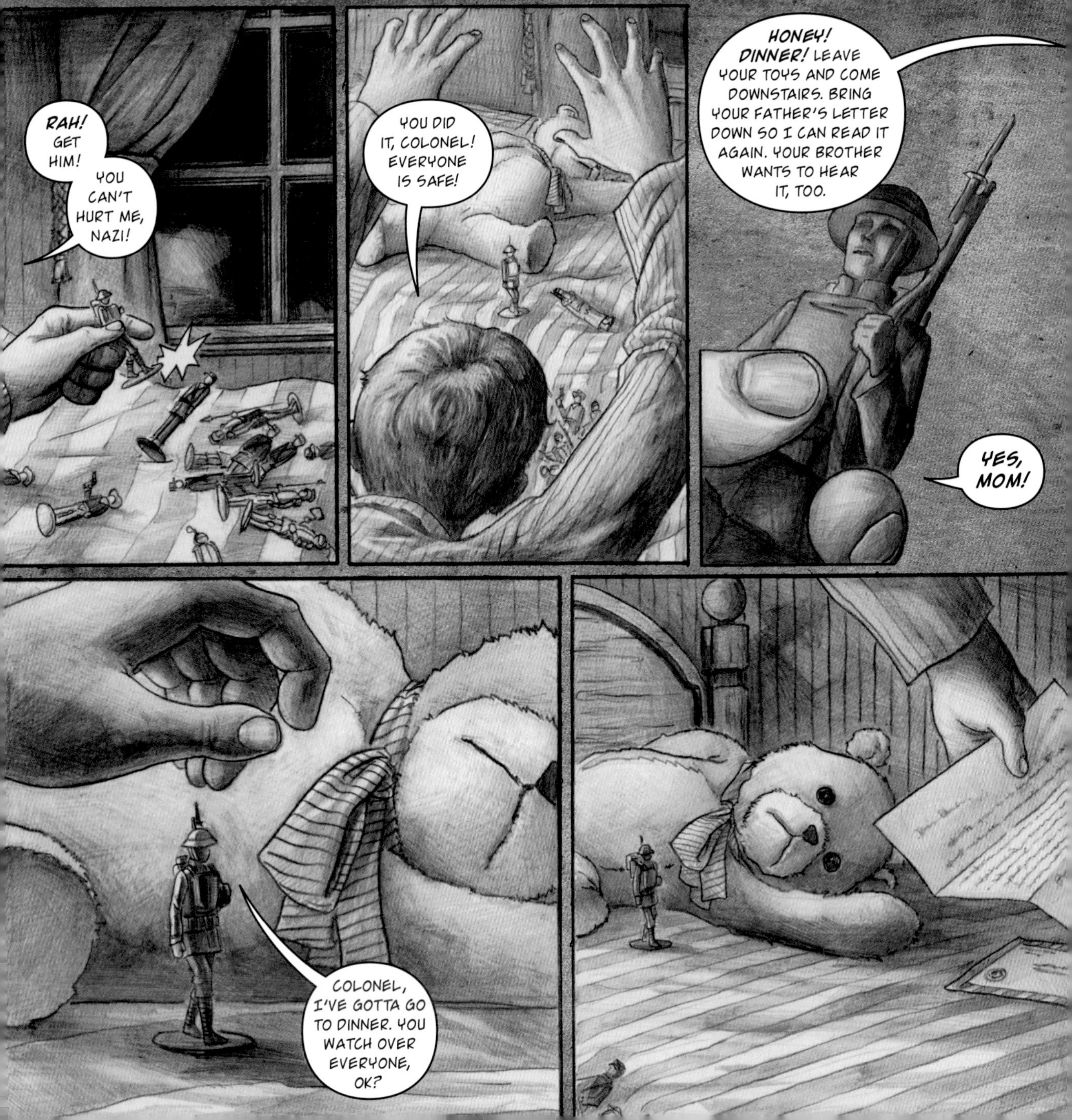
RAH! GET HIM!
YOU CAN'T HURT ME, NAZI!
YOU DID IT, COLONEL! EVERYONE IS SAFE!
HONEY! DINNER! LEAVE YOUR TOYS AND COME DOWNSTAIRS. BRING YOUR FATHER'S LETTER DOWN SO I CAN READ IT AGAIN. YOUR BROTHER WANTS TO HEAR IT, TOO.
YES, MOM!
COLONEL, I'VE GOTTA GO TO DINNER. YOU WATCH OVER EVERYONE, OK?

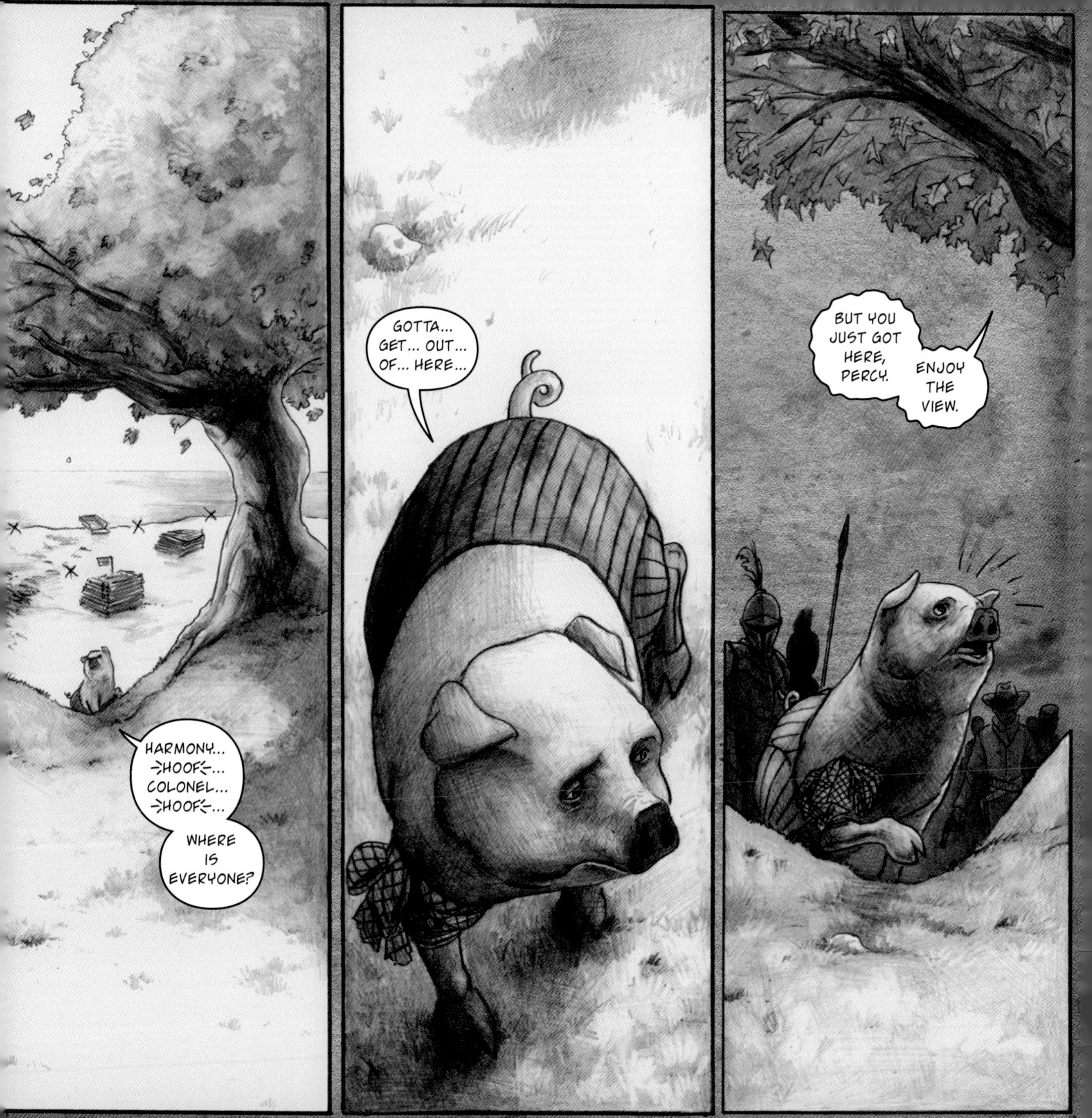
HARMONY... ⇉HOOF⇇... COLONEL... ⇉HOOF⇇...
WHERE IS EVERYONE?
GOTTA... GET... OUT... OF... HERE...
BUT YOU JUST GOT HERE, PERCY.
ENJOY THE VIEW.

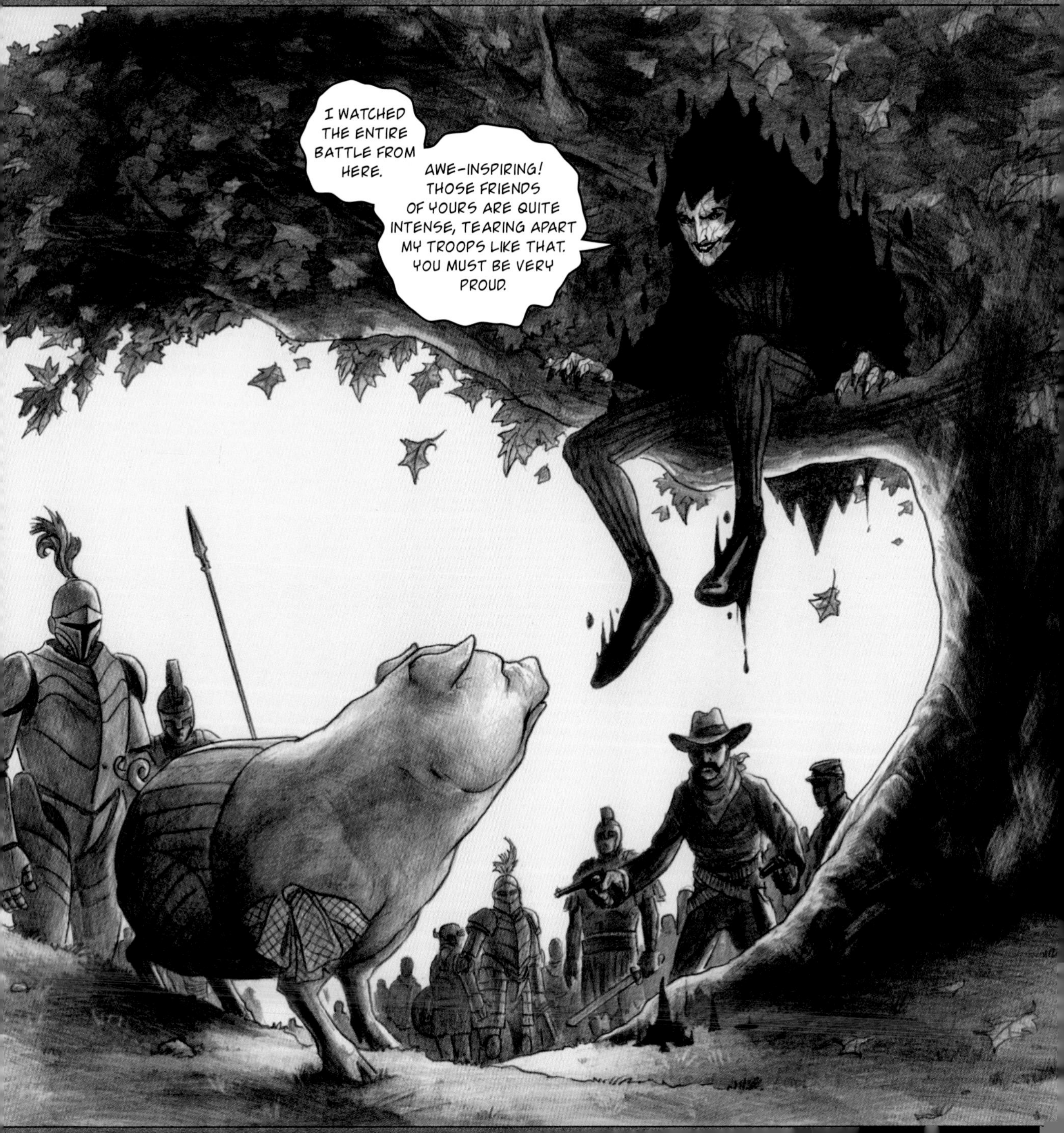
I WATCHED THE ENTIRE BATTLE FROM HERE.
AWE-INSPIRING! THOSE FRIENDS OF YOURS ARE QUITE INTENSE, TEARING APART MY TROOPS LIKE THAT. YOU MUST BE VERY PROUD.

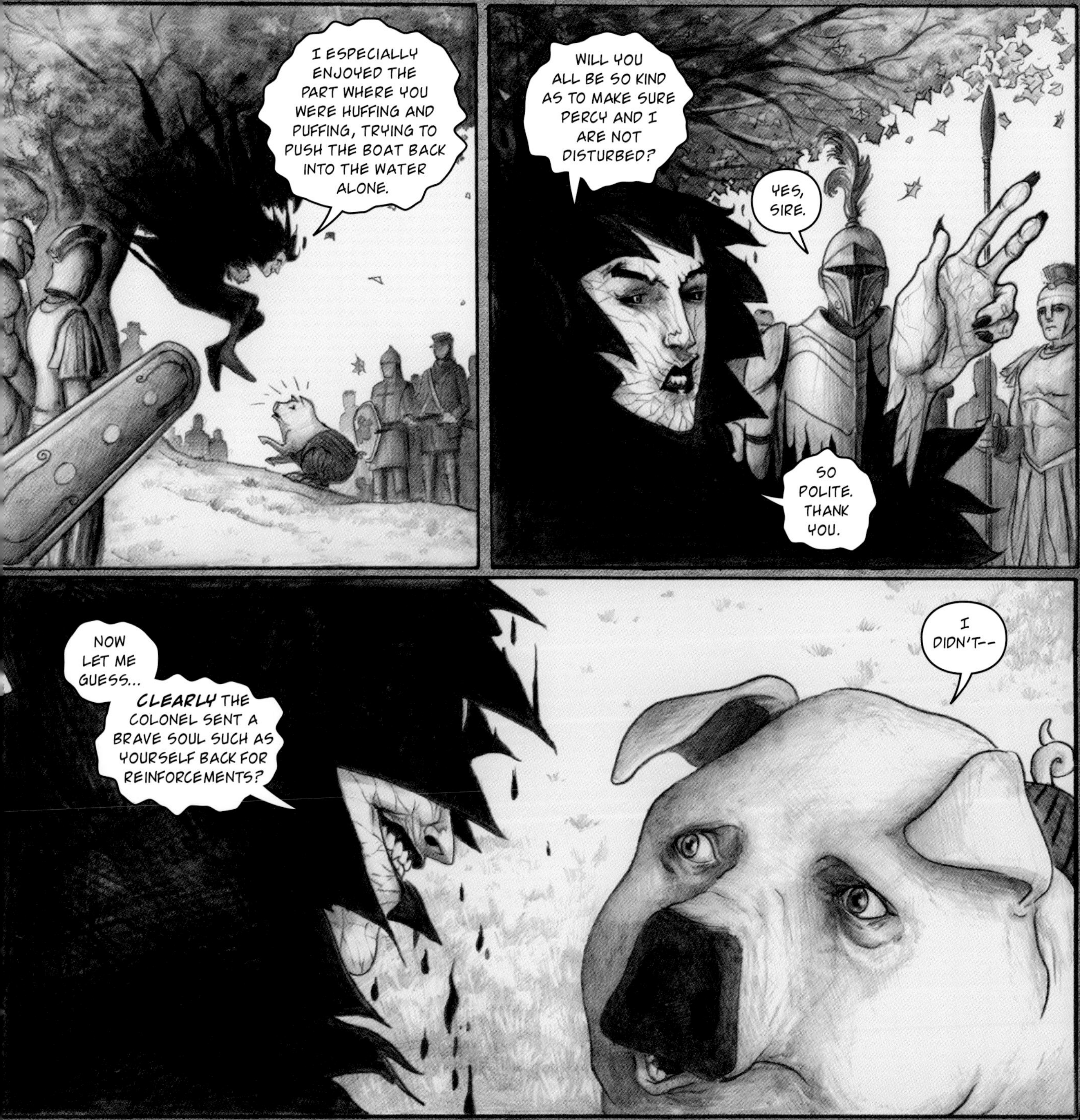
I ESPECIALLY ENJOYED THE PART WHERE YOU WERE HUFFING AND PUFFING, TRYING TO PUSH THE BOAT BACK INTO THE WATER ALONE.
WILL YOU ALL BE SO KIND AS TO MAKE SURE PERCY AND I ARE NOT DISTURBED?
YES, SIRE.
SO POLITE. THANK YOU.
NOW LET ME GUESS...
CLEARLY THE COLONEL SENT A BRAVE SOUL SUCH AS YOURSELF BACK FOR REINFORCEMENTS?
I DIDN'T--

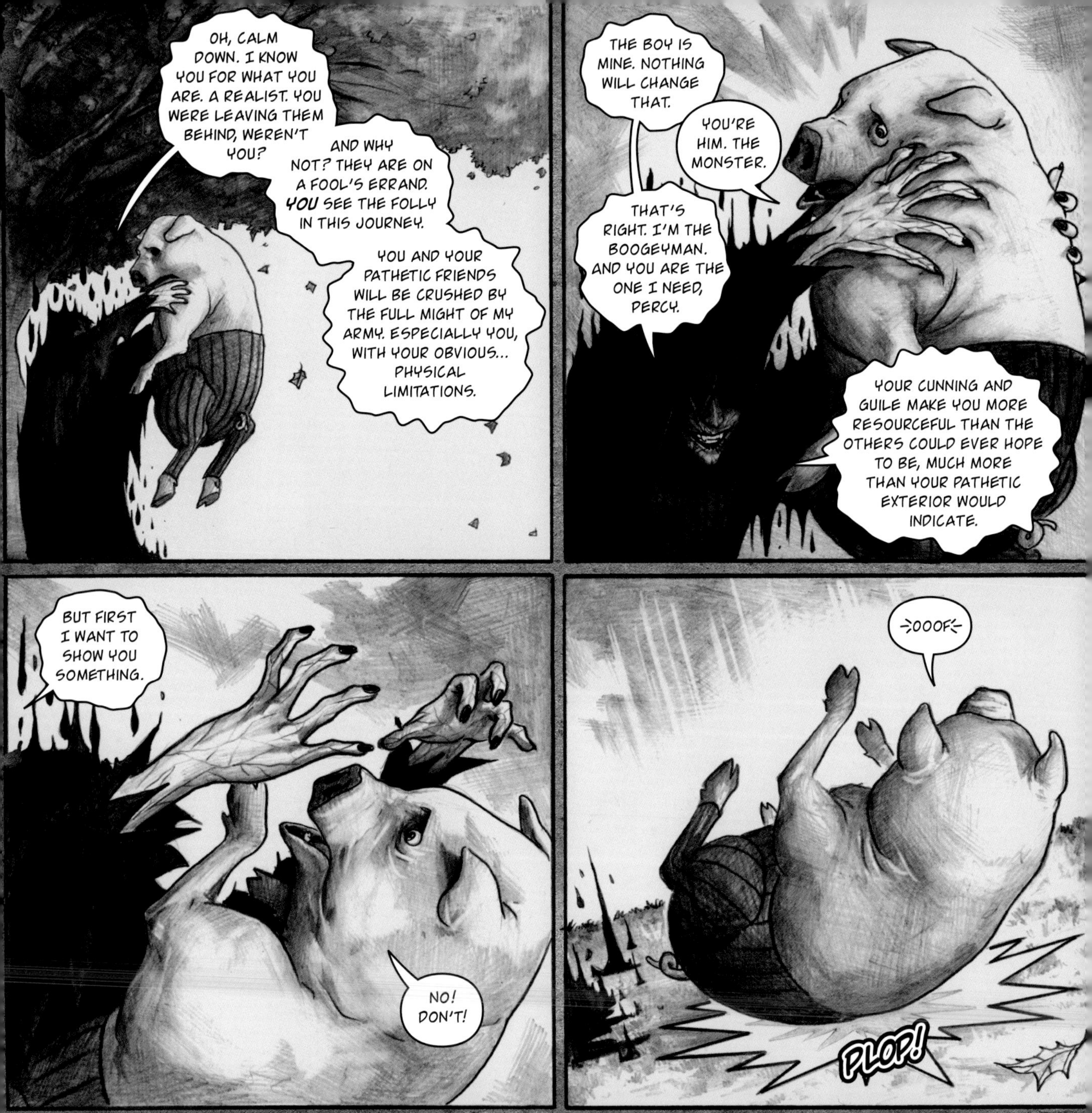
OH, CALM DOWN. I KNOW YOU FOR WHAT YOU ARE. A REALIST. YOU WERE LEAVING THEM BEHIND, WEREN'T YOU?
AND WHY NOT? THEY ARE ON A FOOL'S ERRAND. YOU SEE THE FOLLY IN THIS JOURNEY.
YOU AND YOUR PATHETIC FRIENDS WILL BE CRUSHED BY THE FULL MIGHT OF MY ARMY. ESPECIALLY YOU, WITH YOUR OBVIOUS... PHYSICAL LIMITATIONS.
THE BOY IS MINE. NOTHING WILL CHANGE THAT.
YOU'RE HIM. THE MONSTER.
THAT'S RIGHT. I'M THE BOOGEYMAN. AND YOU ARE THE ONE I NEED, PERCY.
YOUR CUNNING AND GUILE MAKE YOU MORE RESOURCEFUL THAN THE OTHERS COULD EVER HOPE TO BE, MUCH MORE THAN YOUR PATHETIC EXTERIOR WOULD INDICATE.
BUT FIRST I WANT TO SHOW YOU SOMETHING.
NO! DON'T!
OOOF
PLOP!

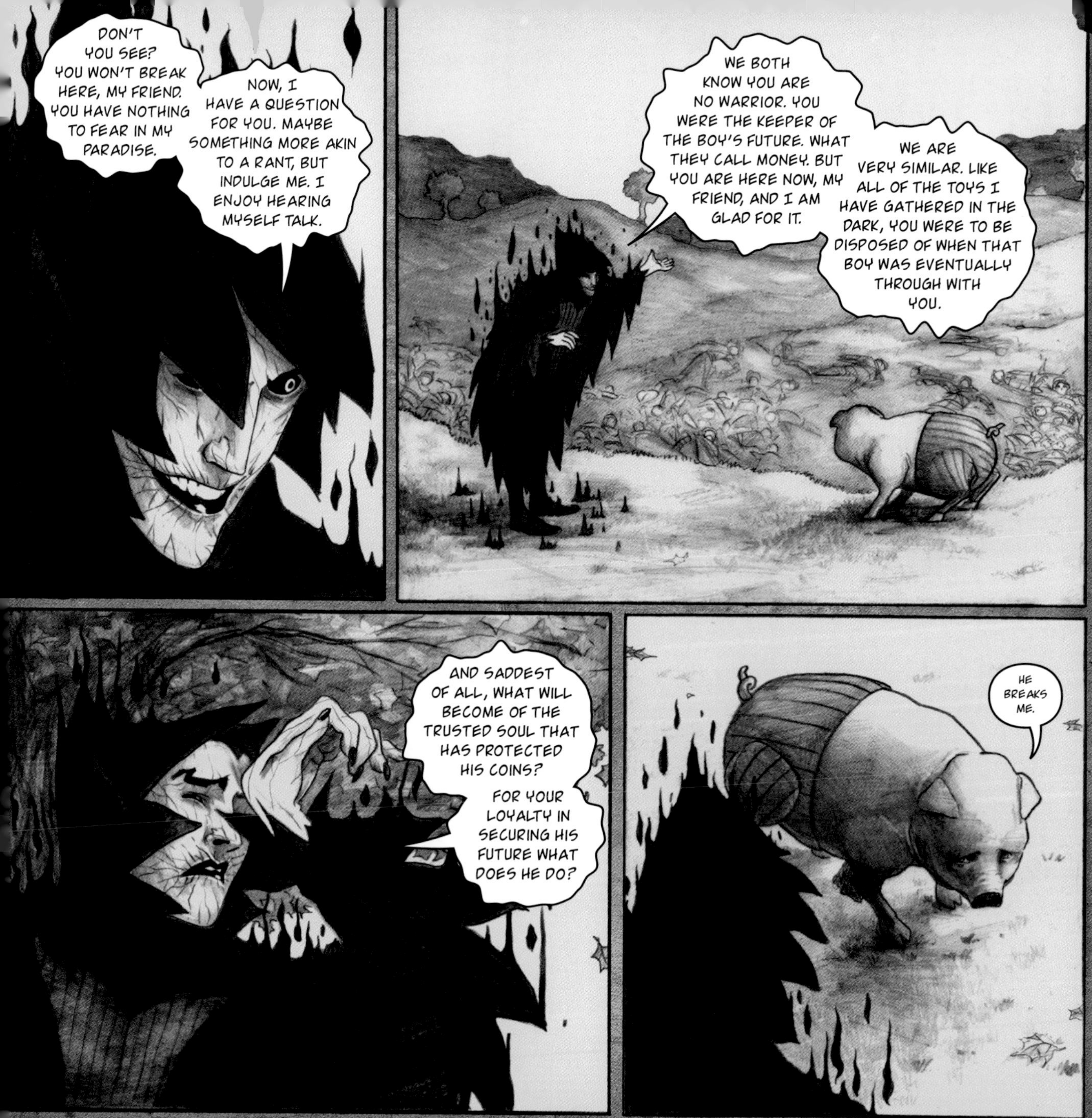
DON'T YOU SEE? YOU WON'T BREAK HERE, MY FRIEND. YOU HAVE NOTHING TO FEAR IN MY PARADISE.
NOW, I HAVE A QUESTION FOR YOU. MAYBE SOMETHING MORE AKIN TO A RANT, BUT INDULGE ME. I ENJOY HEARING MYSELF TALK.
WE BOTH KNOW YOU ARE NO WARRIOR. YOU WERE THE KEEPER OF THE BOY'S FUTURE. WHAT THEY CALL MONEY. BUT YOU ARE HERE NOW, MY FRIEND, AND I AM GLAD FOR IT.
WE ARE VERY SIMILAR. LIKE ALL OF THE TOYS I HAVE GATHERED IN THE DARK, YOU WERE TO BE DISPOSED OF WHEN THAT BOY WAS EVENTUALLY THROUGH WITH YOU.
AND SADDEST OF ALL, WHAT WILL BECOME OF THE TRUSTED SOUL THAT HAS PROTECTED HIS COINS?
FOR YOUR LOYALTY IN SECURING HIS FUTURE WHAT DOES HE DO?
HE BREAKS ME.

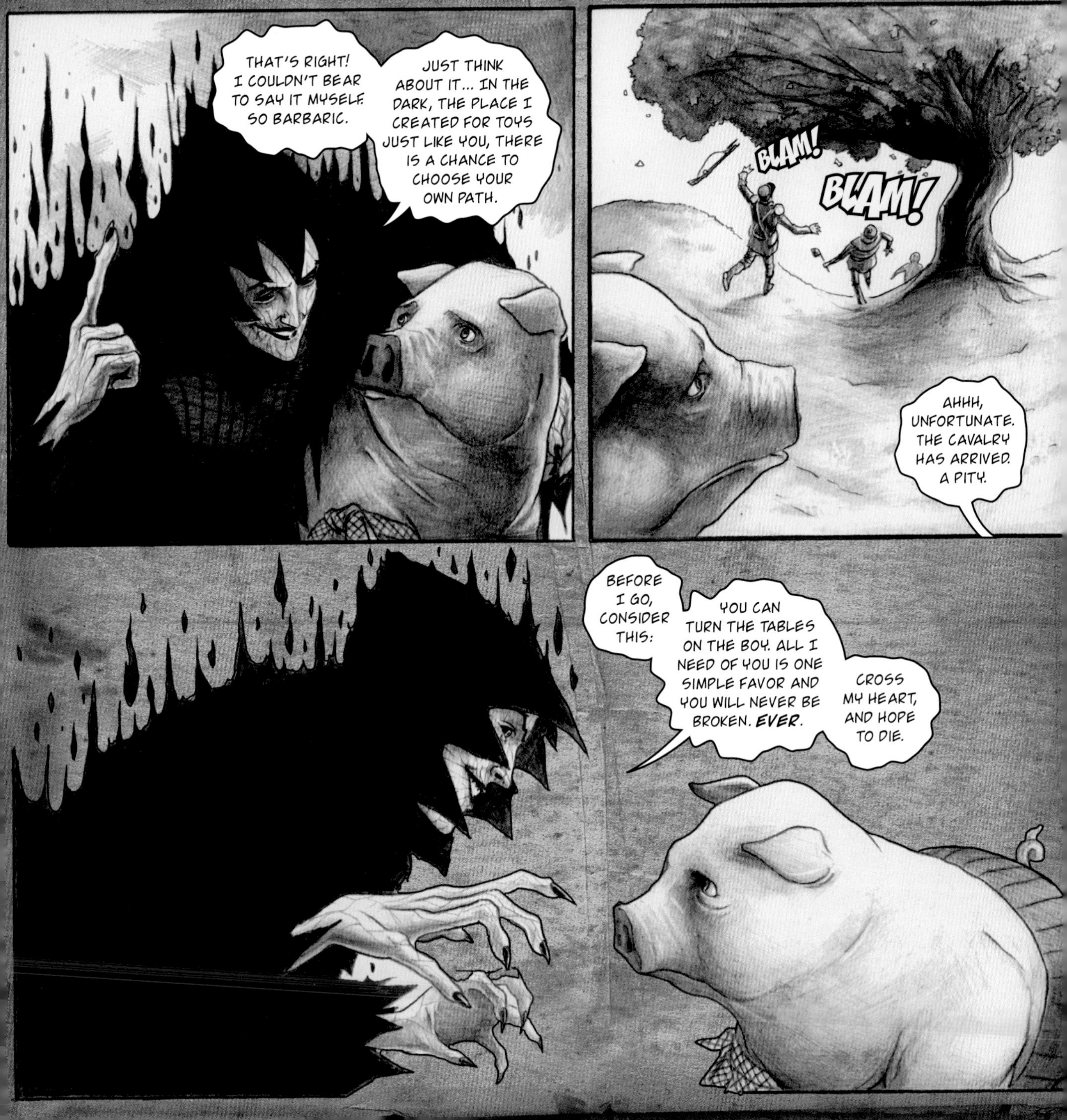
THAT'S RIGHT! I COULDN'T BEAR TO SAY IT MYSELF. SO BARBARIC.
JUST THINK ABOUT IT... IN THE DARK, THE PLACE I CREATED FOR TOYS JUST LIKE YOU, THERE IS A CHANCE TO CHOOSE YOUR OWN PATH.
BLAM!
BLAM!
AHHH, UNFORTUNATE. THE CAVALRY HAS ARRIVED. A PITY.
BEFORE I GO, CONSIDER THIS:
YOU CAN TURN THE TABLES ON THE BOY. ALL I NEED OF YOU IS ONE SIMPLE FAVOR AND YOU WILL NEVER BE BROKEN. ***EVER***.
CROSS MY HEART, AND HOPE TO DIE.

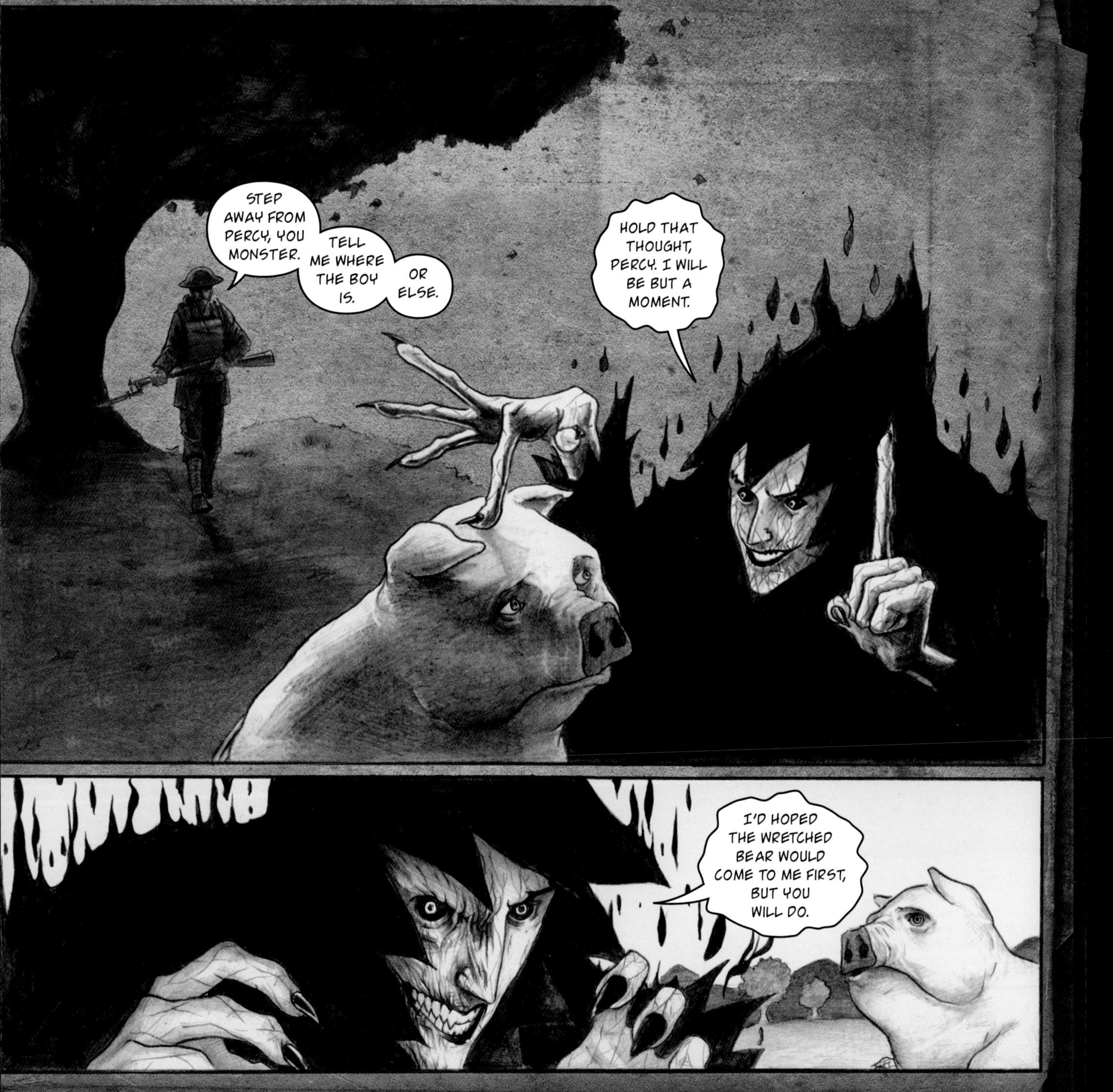
STEP AWAY FROM PERCY, YOU MONSTER.
TELL ME WHERE THE BOY IS.
OR ELSE.
HOLD THAT THOUGHT, PERCY. I WILL BE BUT A MOMENT.
I'D HOPED THE WRETCHED BEAR WOULD COME TO ME FIRST, BUT YOU WILL DO.

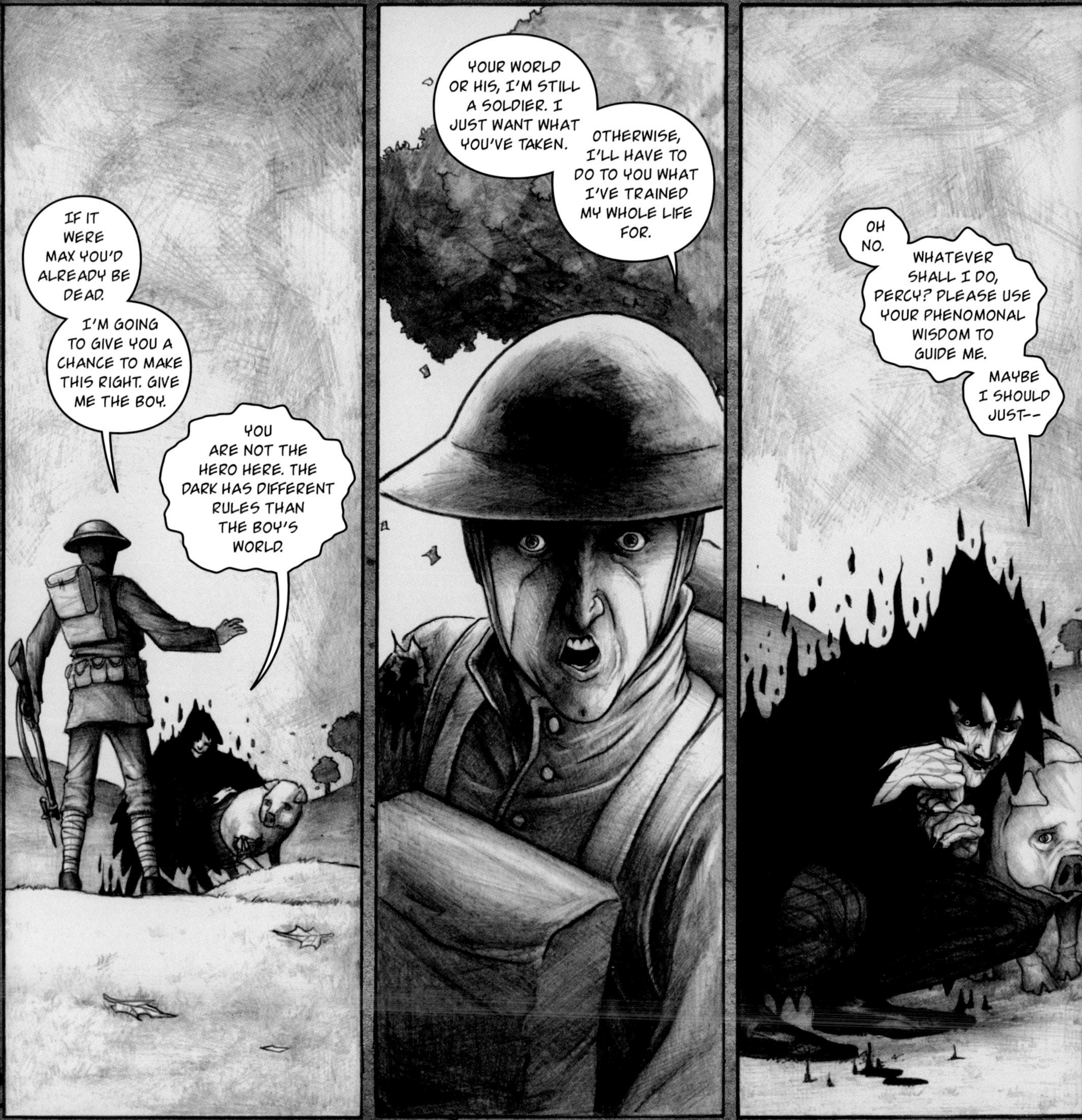
IF IT WERE MAX YOU'D ALREADY BE DEAD.
I'M GOING TO GIVE YOU A CHANCE TO MAKE THIS RIGHT. GIVE ME THE BOY.
YOU ARE NOT THE HERO HERE. THE DARK HAS DIFFERENT RULES THAN THE BOY'S WORLD.
YOUR WORLD OR HIS, I'M STILL A SOLDIER. I JUST WANT WHAT YOU'VE TAKEN.
OTHERWISE, I'LL HAVE TO DO TO YOU WHAT I'VE TRAINED MY WHOLE LIFE FOR.
OH NO.
WHATEVER SHALL I DO, PERCY? PLEASE USE YOUR PHENOMONAL WISDOM TO GUIDE ME.
MAYBE I SHOULD JUST--

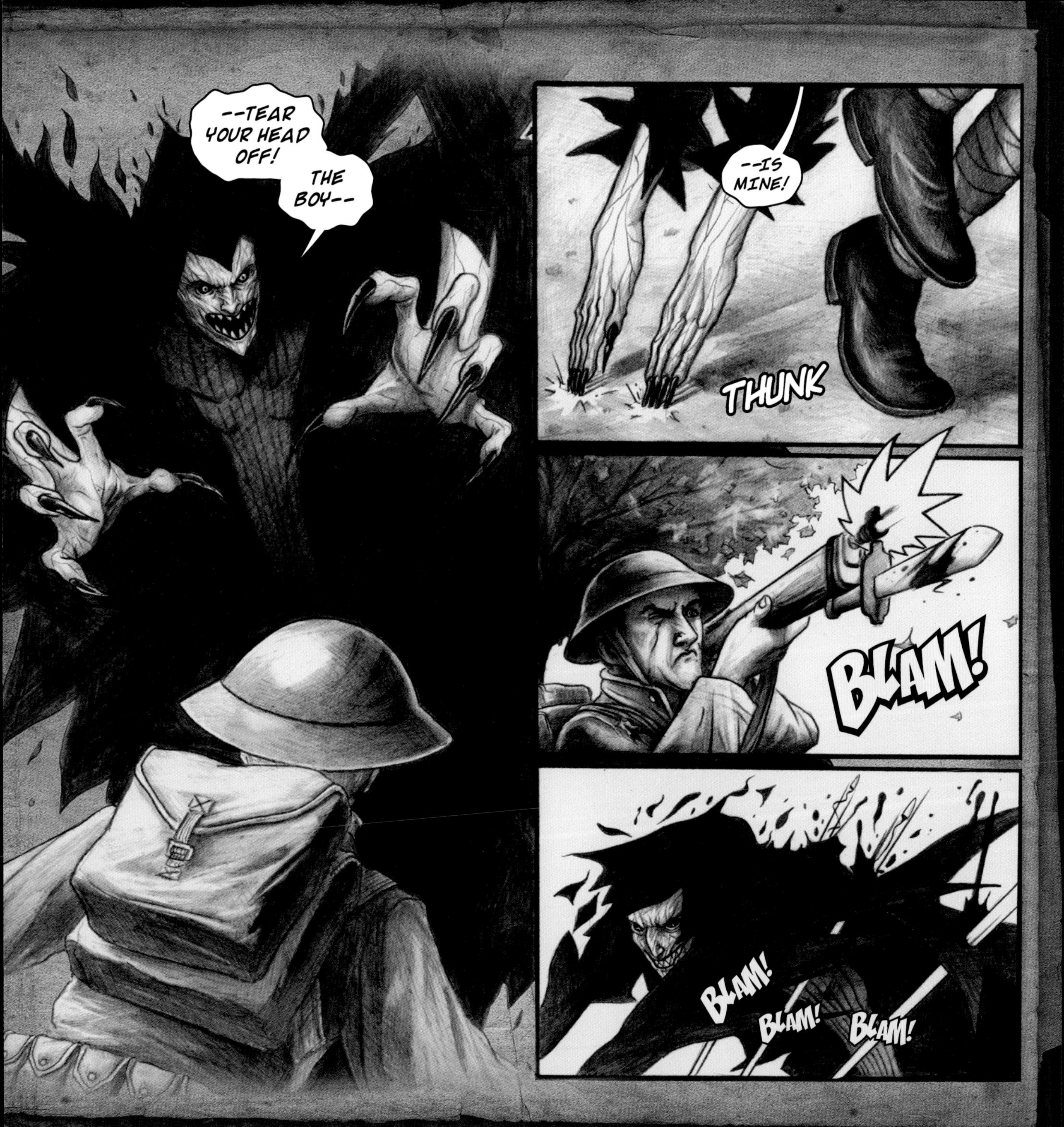
--TEAR YOUR HEAD OFF!
THE BOY--
--IS MINE!
THUNK
BLAM!
BLAM!
BLAM!
BLAM!

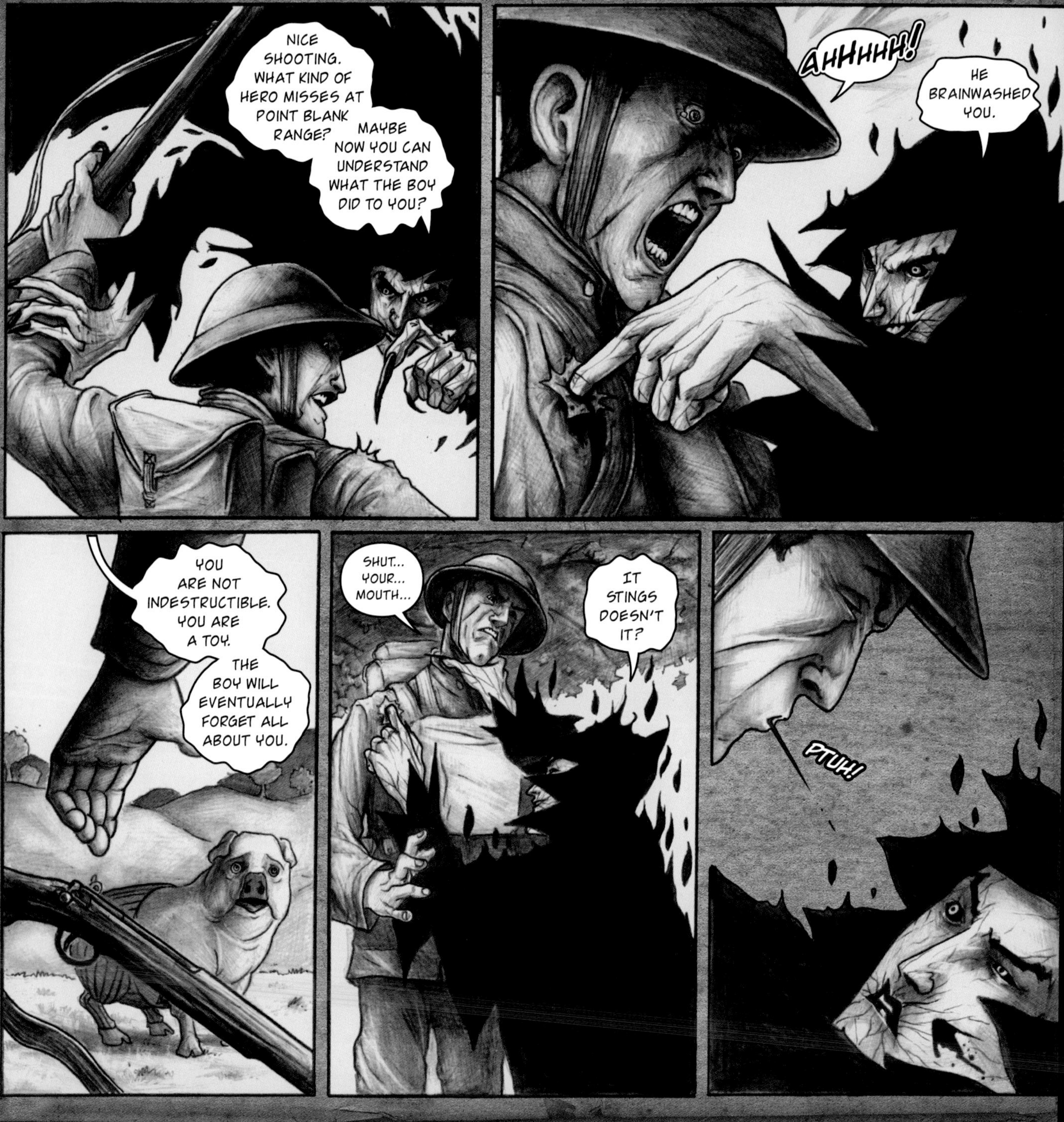
NICE SHOOTING. WHAT KIND OF HERO MISSES AT POINT BLANK RANGE?
MAYBE NOW YOU CAN UNDERSTAND WHAT THE BOY DID TO YOU?
AHHHHH!
HE BRAINWASHED YOU.
YOU ARE NOT INDESTRUCTIBLE. YOU ARE A TOY.
THE BOY WILL EVENTUALLY FORGET ALL ABOUT YOU.
SHUT... YOUR... MOUTH...
IT STINGS DOESN'T IT?
PTUH!

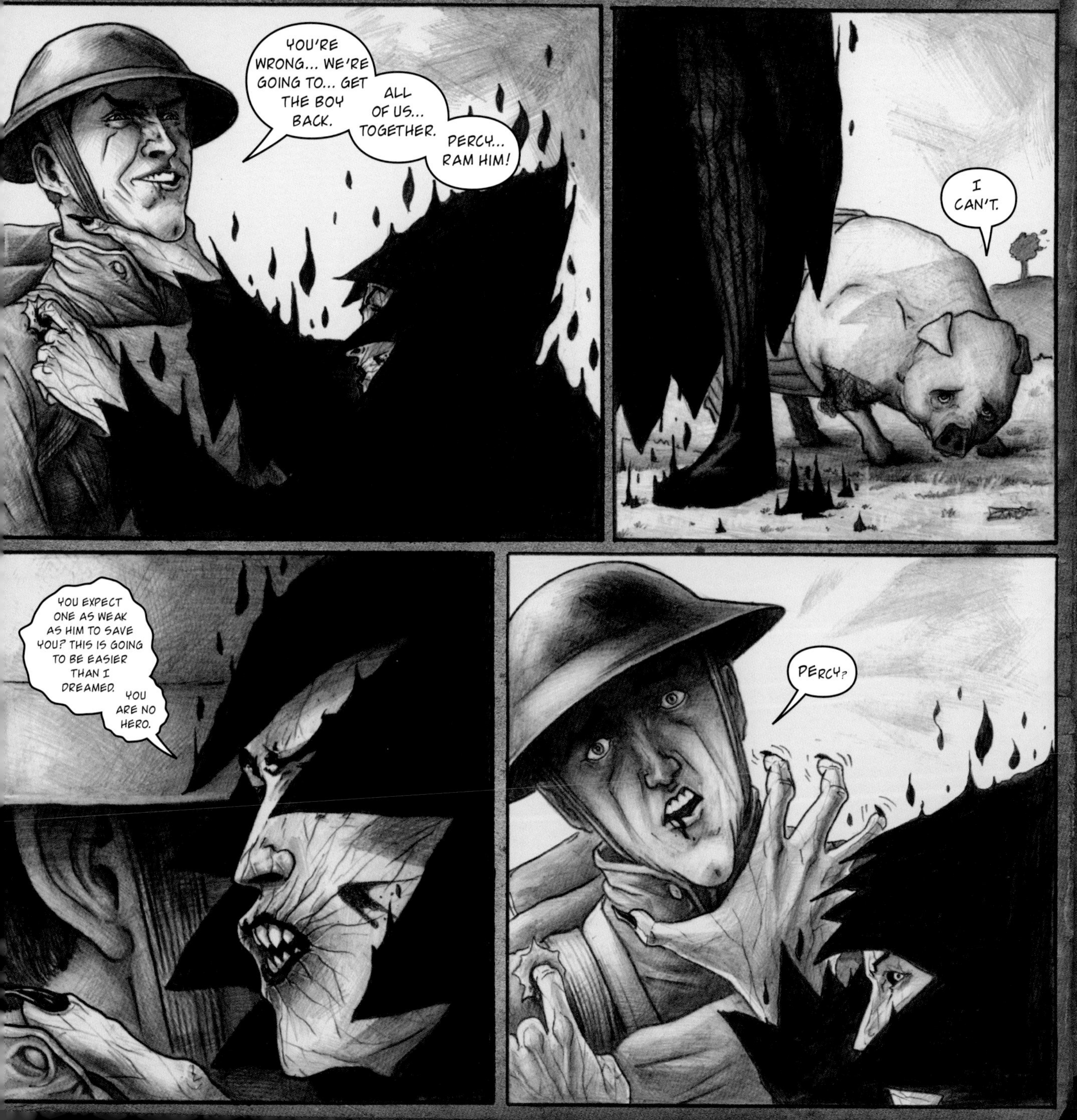
YOU'RE WRONG... WE'RE GOING TO... GET THE BOY BACK.
ALL OF US... TOGETHER.
PERCY... RAM HIM!
I CAN'T.
YOU EXPECT ONE AS WEAK AS HIM TO SAVE YOU? THIS IS GOING TO BE EASIER THAN I DREAMED.
YOU ARE NO HERO.
PERCY?

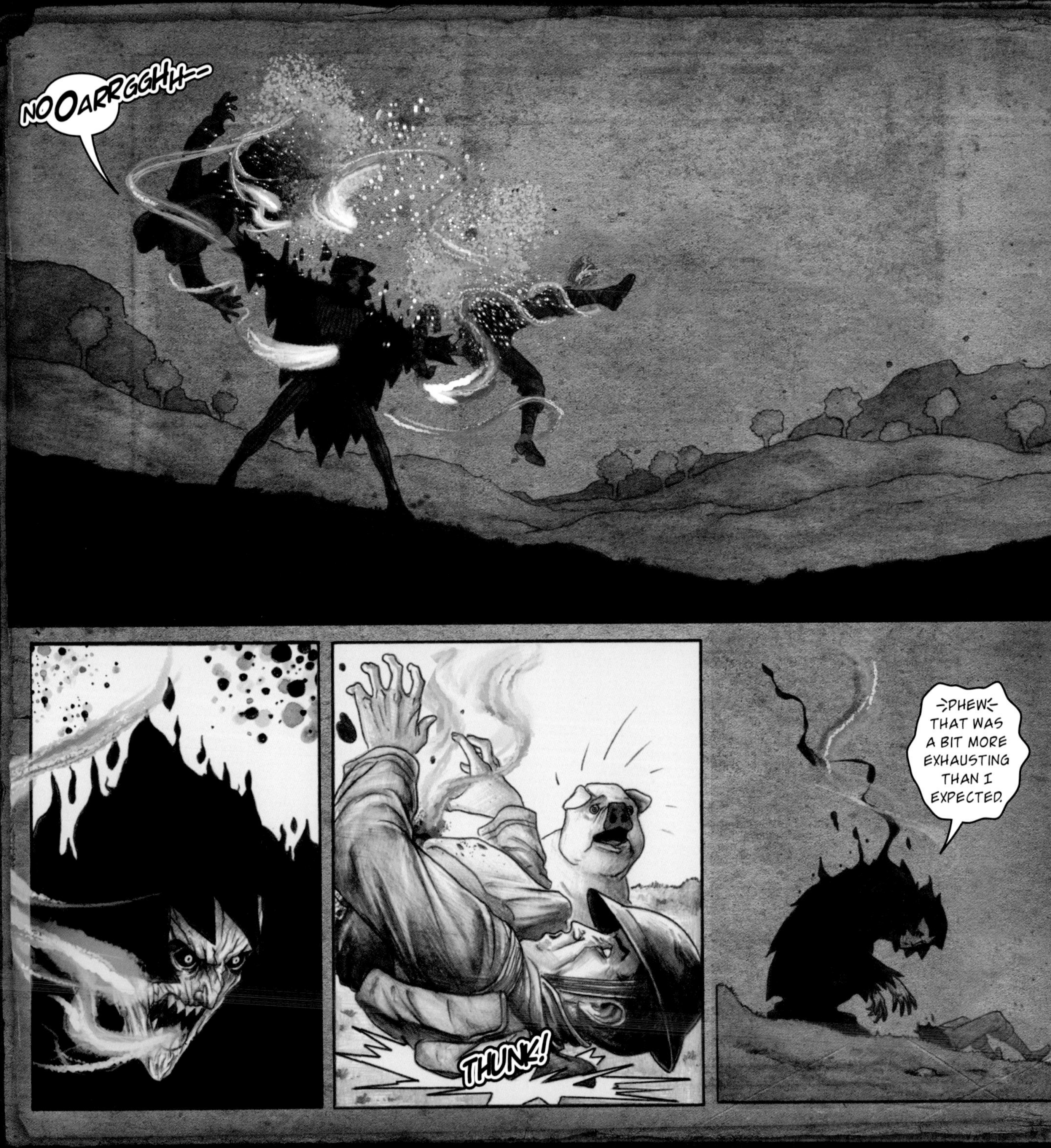
NOOARRGGHH--
THUNK!
PHEW
THAT WAS A BIT MORE EXHAUSTING THAN I EXPECTED.

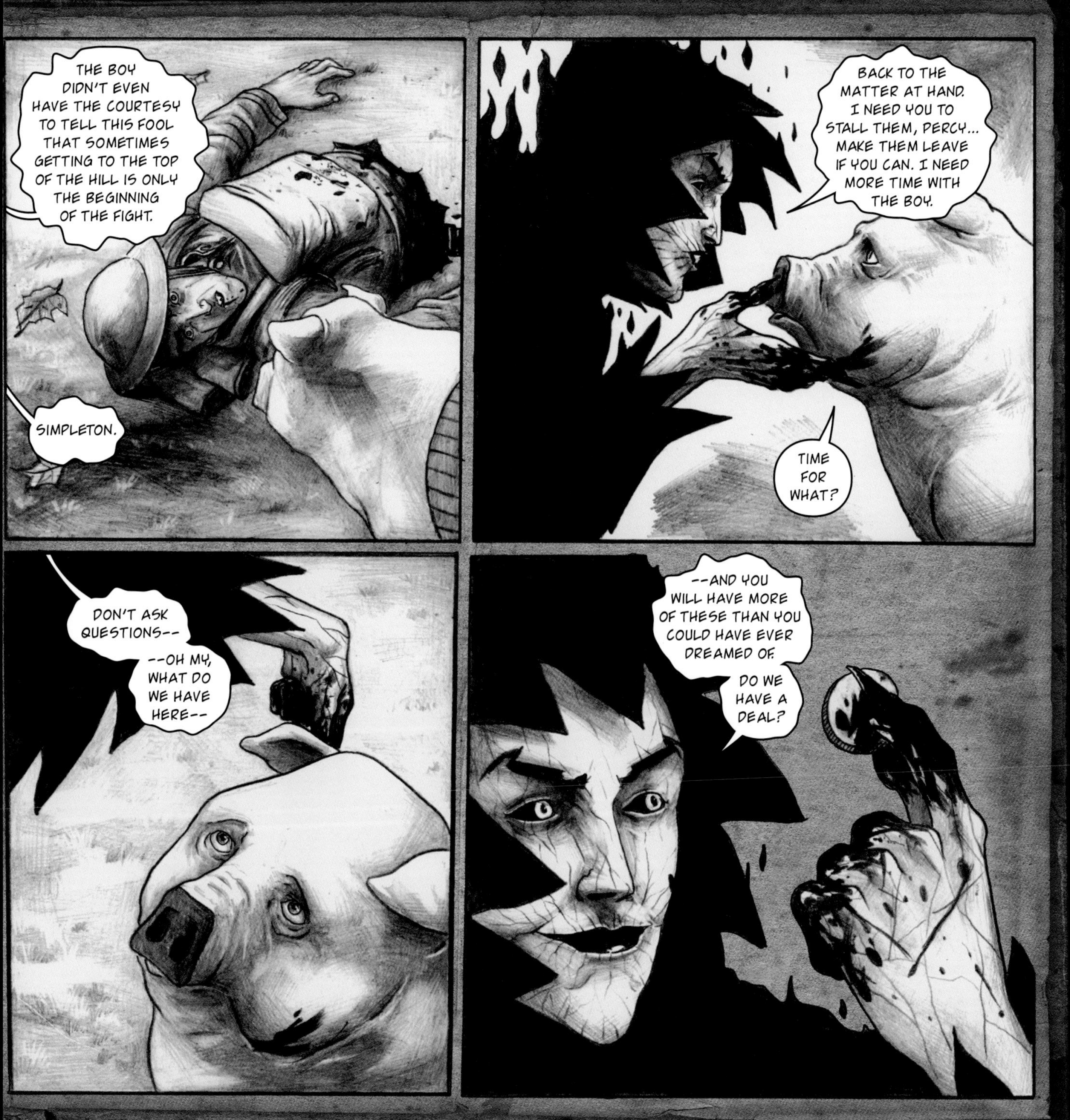
THE BOY DIDN'T EVEN HAVE THE COURTESY TO TELL THIS FOOL THAT SOMETIMES GETTING TO THE TOP OF THE HILL IS ONLY THE BEGINNING OF THE FIGHT.
SIMPLETON.
BACK TO THE MATTER AT HAND. I NEED YOU TO STALL THEM, PERCY... MAKE THEM LEAVE IF YOU CAN. I NEED MORE TIME WITH THE BOY.
TIME FOR WHAT?
DON'T ASK QUESTIONS--
--OH MY, WHAT DO WE HAVE HERE--
--AND YOU WILL HAVE MORE OF THESE THAN YOU COULD HAVE EVER DREAMED OF.
DO WE HAVE A DEAL?

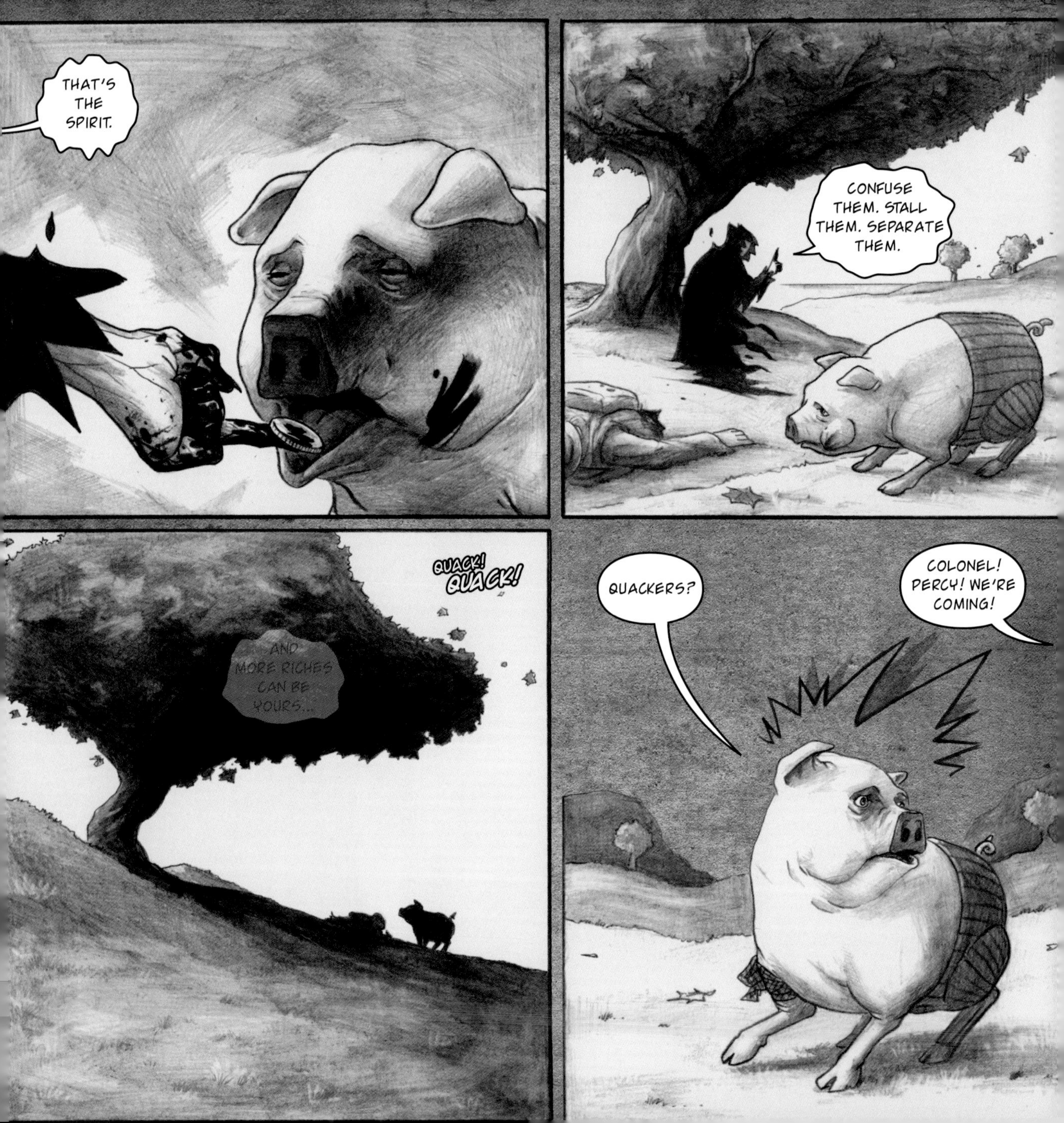
THAT'S THE SPIRIT.
CONFUSE THEM. STALL THEM. SEPARATE THEM.
QUACK! QUACK!
AND MORE RICHES CAN BE YOURS...
QUACKERS?
COLONEL! PERCY! WE'RE COMING!

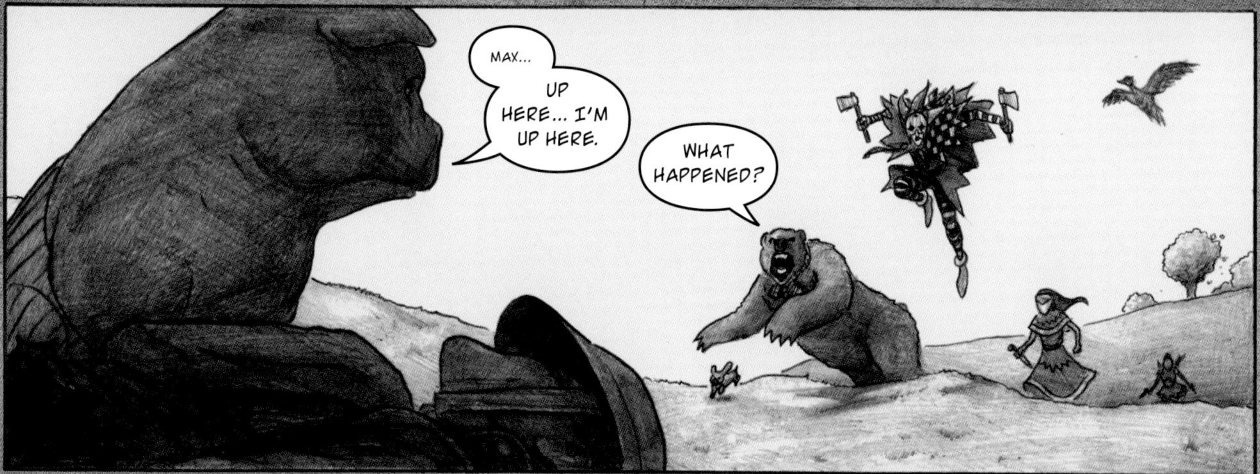
MAX...
UP HERE... I'M UP HERE.
WHAT HAPPENED?

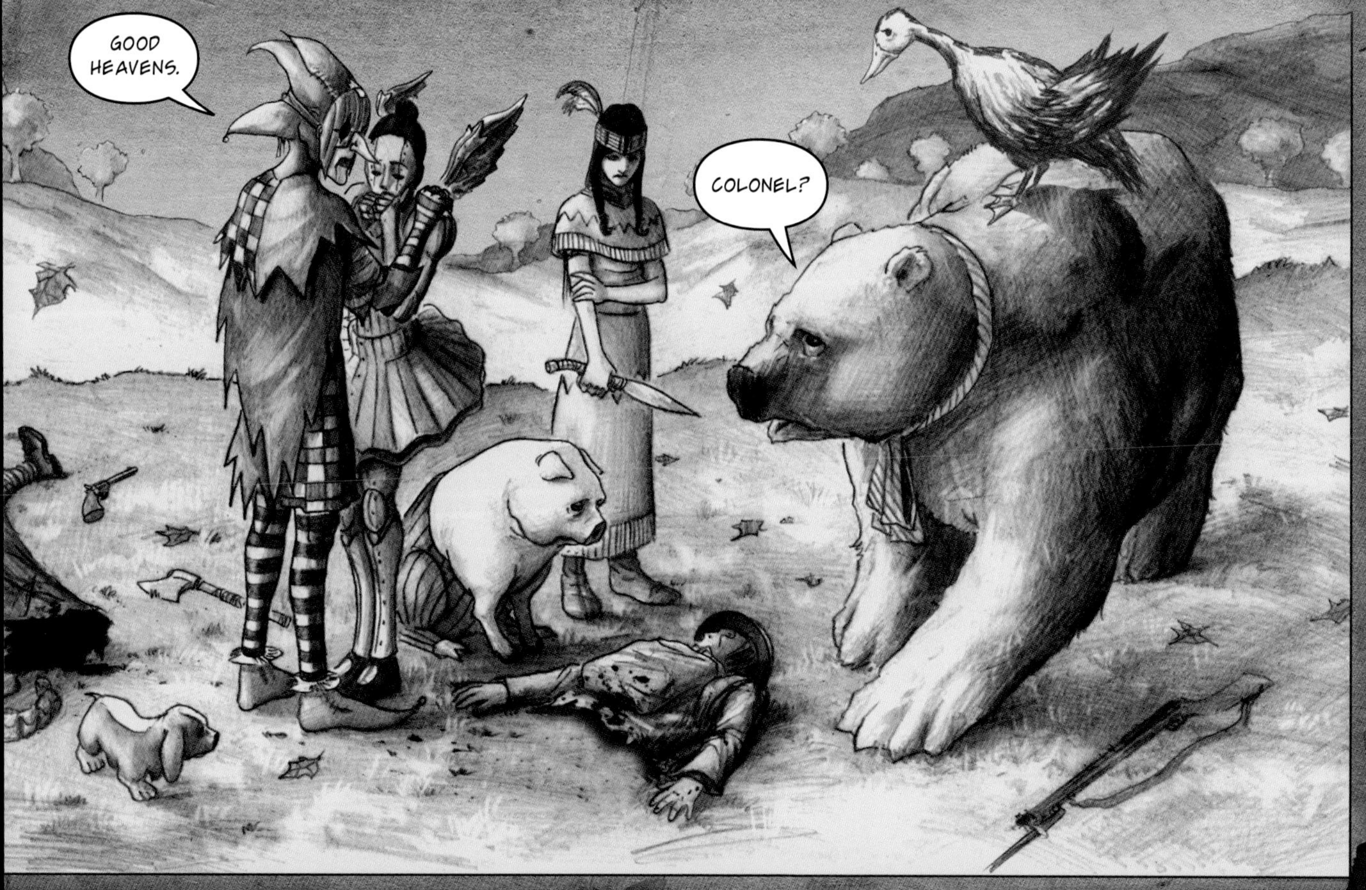
GOOD HEAVENS.
COLONEL?

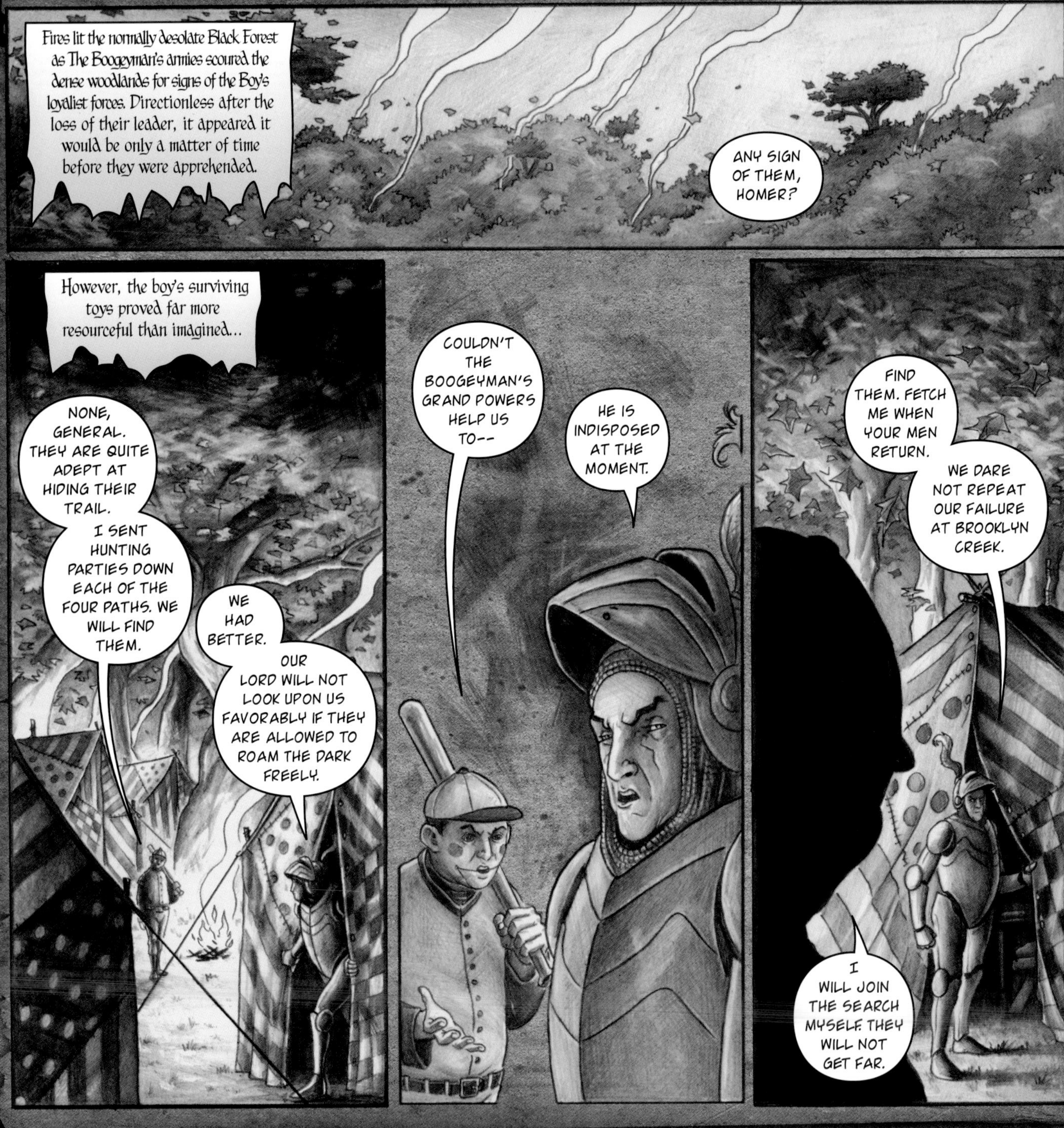
Fires lit the normally desolate Black Forest as The Boogeyman's armies scoured the dense woodlands for signs of the Boy's loyalist forces. Directionless after the loss of their leader, it appeared it would be only a matter of time before they were apprehended.
ANY SIGN OF THEM, HOMER?
However, the boy's surviving toys proved far more resourceful than imagined...
NONE, GENERAL. THEY ARE QUITE ADEPT AT HIDING THEIR TRAIL.
I SENT HUNTING PARTIES DOWN EACH OF THE FOUR PATHS. WE WILL FIND THEM.
WE HAD BETTER.
OUR LORD WILL NOT LOOK UPON US FAVORABLY IF THEY ARE ALLOWED TO ROAM THE DARK FREELY.
COULDN'T THE BOOGEYMAN'S GRAND POWERS HELP US TO--
HE IS INDISPOSED AT THE MOMENT.
FIND THEM. FETCH ME WHEN YOUR MEN RETURN.
WE DARE NOT REPEAT OUR FAILURE AT BROOKLYN CREEK.
I WILL JOIN THE SEARCH MYSELF. THEY WILL NOT GET FAR.

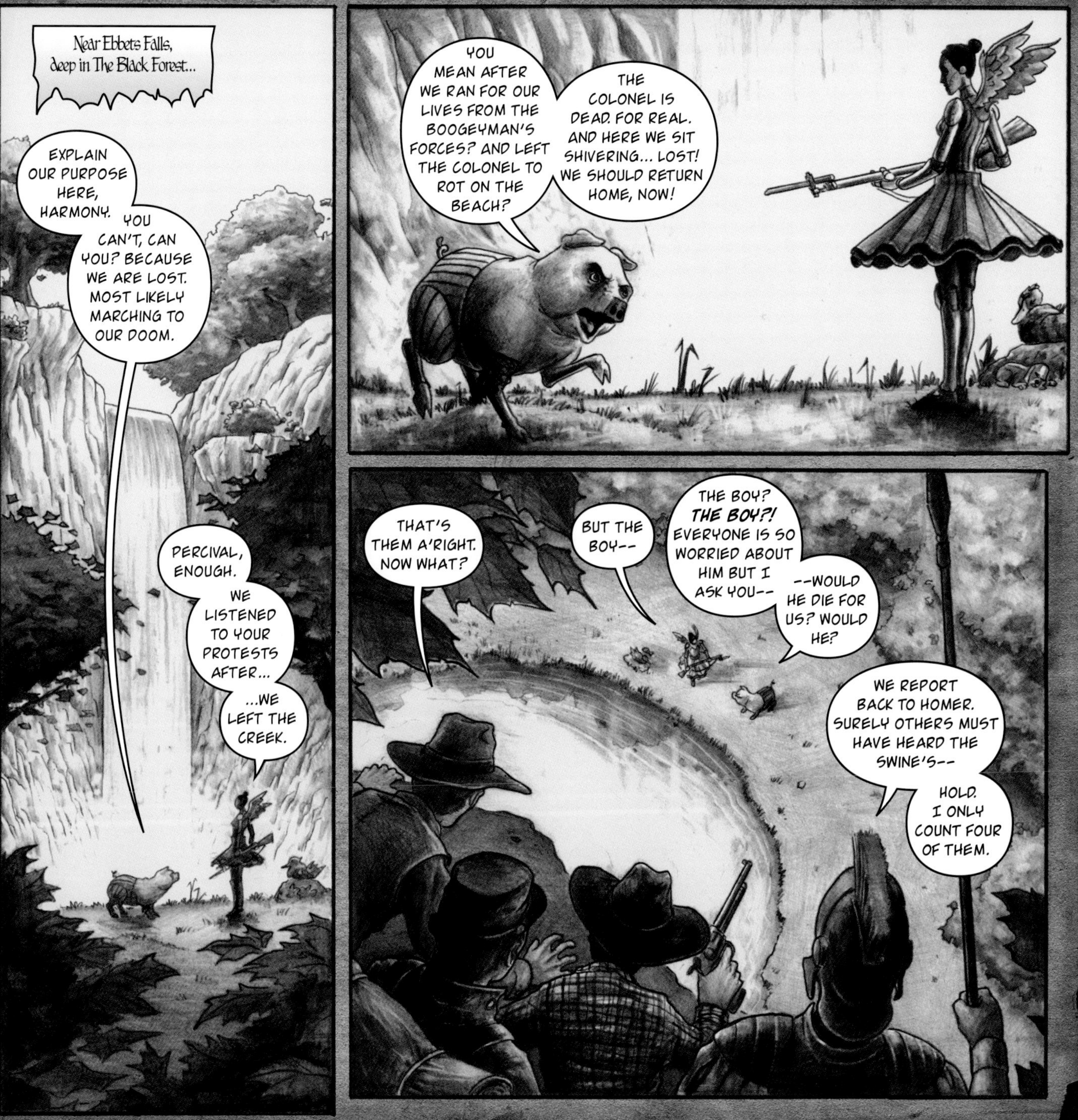
Near Ebbets Falls, deep in The Black Forest...
EXPLAIN OUR PURPOSE HERE, HARMONY.
YOU CAN'T, CAN YOU? BECAUSE WE ARE LOST. MOST LIKELY MARCHING TO OUR DOOM.
PERCIVAL, ENOUGH.
WE LISTENED TO YOUR PROTESTS AFTER...
...WE LEFT THE CREEK.
YOU MEAN AFTER WE RAN FOR OUR LIVES FROM THE BOOGEYMAN'S FORCES? AND LEFT THE COLONEL TO ROT ON THE BEACH?
THE COLONEL IS DEAD. FOR REAL. AND HERE WE SIT SHIVERING... LOST! WE SHOULD RETURN HOME, NOW!
THAT'S THEM A'RIGHT. NOW WHAT?
BUT THE BOY--
THE BOY? ***THE BOY?!*** EVERYONE IS SO WORRIED ABOUT HIM BUT I ASK YOU--
--WOULD HE DIE FOR US? WOULD HE?
WE REPORT BACK TO HOMER. SURELY OTHERS MUST HAVE HEARD THE SWINE'S--
HOLD. I ONLY COUNT FOUR OF THEM.

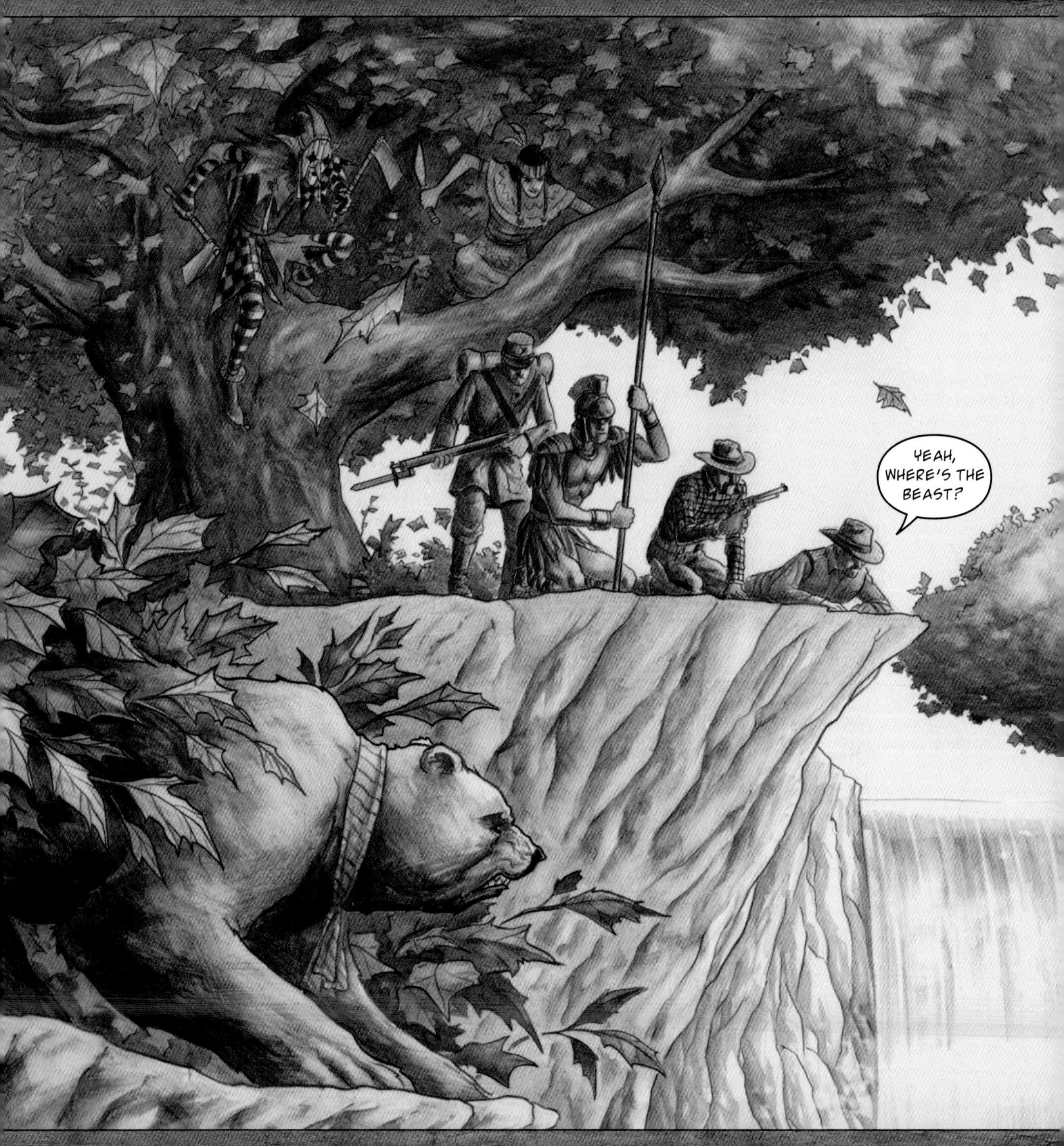
YEAH, WHERE'S THE BEAST?

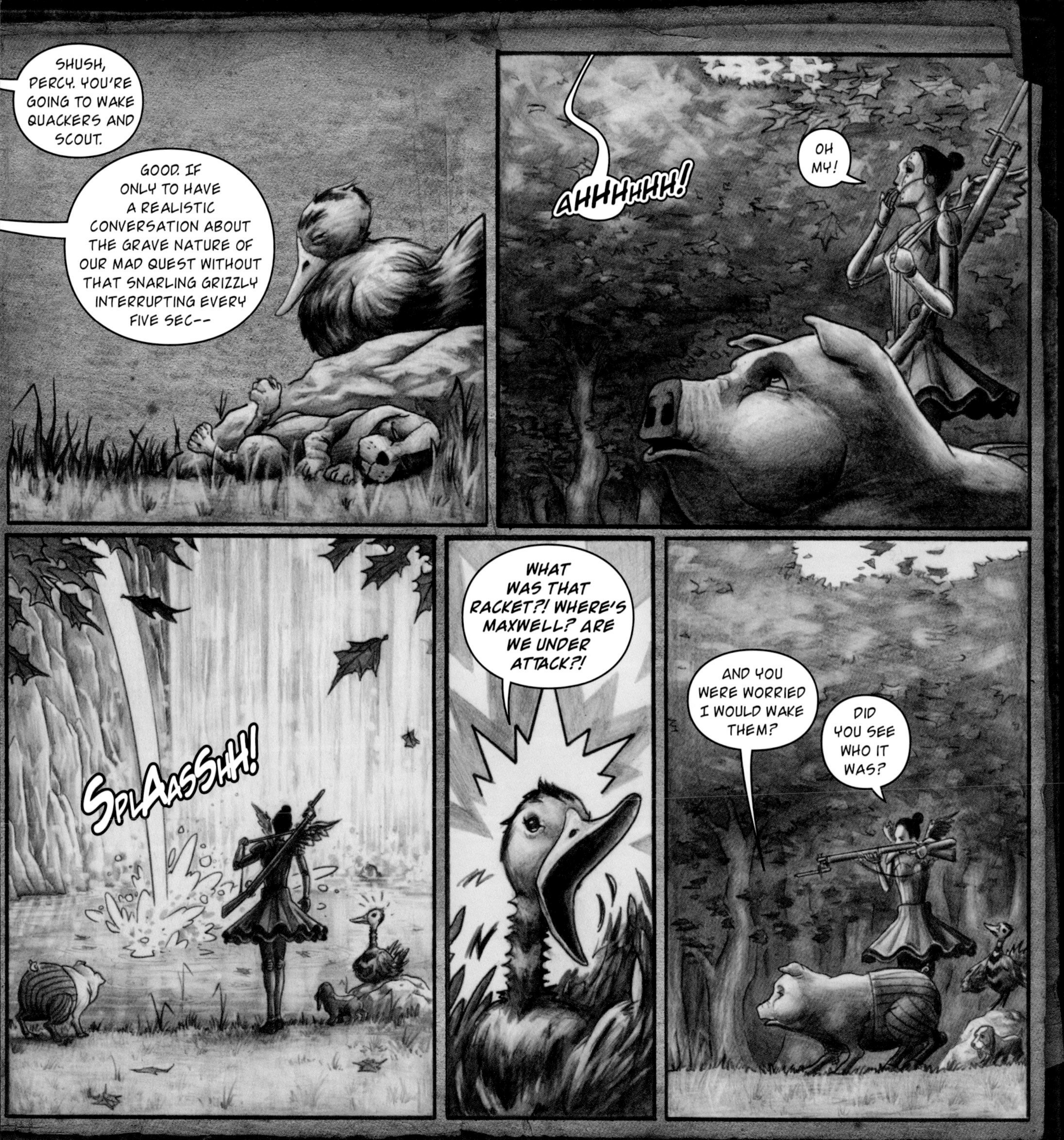
SHUSH, PERCY. YOU'RE GOING TO WAKE QUACKERS AND SCOUT.
GOOD. IF ONLY TO HAVE A REALISTIC CONVERSATION ABOUT THE GRAVE NATURE OF OUR MAD QUEST WITHOUT THAT SNARLING GRIZZLY INTERRUPTING EVERY FIVE SEC--
AHHHHHH!
OH MY!
SPLAASSHH!
WHAT WAS THAT RACKET?! WHERE'S MAXWELL? ARE WE UNDER ATTACK?!
AND YOU WERE WORRIED I WOULD WAKE THEM?
DID YOU SEE WHO IT WAS?

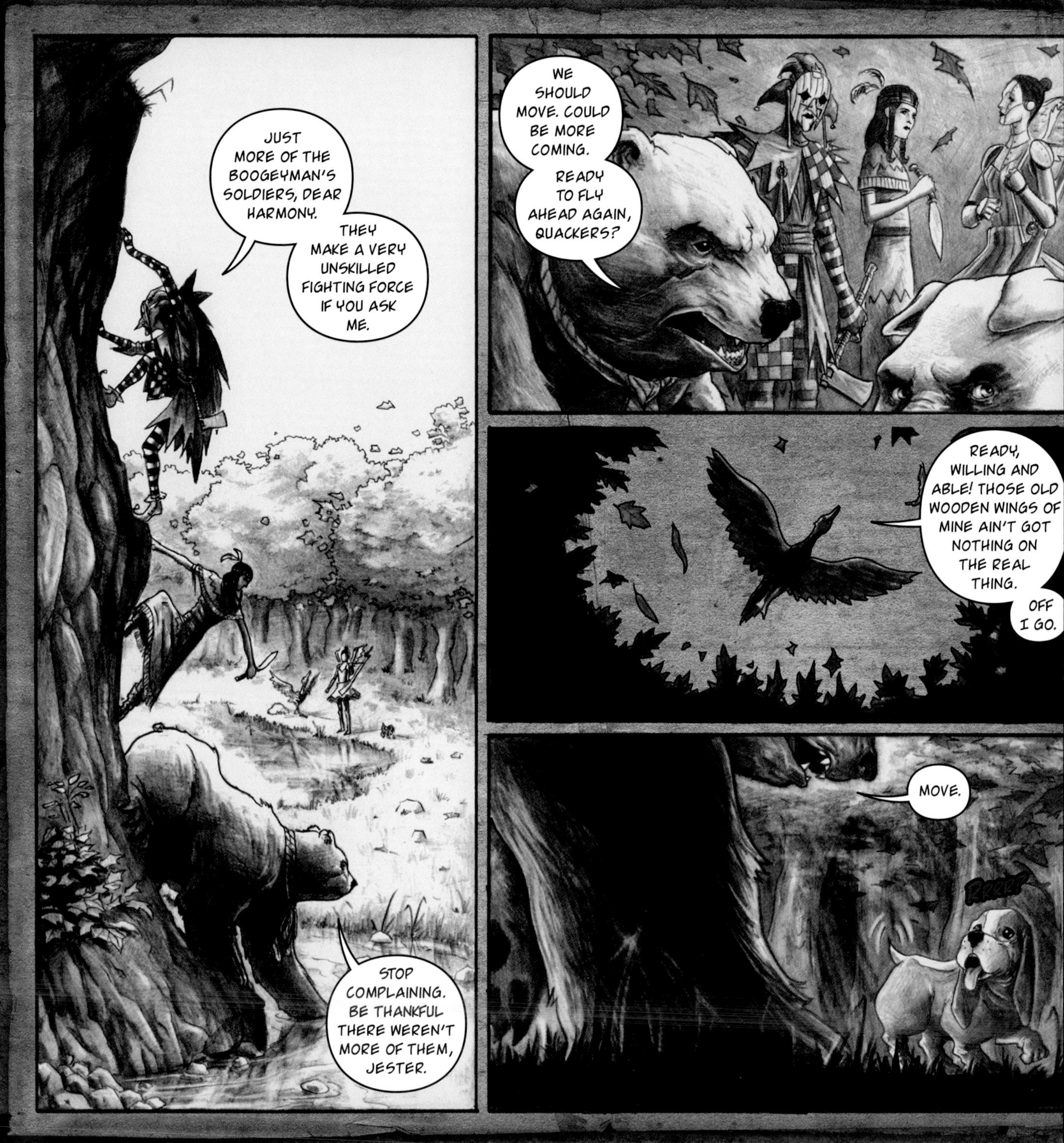
JUST MORE OF THE BOOGEYMAN'S SOLDIERS, DEAR HARMONY.
THEY MAKE A VERY UNSKILLED FIGHTING FORCE IF YOU ASK ME.
STOP COMPLAINING. BE THANKFUL THERE WEREN'T MORE OF THEM, JESTER.
WE SHOULD MOVE. COULD BE MORE COMING.
READY TO FLY AHEAD AGAIN, QUACKERS?
READY, WILLING AND ABLE! THOSE OLD WOODEN WINGS OF MINE AIN'T GOT NOTHING ON THE REAL THING.
OFF I GO.
MOVE.

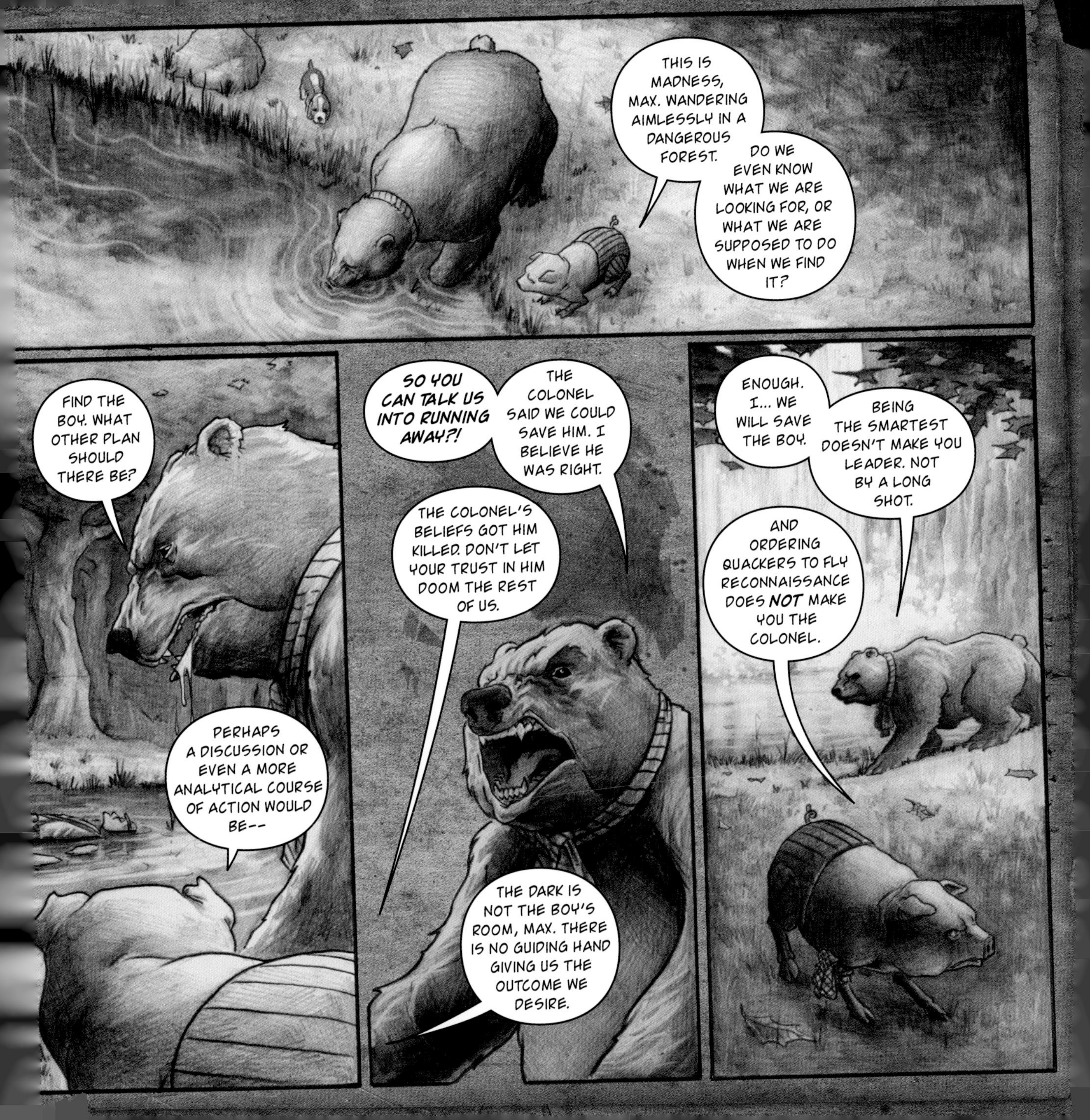
THIS IS MADNESS, MAX. WANDERING AIMLESSLY IN A DANGEROUS FOREST.
DO WE EVEN KNOW WHAT WE ARE LOOKING FOR, OR WHAT WE ARE SUPPOSED TO DO WHEN WE FIND IT?
FIND THE BOY. WHAT OTHER PLAN SHOULD THERE BE?
PERHAPS A DISCUSSION OR EVEN A MORE ANALYTICAL COURSE OF ACTION WOULD BE--
SO YOU CAN TALK US INTO RUNNING AWAY?!
THE COLONEL SAID WE COULD SAVE HIM. I BELIEVE HE WAS RIGHT.
THE COLONEL'S BELIEFS GOT HIM KILLED. DON'T LET YOUR TRUST IN HIM DOOM THE REST OF US.
THE DARK IS NOT THE BOY'S ROOM, MAX. THERE IS NO GUIDING HAND GIVING US THE OUTCOME WE DESIRE.
ENOUGH. I... WE WILL SAVE THE BOY.
BEING THE SMARTEST DOESN'T MAKE YOU LEADER. NOT BY A LONG SHOT.
AND ORDERING QUACKERS TO FLY RECONNAISSANCE DOES NOT MAKE YOU THE COLONEL.

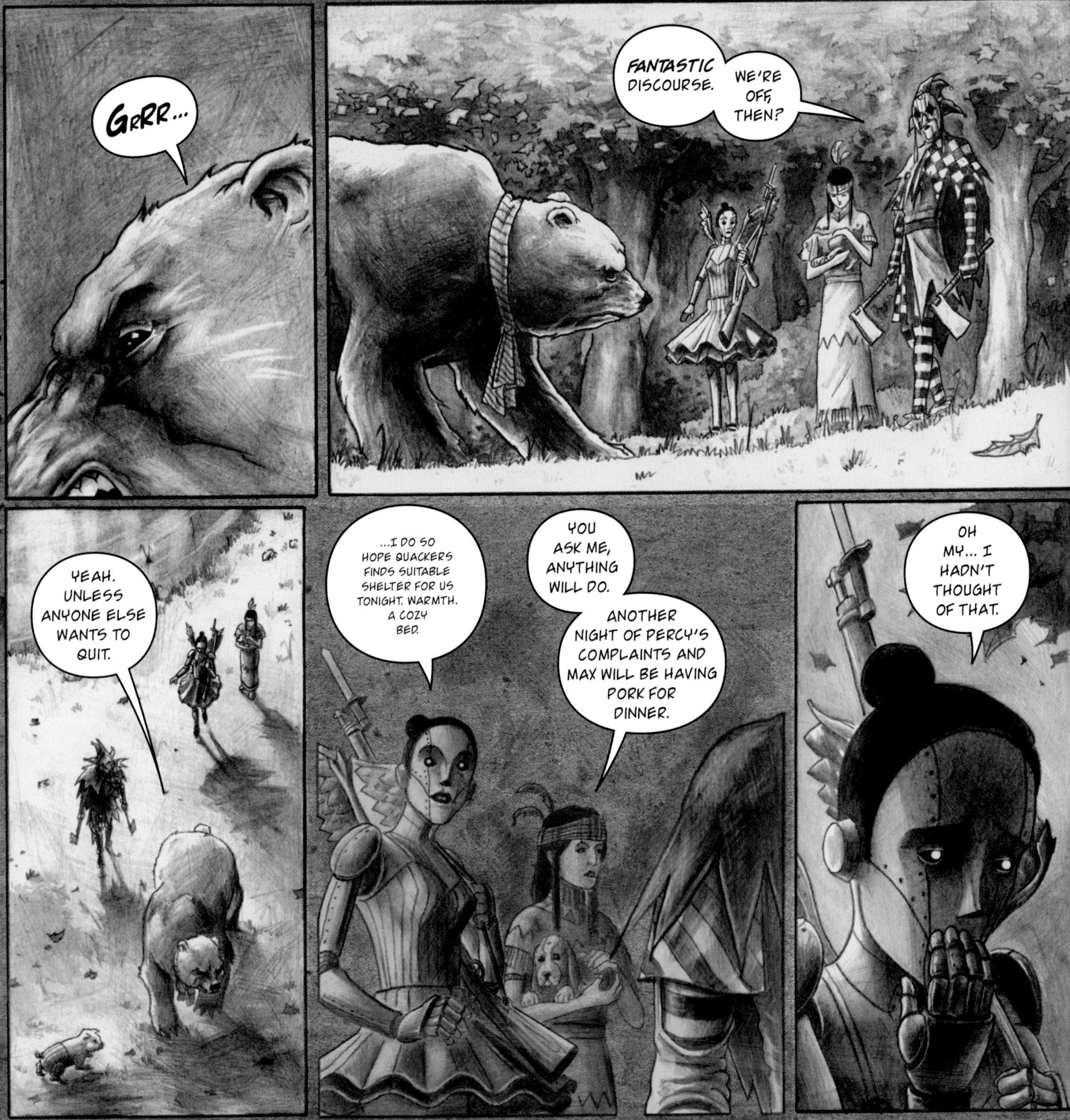
GRRR...
FANTASTIC DISCOURSE.
WE'RE OFF, THEN?
YEAH. UNLESS ANYONE ELSE WANTS TO QUIT.
...I DO SO HOPE QUACKERS FINDS SUITABLE SHELTER FOR US TONIGHT. WARMTH. A COZY BED.
YOU ASK ME, ANYTHING WILL DO.
ANOTHER NIGHT OF PERCY'S COMPLAINTS AND MAX WILL BE HAVING PORK FOR DINNER.
OH MY... I HADN'T THOUGHT OF THAT.

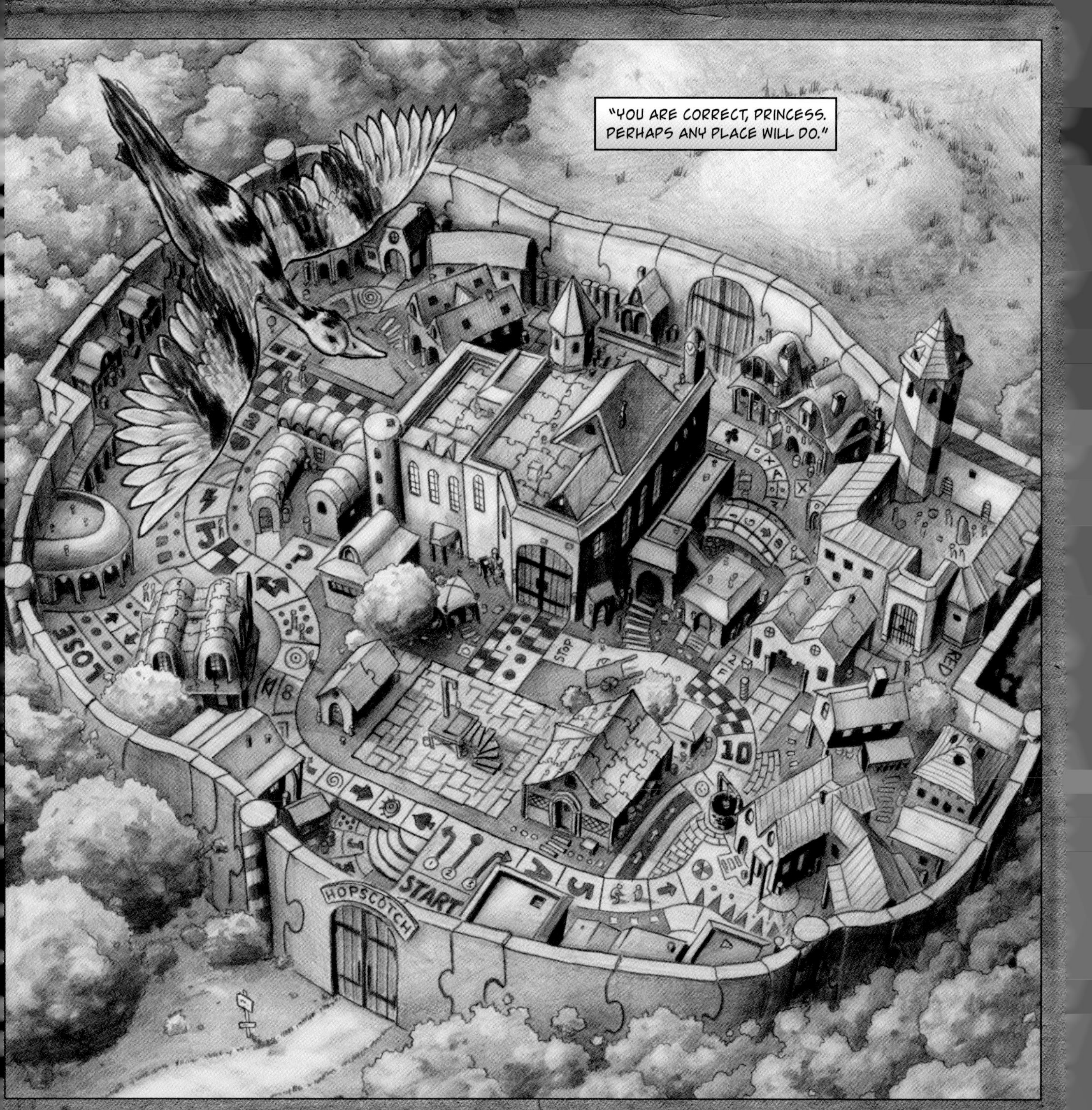
"YOU ARE CORRECT, PRINCESS. PERHAPS ANY PLACE WILL DO."
HOPSCOTCH
START
LOSE
STOP
RED
10

Chapter 2:
The Town of Hopscotch

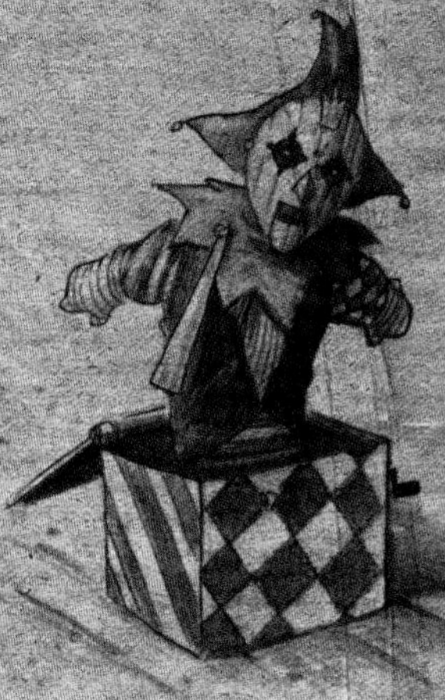

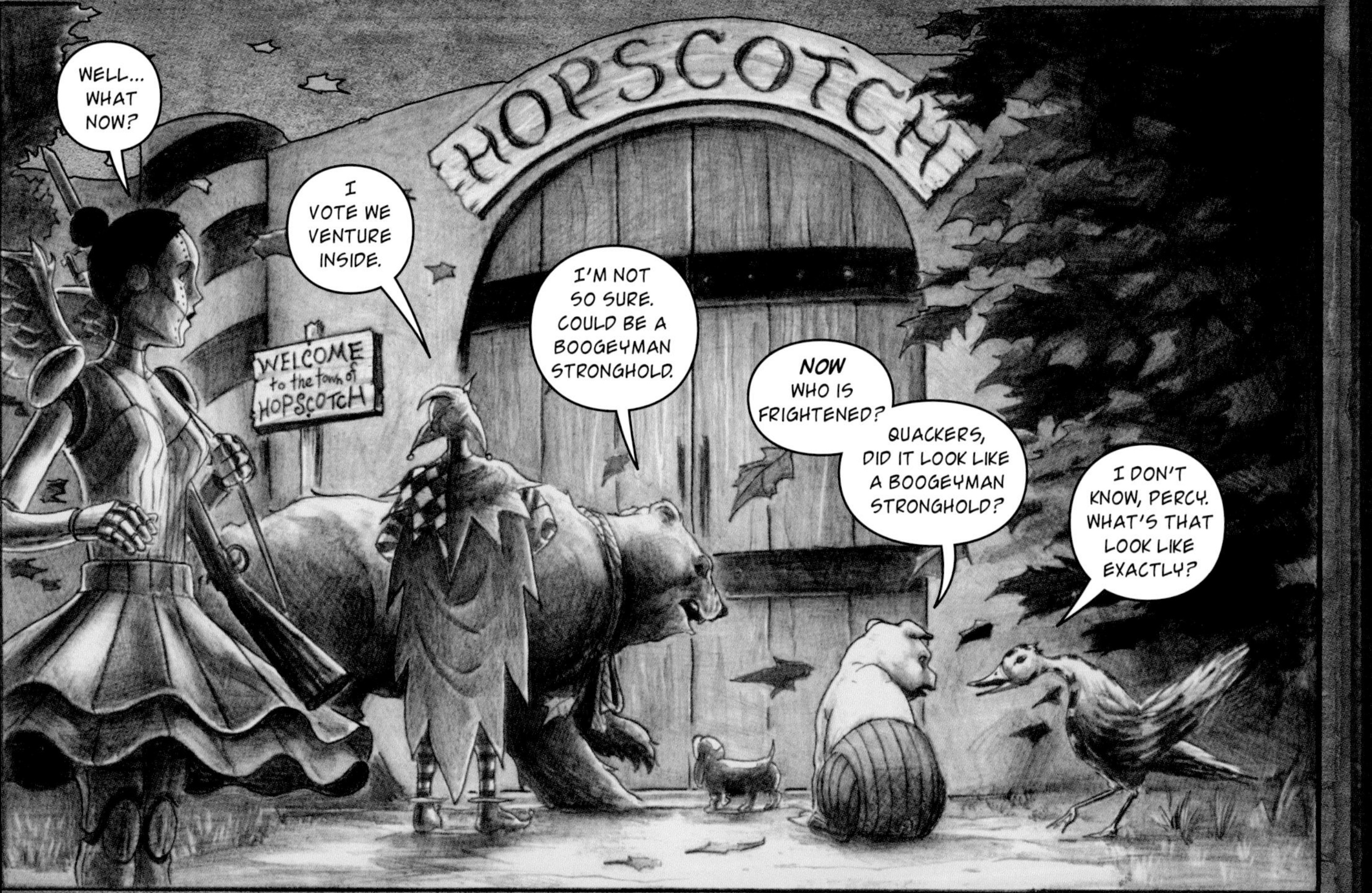
HOPSCOTCH
WELL... WHAT NOW?
I VOTE WE VENTURE INSIDE.
WELCOME to the town of HOPSCOTCH
I'M NOT SO SURE. COULD BE A BOOGEYMAN STRONGHOLD.
NOW WHO IS FRIGHTENED?
QUACKERS, DID IT LOOK LIKE A BOOGEYMAN STRONGHOLD?
I DON'T KNOW, PERCY. WHAT'S THAT LOOK LIKE EXACTLY?

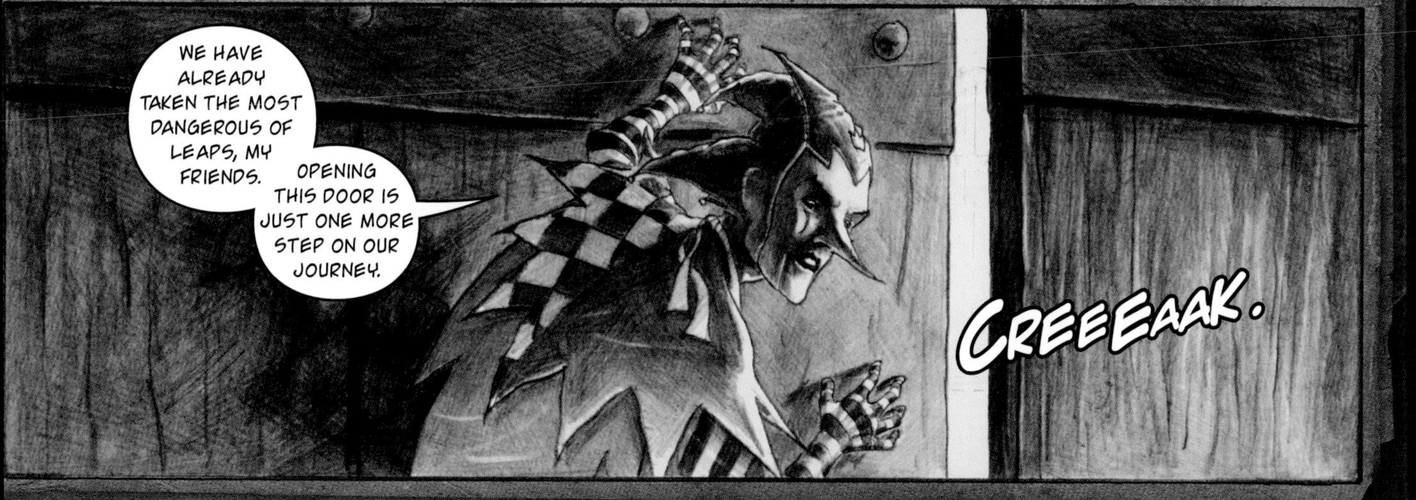
WE HAVE ALREADY TAKEN THE MOST DANGEROUS OF LEAPS, MY FRIENDS.
OPENING THIS DOOR IS JUST ONE MORE STEP ON OUR JOURNEY.
CREEEAAK.

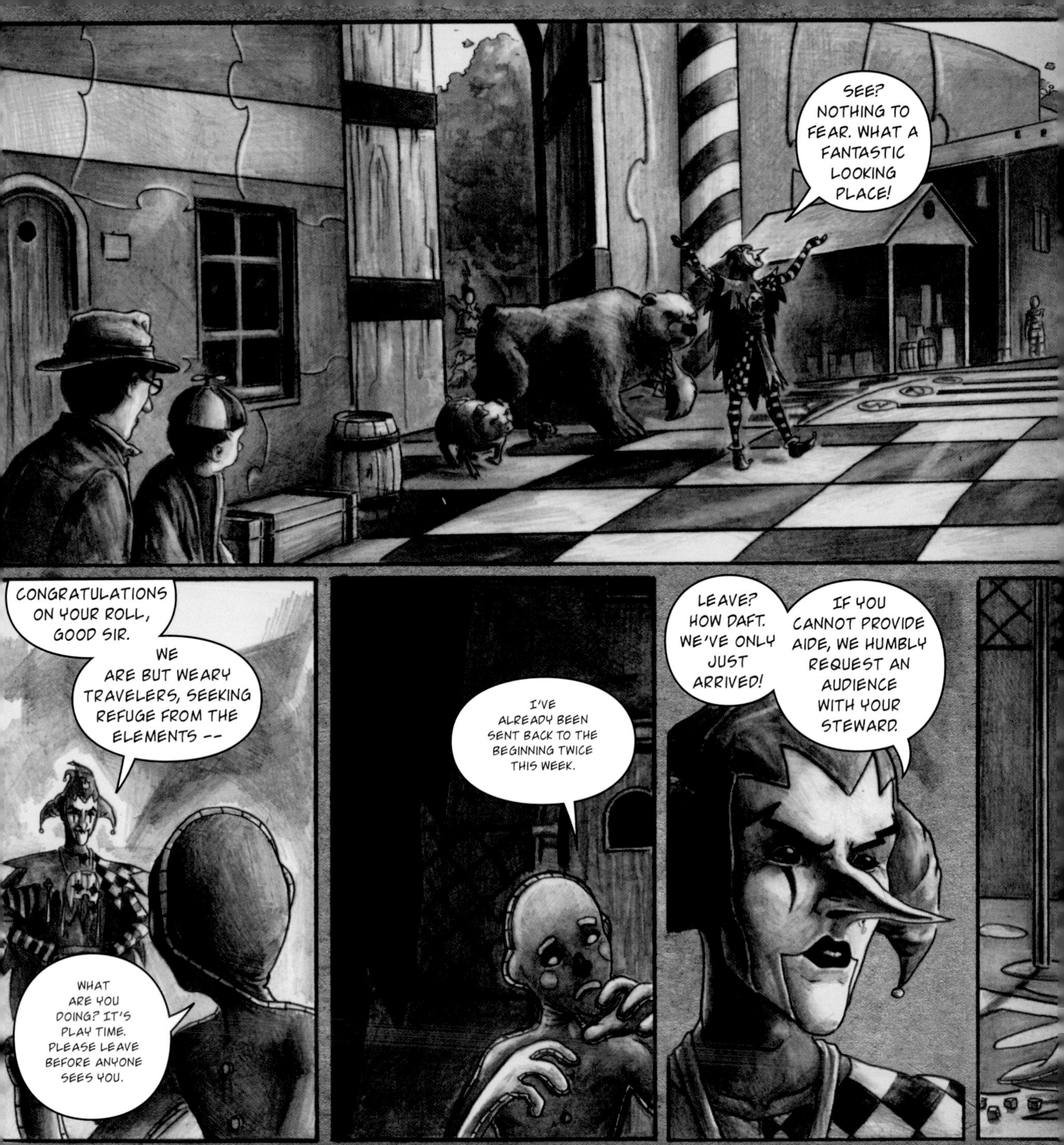
SEE? NOTHING TO FEAR. WHAT A FANTASTIC LOOKING PLACE!
CONGRATULATIONS ON YOUR ROLL, GOOD SIR.
WE ARE BUT WEARY TRAVELERS, SEEKING REFUGE FROM THE ELEMENTS --
WHAT ARE YOU DOING? IT'S PLAY TIME. PLEASE LEAVE BEFORE ANYONE SEES YOU.
I'VE ALREADY BEEN SENT BACK TO THE BEGINNING TWICE THIS WEEK.
LEAVE? HOW DAFT. WE'VE ONLY JUST ARRIVED!
IF YOU CANNOT PROVIDE AIDE, WE HUMBLY REQUEST AN AUDIENCE WITH YOUR STEWARD.

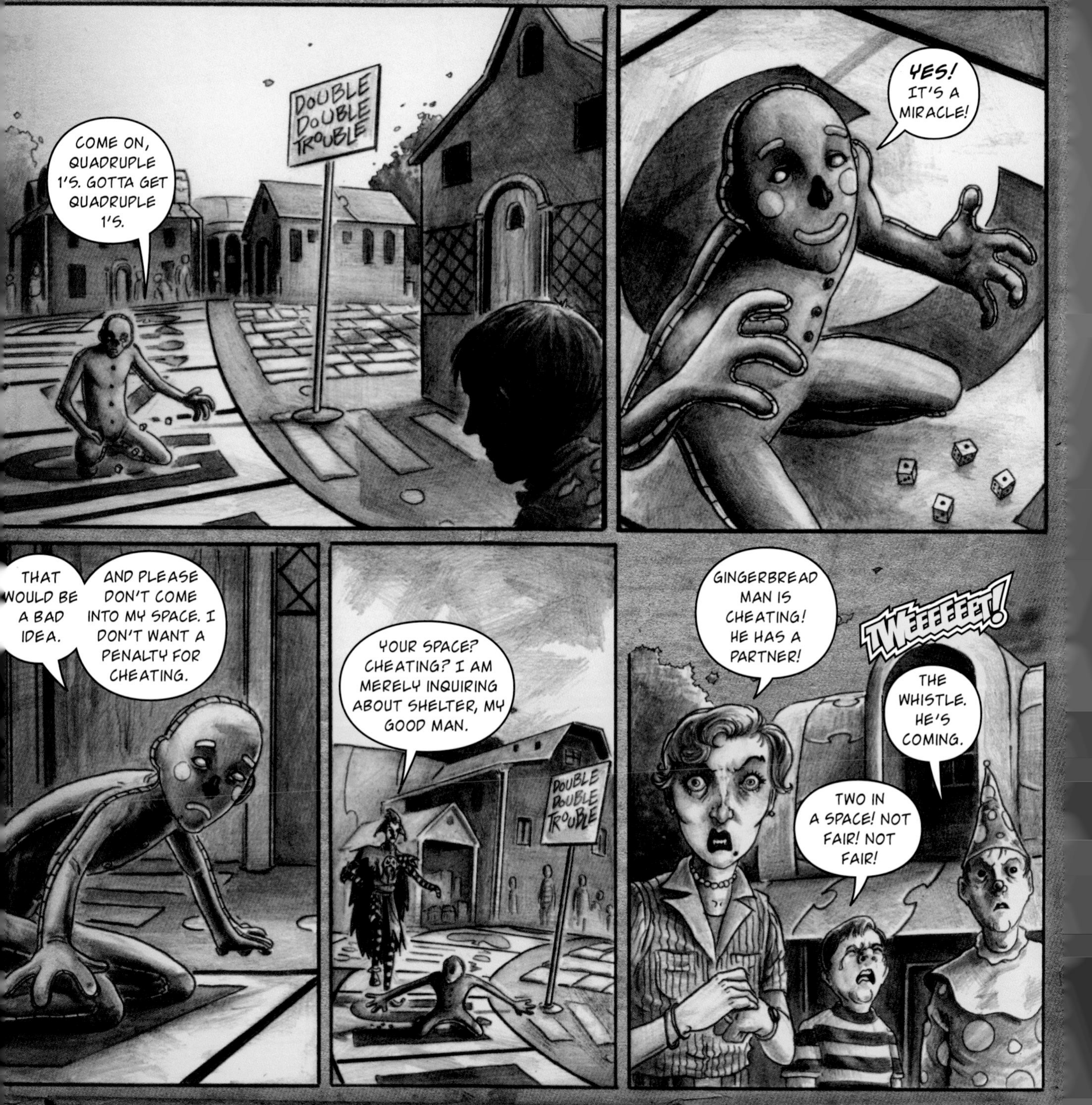
DOUBLE DOUBLE TROUBLE
COME ON, QUADRUPLE 1'S. GOTTA GET QUADRUPLE 1'S.
YES! IT'S A MIRACLE!
THAT WOULD BE A BAD IDEA.
AND PLEASE DON'T COME INTO MY SPACE. I DON'T WANT A PENALTY FOR CHEATING.
YOUR SPACE? CHEATING? I AM MERELY INQUIRING ABOUT SHELTER, MY GOOD MAN.
DOUBLE DOUBLE TROUBLE
GINGERBREAD MAN IS CHEATING! HE HAS A PARTNER!
TWEEEEEET!
THE WHISTLE. HE'S COMING.
TWO IN A SPACE! NOT FAIR! NOT FAIR!

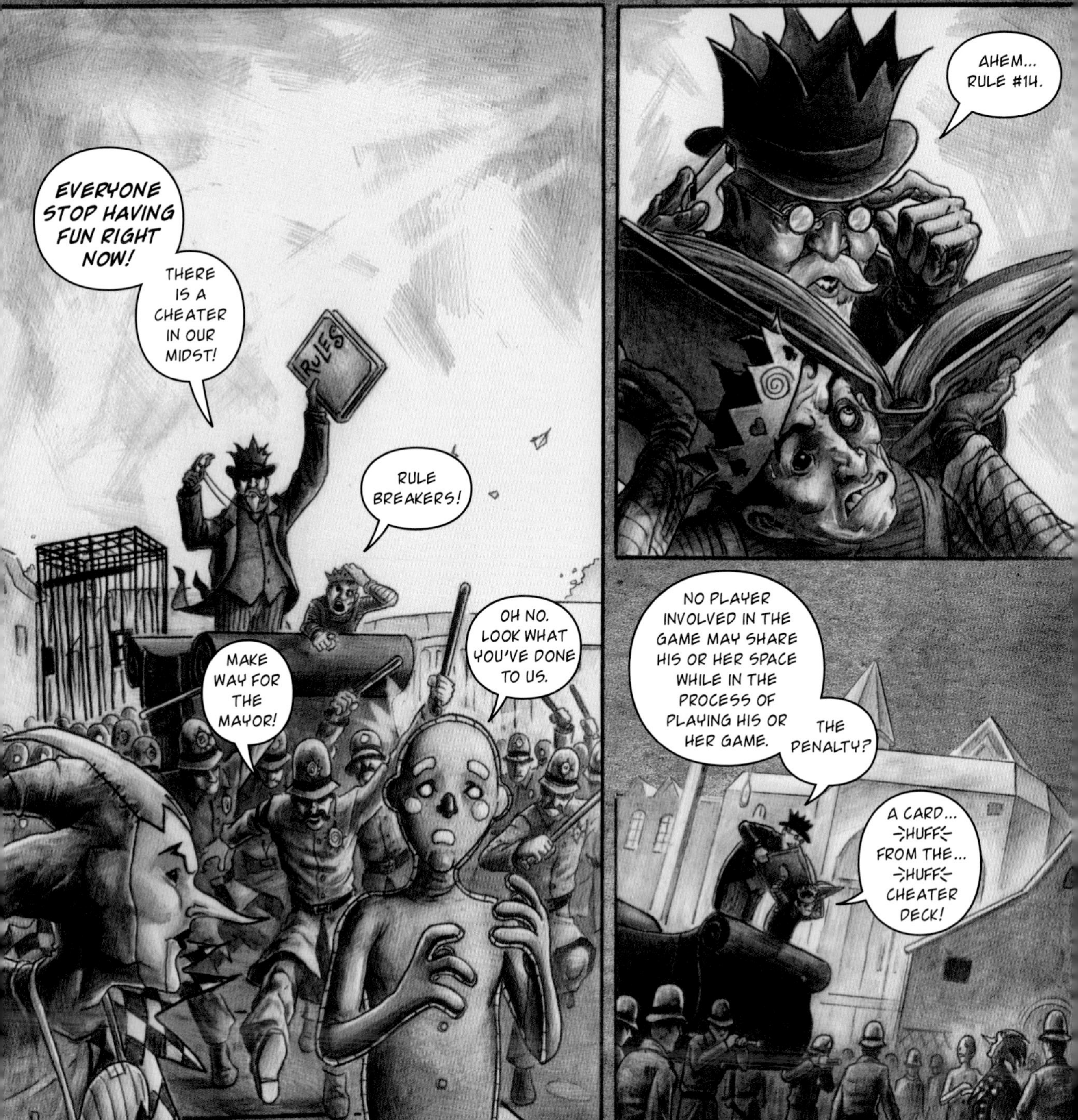
EVERYONE STOP HAVING FUN RIGHT NOW!
THERE IS A CHEATER IN OUR MIDST!
RULES
RULE BREAKERS!
MAKE WAY FOR THE MAYOR!
OH NO. LOOK WHAT YOU'VE DONE TO US.
AHEM... RULE #14.
NO PLAYER INVOLVED IN THE GAME MAY SHARE HIS OR HER SPACE WHILE IN THE PROCESS OF PLAYING HIS OR HER GAME.
THE PENALTY?
A CARD... HUFF FROM THE... HUFF CHEATER DECK!

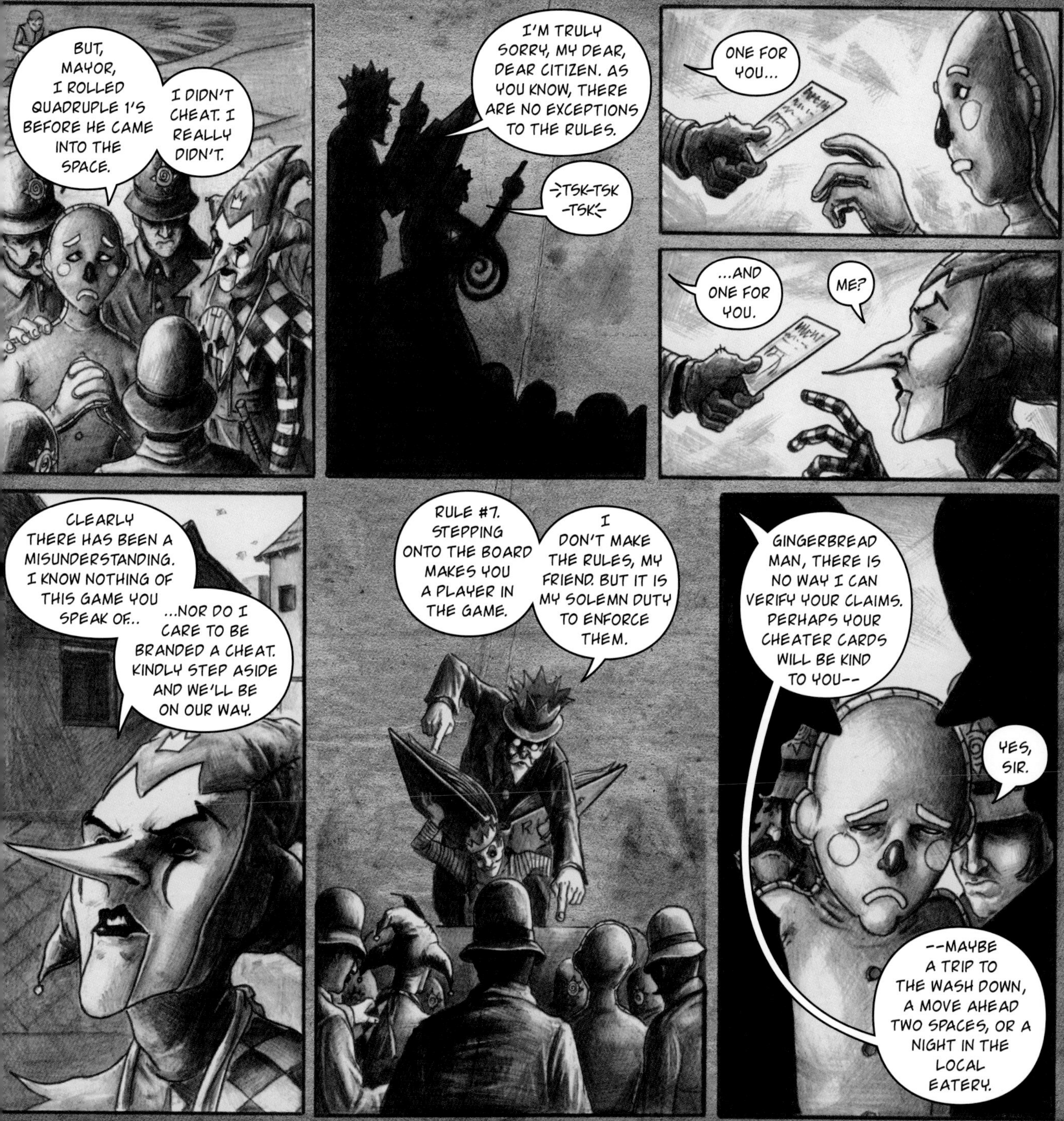
BUT, MAYOR, I ROLLED QUADRUPLE 1'S BEFORE HE CAME INTO THE SPACE.
I DIDN'T CHEAT. I REALLY DIDN'T.
I'M TRULY SORRY, MY DEAR, DEAR CITIZEN. AS YOU KNOW, THERE ARE NO EXCEPTIONS TO THE RULES.
TSK-TSK -TSK
ONE FOR YOU...
...AND ONE FOR YOU.
ME?
CLEARLY THERE HAS BEEN A MISUNDERSTANDING. I KNOW NOTHING OF THIS GAME YOU SPEAK OF..
...NOR DO I CARE TO BE BRANDED A CHEAT. KINDLY STEP ASIDE AND WE'LL BE ON OUR WAY.
RULE #7. STEPPING ONTO THE BOARD MAKES YOU A PLAYER IN THE GAME.
I DON'T MAKE THE RULES, MY FRIEND. BUT IT IS MY SOLEMN DUTY TO ENFORCE THEM.
GINGERBREAD MAN, THERE IS NO WAY I CAN VERIFY YOUR CLAIMS. PERHAPS YOUR CHEATER CARDS WILL BE KIND TO YOU--
YES, SIR.
--MAYBE A TRIP TO THE WASH DOWN, A MOVE AHEAD TWO SPACES, OR A NIGHT IN THE LOCAL EATERY.

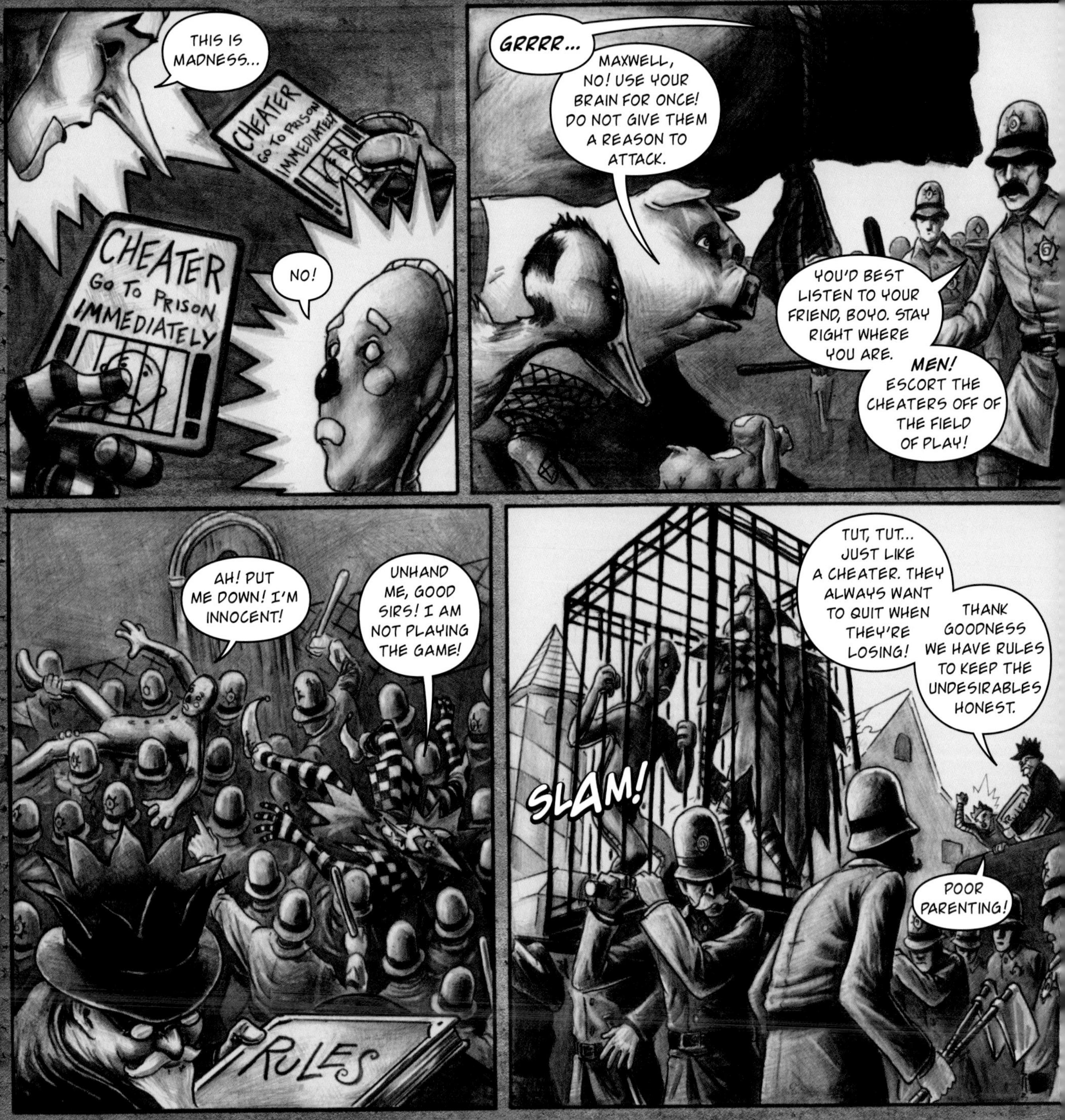
THIS IS MADNESS...
CHEATER GO TO PRISON IMMEDIATELY
CHEATER GO TO PRISON IMMEDIATELY
NO!
GRRRR...
MAXWELL, NO! USE YOUR BRAIN FOR ONCE! DO NOT GIVE THEM A REASON TO ATTACK.
YOU'D BEST LISTEN TO YOUR FRIEND, BOYO. STAY RIGHT WHERE YOU ARE.
MEN! ESCORT THE CHEATERS OFF OF THE FIELD OF PLAY!
AH! PUT ME DOWN! I'M INNOCENT!
UNHAND ME, GOOD SIRS! I AM NOT PLAYING THE GAME!
RULES
TUT, TUT... JUST LIKE A CHEATER. THEY ALWAYS WANT TO QUIT WHEN THEY'RE LOSING!
THANK GOODNESS WE HAVE RULES TO KEEP THE UNDESIRABLES HONEST.
SLAM!
POOR PARENTING!

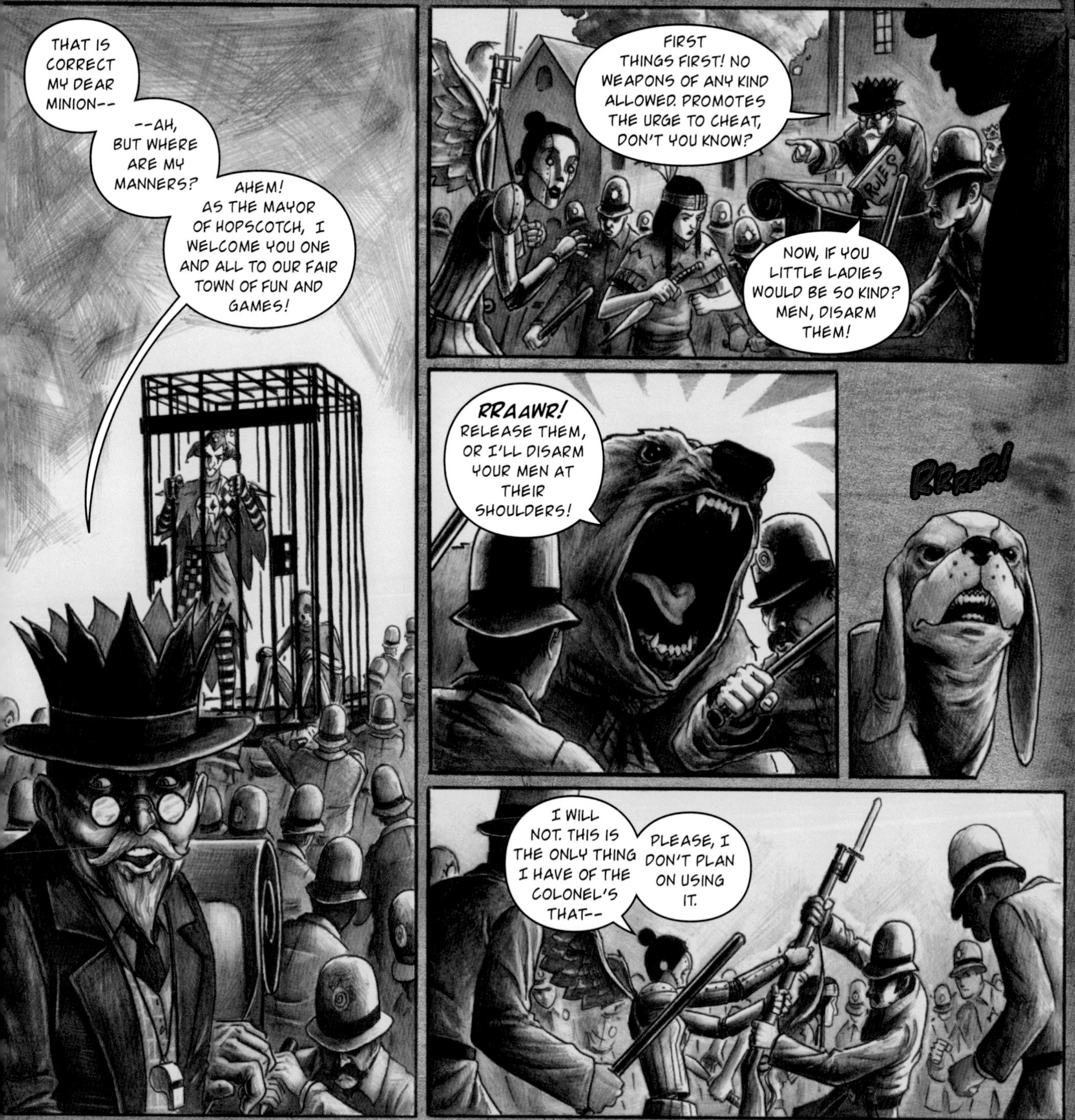
THAT IS CORRECT MY DEAR MINION--
--AH, BUT WHERE ARE MY MANNERS?
AHEM! AS THE MAYOR OF HOPSCOTCH, I WELCOME YOU ONE AND ALL TO OUR FAIR TOWN OF FUN AND GAMES!
FIRST THINGS FIRST! NO WEAPONS OF ANY KIND ALLOWED. PROMOTES THE URGE TO CHEAT, DON'T YOU KNOW?
RULES
NOW, IF YOU LITTLE LADIES WOULD BE SO KIND? MEN, DISARM THEM!
RRAAWR! RELEASE THEM, OR I'LL DISARM YOUR MEN AT THEIR SHOULDERS!
RRRRR!
I WILL NOT. THIS IS THE ONLY THING I HAVE OF THE COLONEL'S THAT--
PLEASE, I DON'T PLAN ON USING IT.

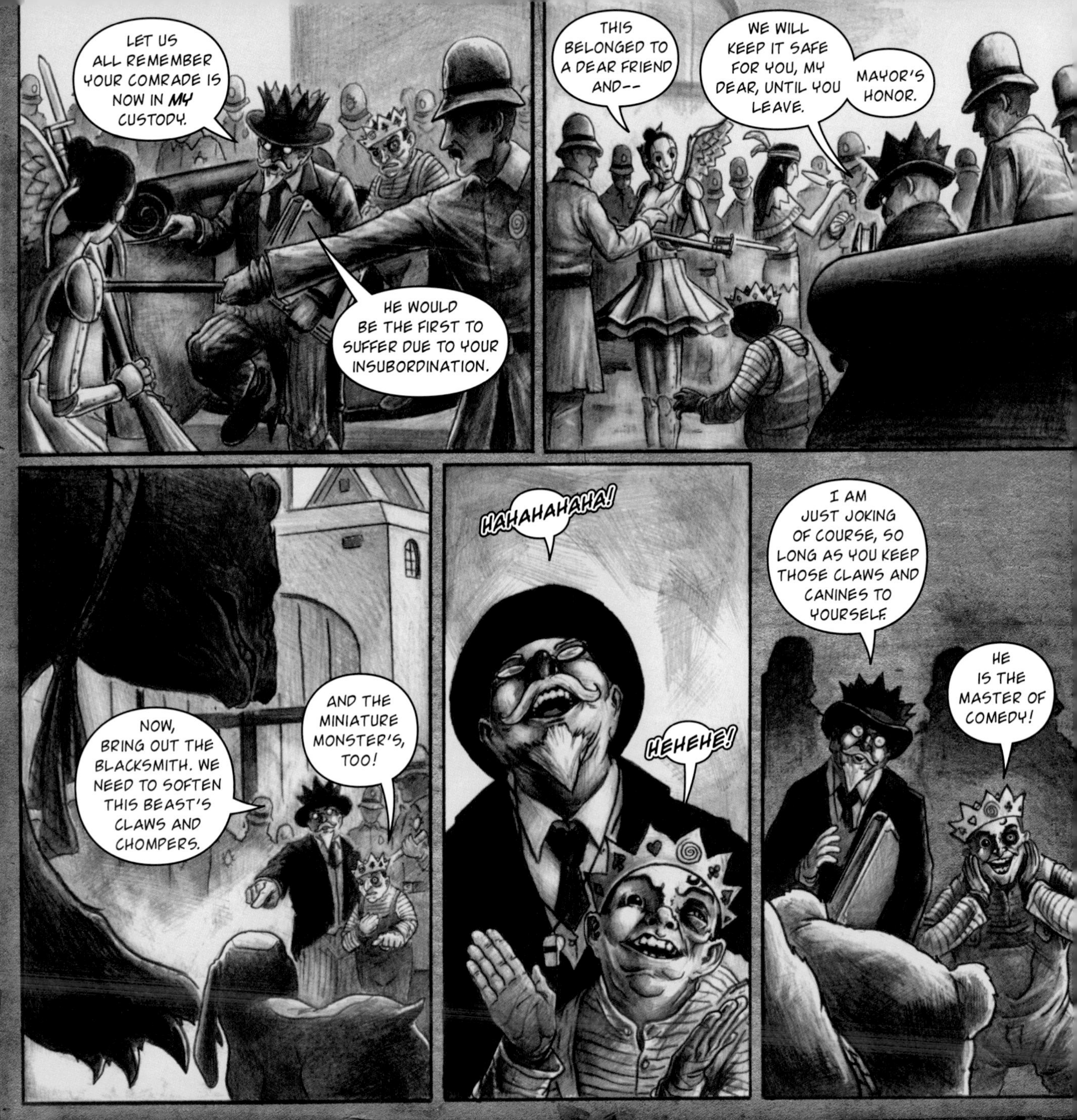
LET US ALL REMEMBER YOUR COMRADE IS NOW IN MY CUSTODY.
HE WOULD BE THE FIRST TO SUFFER DUE TO YOUR INSUBORDINATION.
THIS BELONGED TO A DEAR FRIEND AND--
WE WILL KEEP IT SAFE FOR YOU, MY DEAR, UNTIL YOU LEAVE.
MAYOR'S HONOR.
NOW, BRING OUT THE BLACKSMITH. WE NEED TO SOFTEN THIS BEAST'S CLAWS AND CHOMPERS.
AND THE MINIATURE MONSTER'S, TOO!
HAHAHAHAHA!
HEHEHE!
I AM JUST JOKING OF COURSE, SO LONG AS YOU KEEP THOSE CLAWS AND CANINES TO YOURSELF.
HE IS THE MASTER OF COMEDY!

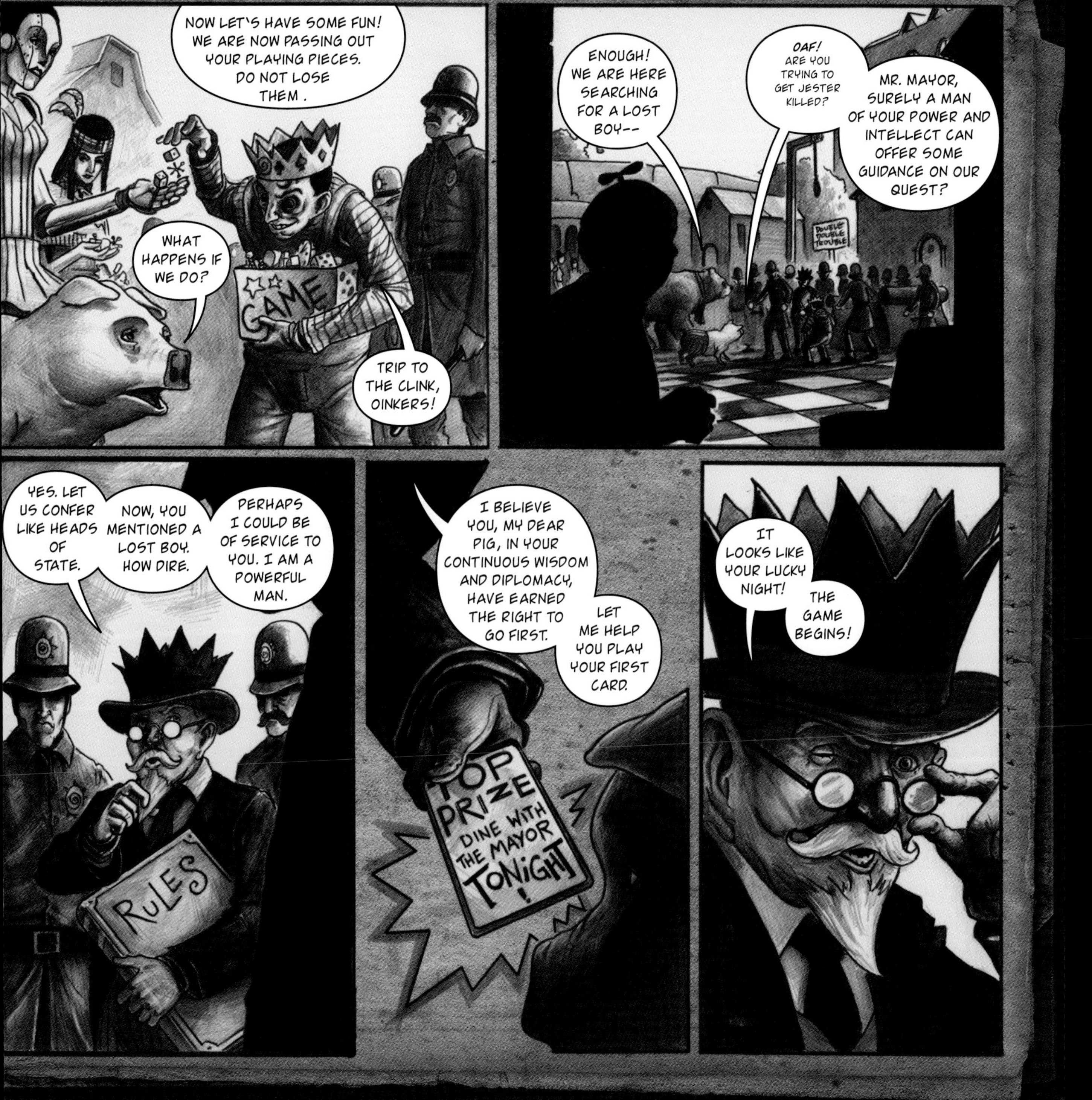
NOW LET'S HAVE SOME FUN! WE ARE NOW PASSING OUT YOUR PLAYING PIECES. DO NOT LOSE THEM .
GAME
WHAT HAPPENS IF WE DO?
TRIP TO THE CLINK, OINKERS!
ENOUGH! WE ARE HERE SEARCHING FOR A LOST BOY--
OAF! ARE YOU TRYING TO GET JESTER KILLED?
MR. MAYOR, SURELY A MAN OF YOUR POWER AND INTELLECT CAN OFFER SOME GUIDANCE ON OUR QUEST?
DOUBLE DOUBLE TROUBLE
YES. LET US CONFER LIKE HEADS OF STATE.
NOW, YOU MENTIONED A LOST BOY. HOW DIRE.
PERHAPS I COULD BE OF SERVICE TO YOU. I AM A POWERFUL MAN.
RULES
I BELIEVE YOU, MY DEAR PIG, IN YOUR CONTINUOUS WISDOM AND DIPLOMACY, HAVE EARNED THE RIGHT TO GO FIRST.
LET ME HELP YOU PLAY YOUR FIRST CARD.
TOP PRIZE DINE WITH THE MAYOR TONIGHT !
IT LOOKS LIKE YOUR LUCKY NIGHT!
THE GAME BEGINS!

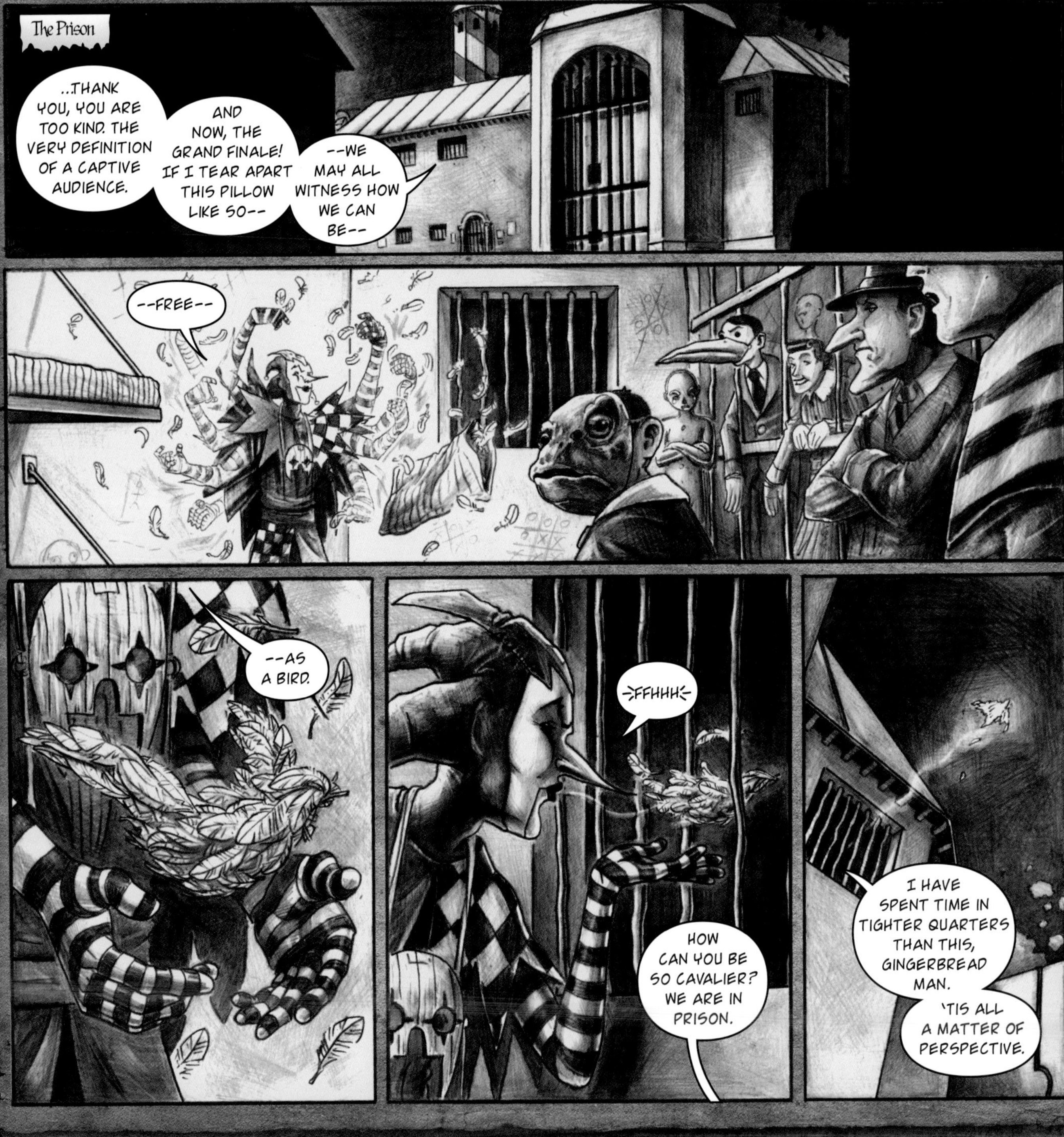
The Prison
...THANK YOU, YOU ARE TOO KIND. THE VERY DEFINITION OF A CAPTIVE AUDIENCE.
AND NOW, THE GRAND FINALE! IF I TEAR APART THIS PILLOW LIKE SO--
--WE MAY ALL WITNESS HOW WE CAN BE--
--FREE--
--AS A BIRD.
FFHHH
HOW CAN YOU BE SO CAVALIER? WE ARE IN PRISON.
I HAVE SPENT TIME IN TIGHTER QUARTERS THAN THIS, GINGERBREAD MAN.
'TIS ALL A MATTER OF PERSPECTIVE.

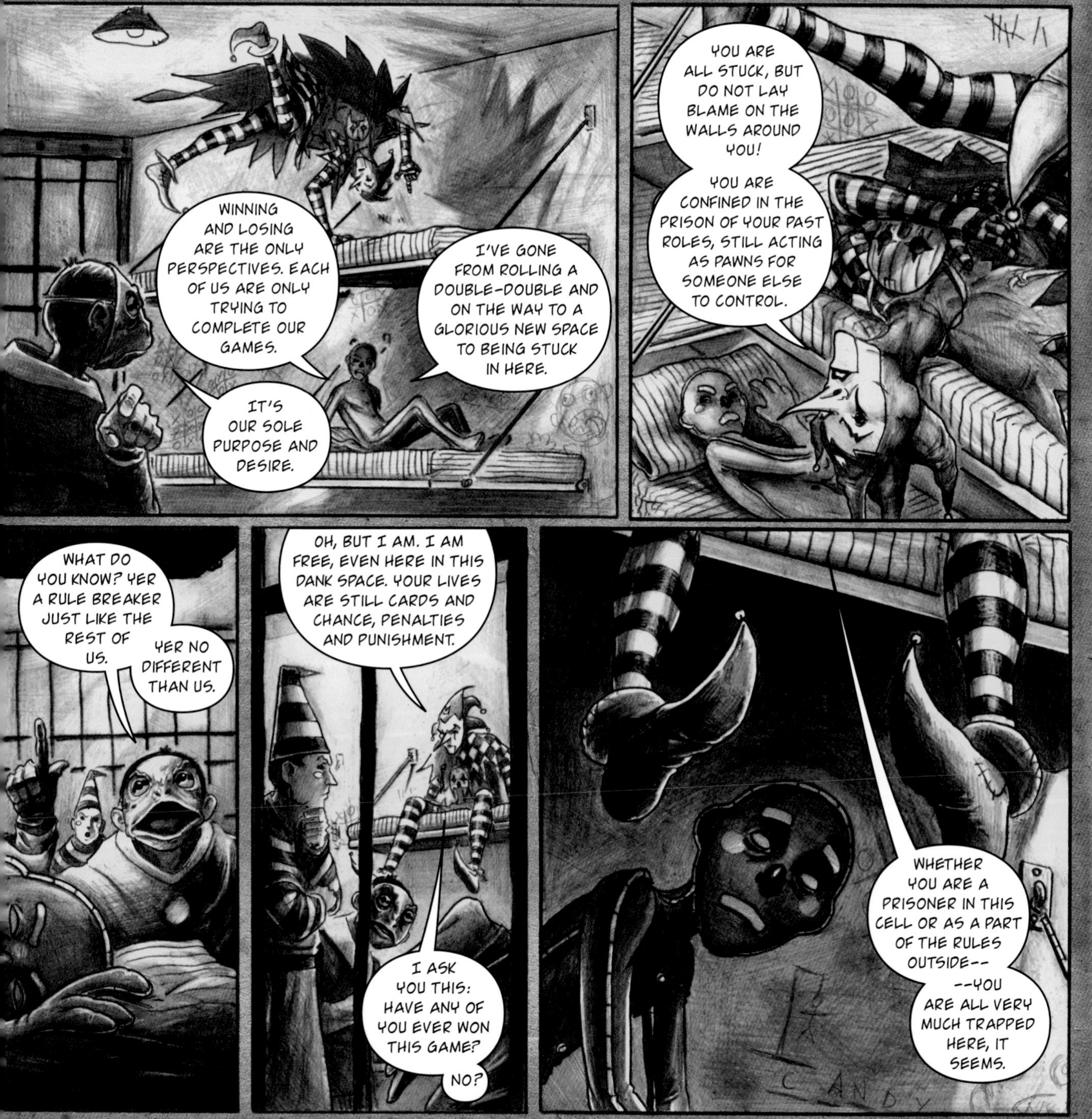
WINNING AND LOSING ARE THE ONLY PERSPECTIVES. EACH OF US ARE ONLY TRYING TO COMPLETE OUR GAMES.
IT'S OUR SOLE PURPOSE AND DESIRE.
I'VE GONE FROM ROLLING A DOUBLE-DOUBLE AND ON THE WAY TO A GLORIOUS NEW SPACE TO BEING STUCK IN HERE.
YOU ARE ALL STUCK, BUT DO NOT LAY BLAME ON THE WALLS AROUND YOU!
YOU ARE CONFINED IN THE PRISON OF YOUR PAST ROLES, STILL ACTING AS PAWNS FOR SOMEONE ELSE TO CONTROL.
WHAT DO YOU KNOW? YER A RULE BREAKER JUST LIKE THE REST OF US.
YER NO DIFFERENT THAN US.
OH, BUT I AM. I AM FREE, EVEN HERE IN THIS DANK SPACE. YOUR LIVES ARE STILL CARDS AND CHANCE, PENALTIES AND PUNISHMENT.
I ASK YOU THIS: HAVE ANY OF YOU EVER WON THIS GAME?
NO?
WHETHER YOU ARE A PRISONER IN THIS CELL OR AS A PART OF THE RULES OUTSIDE--
--YOU ARE ALL VERY MUCH TRAPPED HERE, IT SEEMS.
CANDY

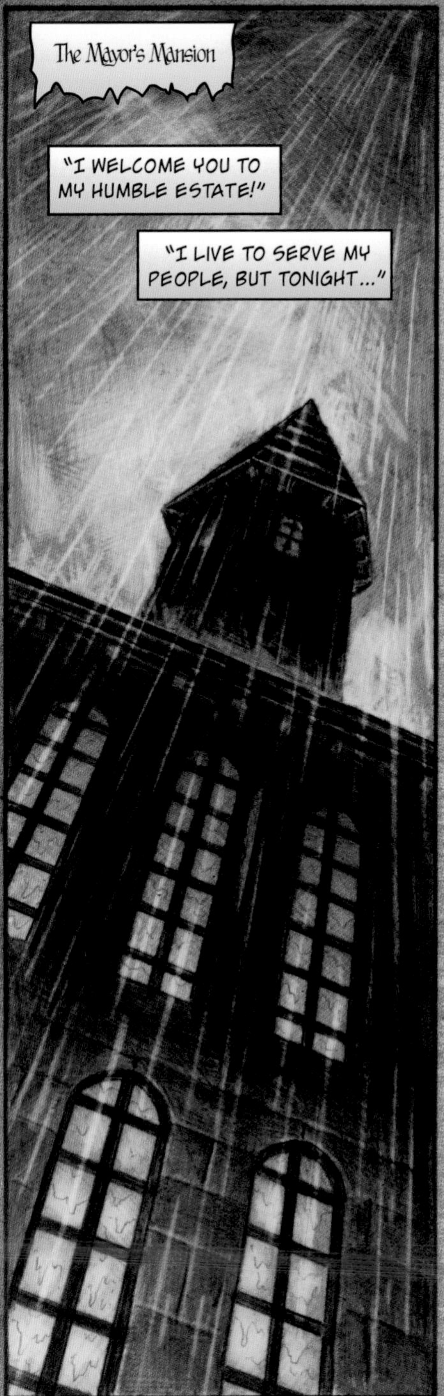
The Mayor's Mansion
"I WELCOME YOU TO MY HUMBLE ESTATE!"
"I LIVE TO SERVE MY PEOPLE, BUT TONIGHT..."

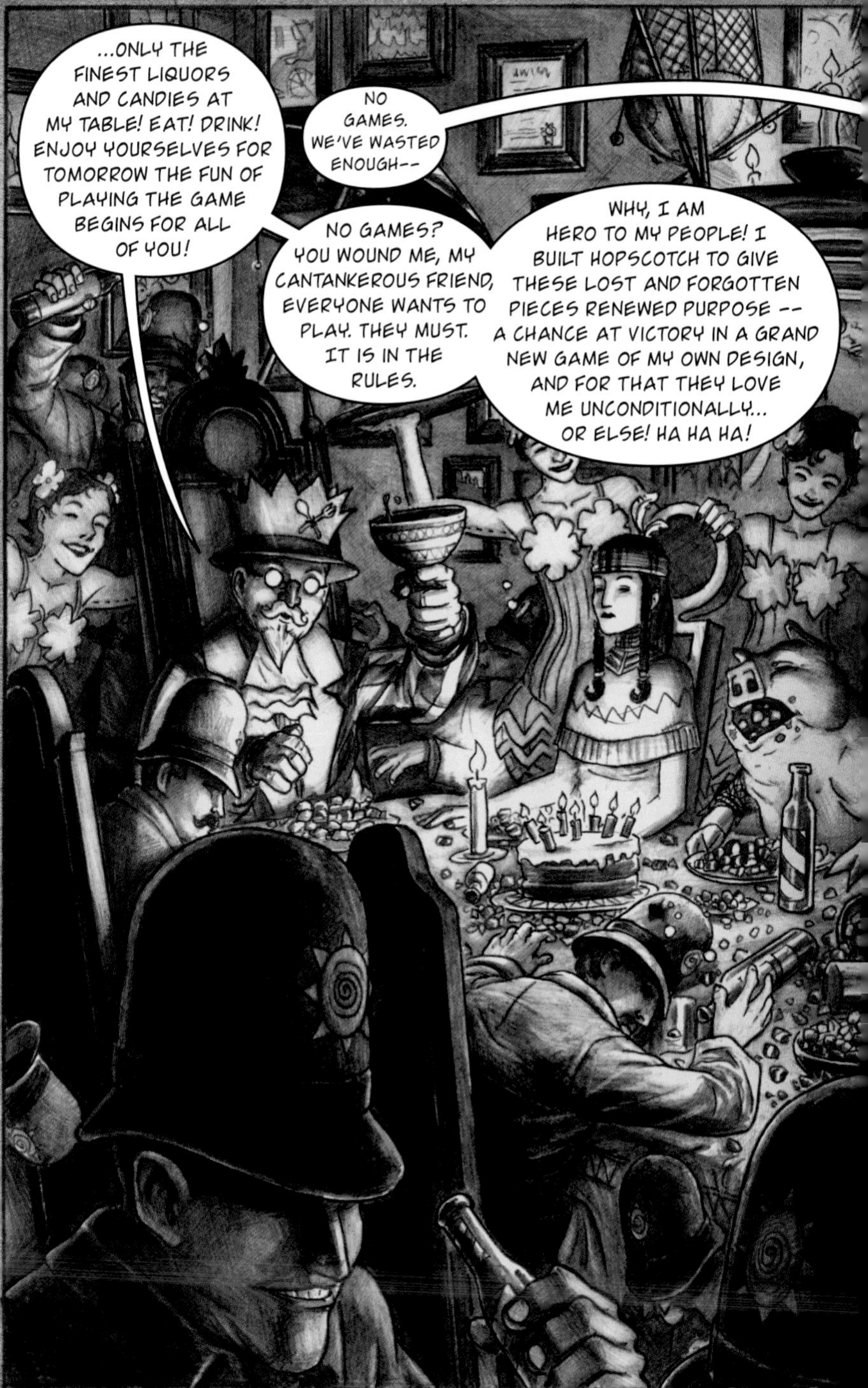
...ONLY THE FINEST LIQUORS AND CANDIES AT MY TABLE! EAT! DRINK! ENJOY YOURSELVES FOR TOMORROW THE FUN OF PLAYING THE GAME BEGINS FOR ALL OF YOU!
NO GAMES. WE'VE WASTED ENOUGH--
NO GAMES? YOU WOUND ME, MY CANTANKEROUS FRIEND, EVERYONE WANTS TO PLAY. THEY MUST. IT IS IN THE RULES.
WHY, I AM HERO TO MY PEOPLE! I BUILT HOPSCOTCH TO GIVE THESE LOST AND FORGOTTEN PIECES RENEWED PURPOSE -- A CHANCE AT VICTORY IN A GRAND NEW GAME OF MY OWN DESIGN, AND FOR THAT THEY LOVE ME UNCONDITIONALLY... OR ELSE! HA HA HA!

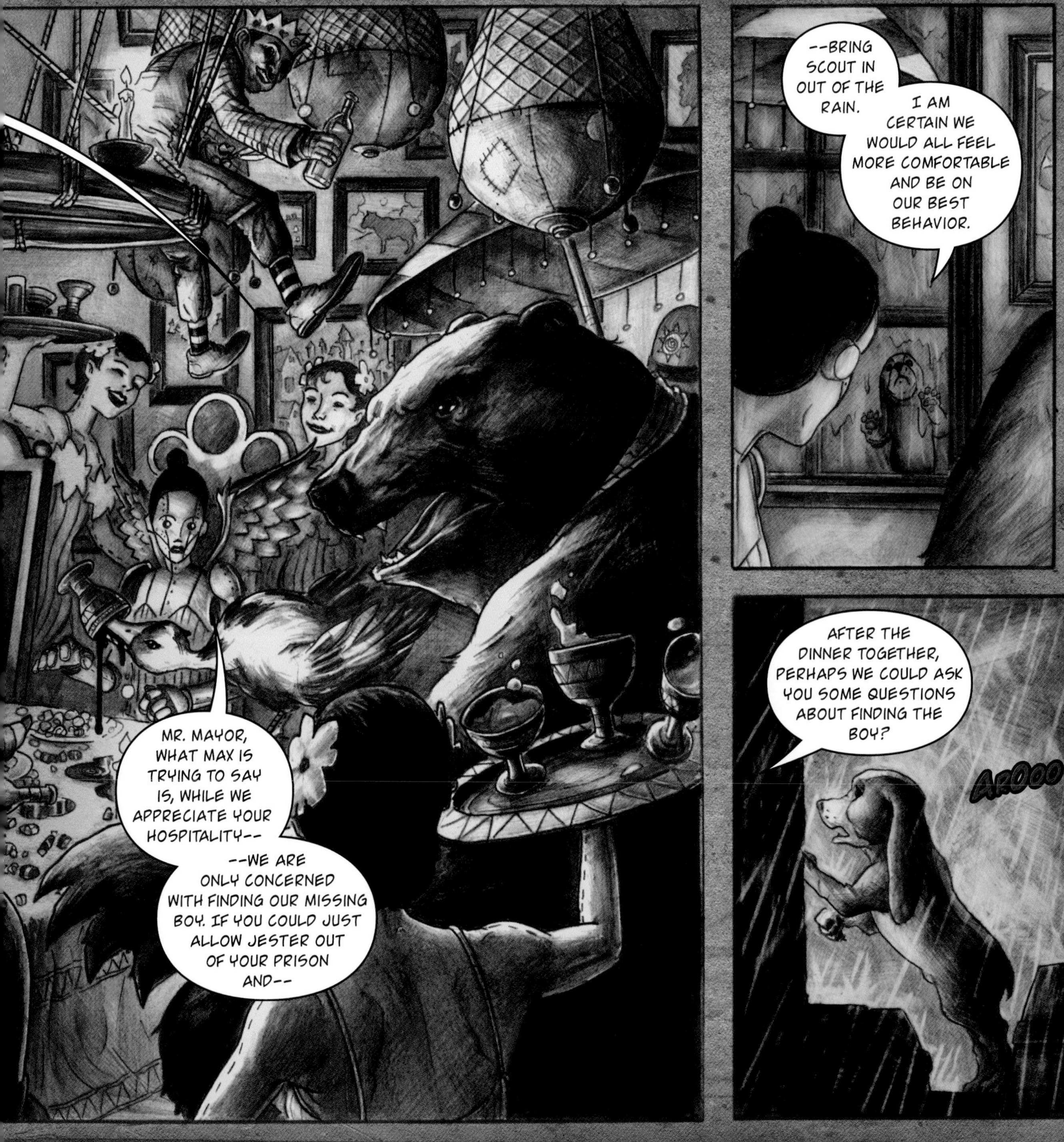
MR. MAYOR, WHAT MAX IS TRYING TO SAY IS, WHILE WE APPRECIATE YOUR HOSPITALITY--
--WE ARE ONLY CONCERNED WITH FINDING OUR MISSING BOY. IF YOU COULD JUST ALLOW JESTER OUT OF YOUR PRISON AND--
--BRING SCOUT IN OUT OF THE RAIN.
I AM CERTAIN WE WOULD ALL FEEL MORE COMFORTABLE AND BE ON OUR BEST BEHAVIOR.
AFTER THE DINNER TOGETHER, PERHAPS WE COULD ASK YOU SOME QUESTIONS ABOUT FINDING THE BOY?
AROOO

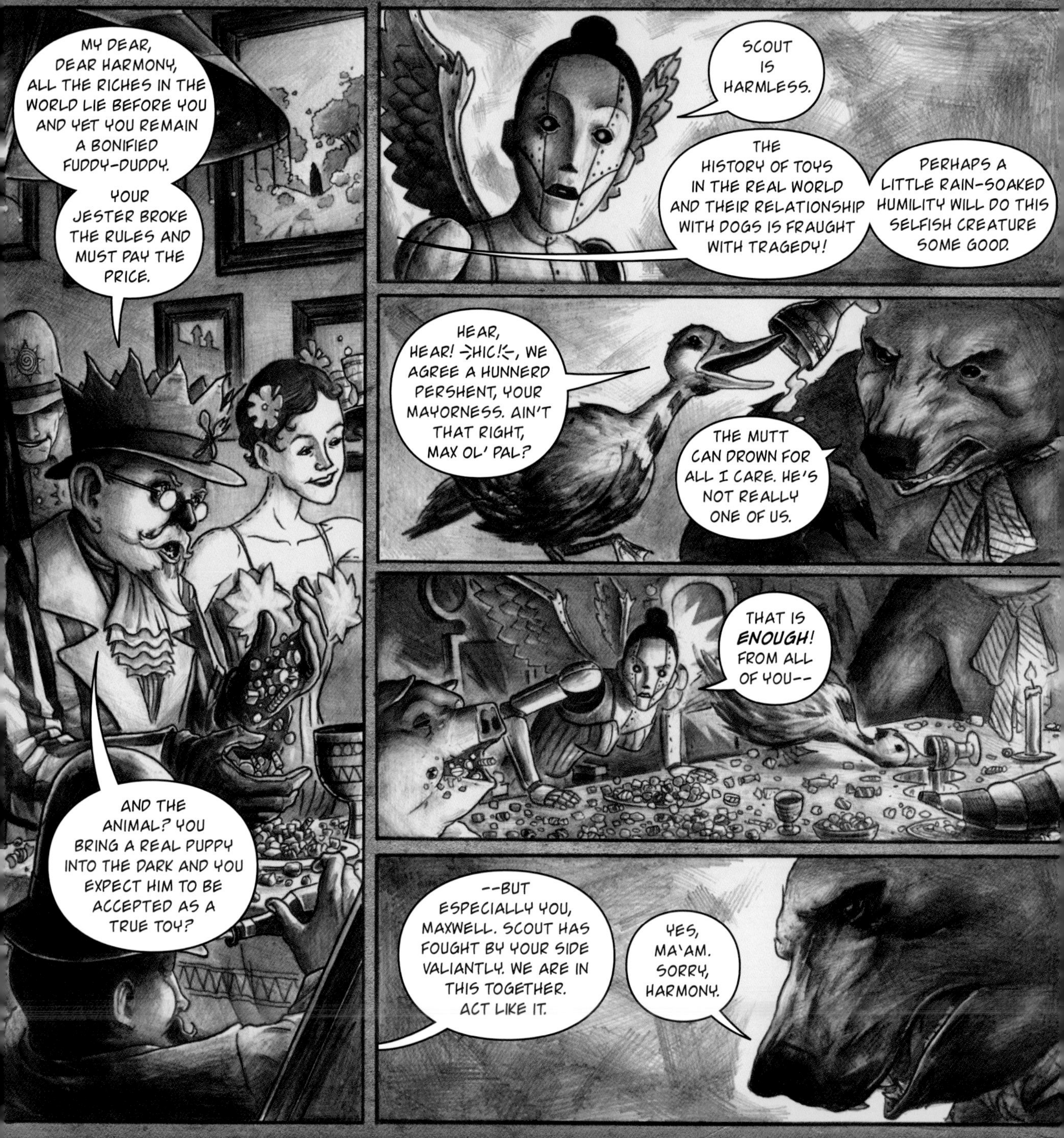
MY DEAR, DEAR HARMONY, ALL THE RICHES IN THE WORLD LIE BEFORE YOU AND YET YOU REMAIN A BONIFIED FUDDY-DUDDY.
YOUR JESTER BROKE THE RULES AND MUST PAY THE PRICE.
AND THE ANIMAL? YOU BRING A REAL PUPPY INTO THE DARK AND YOU EXPECT HIM TO BE ACCEPTED AS A TRUE TOY?
SCOUT IS HARMLESS.
THE HISTORY OF TOYS IN THE REAL WORLD AND THEIR RELATIONSHIP WITH DOGS IS FRAUGHT WITH TRAGEDY!
PERHAPS A LITTLE RAIN-SOAKED HUMILITY WILL DO THIS SELFISH CREATURE SOME GOOD.
HEAR, HEAR! *HIC!*, WE AGREE A HUNNERD PERSHENT, YOUR MAYORNESS. AIN'T THAT RIGHT, MAX OL' PAL?
THE MUTT CAN DROWN FOR ALL I CARE. HE'S NOT REALLY ONE OF US.
THAT IS **ENOUGH**! FROM ALL OF YOU--
--BUT ESPECIALLY YOU, MAXWELL. SCOUT HAS FOUGHT BY YOUR SIDE VALIANTLY. WE ARE IN THIS TOGETHER. ACT LIKE IT.
YES, MA'AM. SORRY, HARMONY.

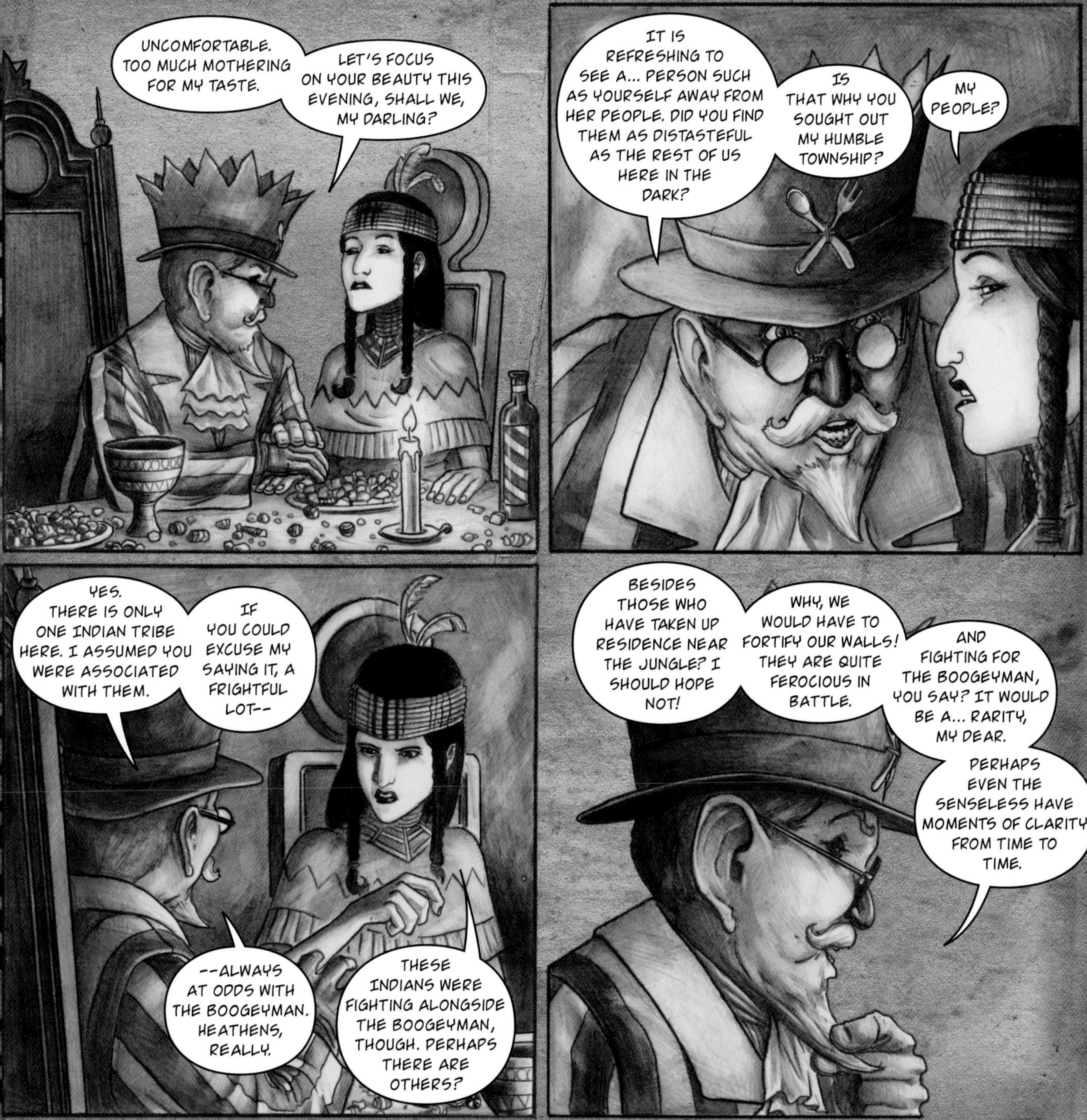
UNCOMFORTABLE. TOO MUCH MOTHERING FOR MY TASTE.
LET'S FOCUS ON YOUR BEAUTY THIS EVENING, SHALL WE, MY DARLING?
IT IS REFRESHING TO SEE A... PERSON SUCH AS YOURSELF AWAY FROM HER PEOPLE. DID YOU FIND THEM AS DISTASTEFUL AS THE REST OF US HERE IN THE DARK?
IS THAT WHY YOU SOUGHT OUT MY HUMBLE TOWNSHIP?
MY PEOPLE?
YES. THERE IS ONLY ONE INDIAN TRIBE HERE. I ASSUMED YOU WERE ASSOCIATED WITH THEM.
IF YOU COULD EXCUSE MY SAYING IT, A FRIGHTFUL LOT--
--ALWAYS AT ODDS WITH THE BOOGEYMAN. HEATHENS, REALLY.
THESE INDIANS WERE FIGHTING ALONGSIDE THE BOOGEYMAN, THOUGH. PERHAPS THERE ARE OTHERS?
BESIDES THOSE WHO HAVE TAKEN UP RESIDENCE NEAR THE JUNGLE? I SHOULD HOPE NOT!
WHY, WE WOULD HAVE TO FORTIFY OUR WALLS! THEY ARE QUITE FEROCIOUS IN BATTLE.
AND FIGHTING FOR THE BOOGEYMAN, YOU SAY? IT WOULD BE A... RARITY, MY DEAR.
PERHAPS EVEN THE SENSELESS HAVE MOMENTS OF CLARITY FROM TIME TO TIME.

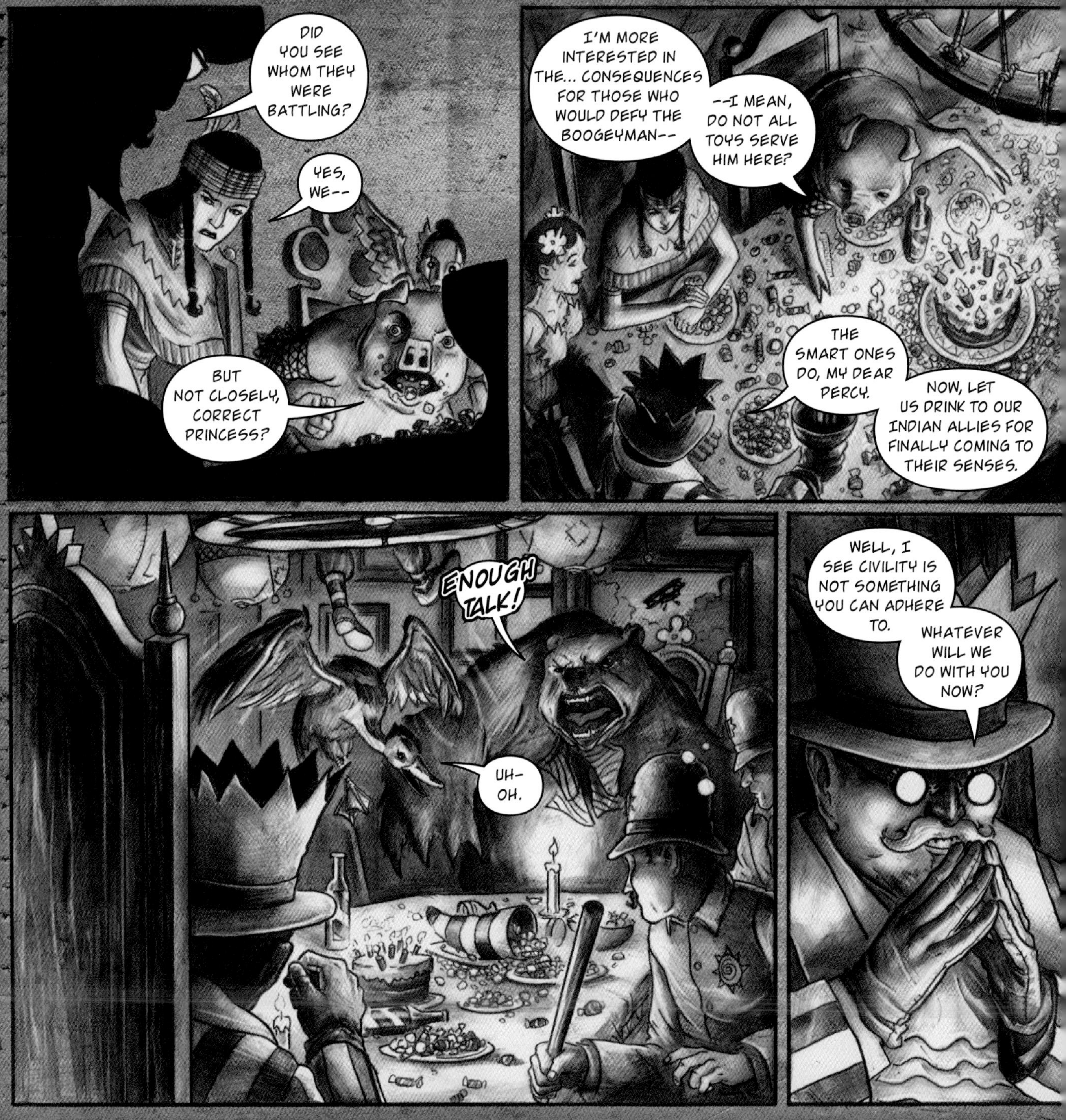
DID YOU SEE WHOM THEY WERE BATTLING?
YES, WE--
BUT NOT CLOSELY, CORRECT PRINCESS?
I'M MORE INTERESTED IN THE... CONSEQUENCES FOR THOSE WHO WOULD DEFY THE BOOGEYMAN--
--I MEAN, DO NOT ALL TOYS SERVE HIM HERE?
THE SMART ONES DO, MY DEAR PERCY.
NOW, LET US DRINK TO OUR INDIAN ALLIES FOR FINALLY COMING TO THEIR SENSES.
ENOUGH TALK!
UH-OH.
WELL, I SEE CIVILITY IS NOT SOMETHING YOU CAN ADHERE TO.
WHATEVER WILL WE DO WITH YOU NOW?

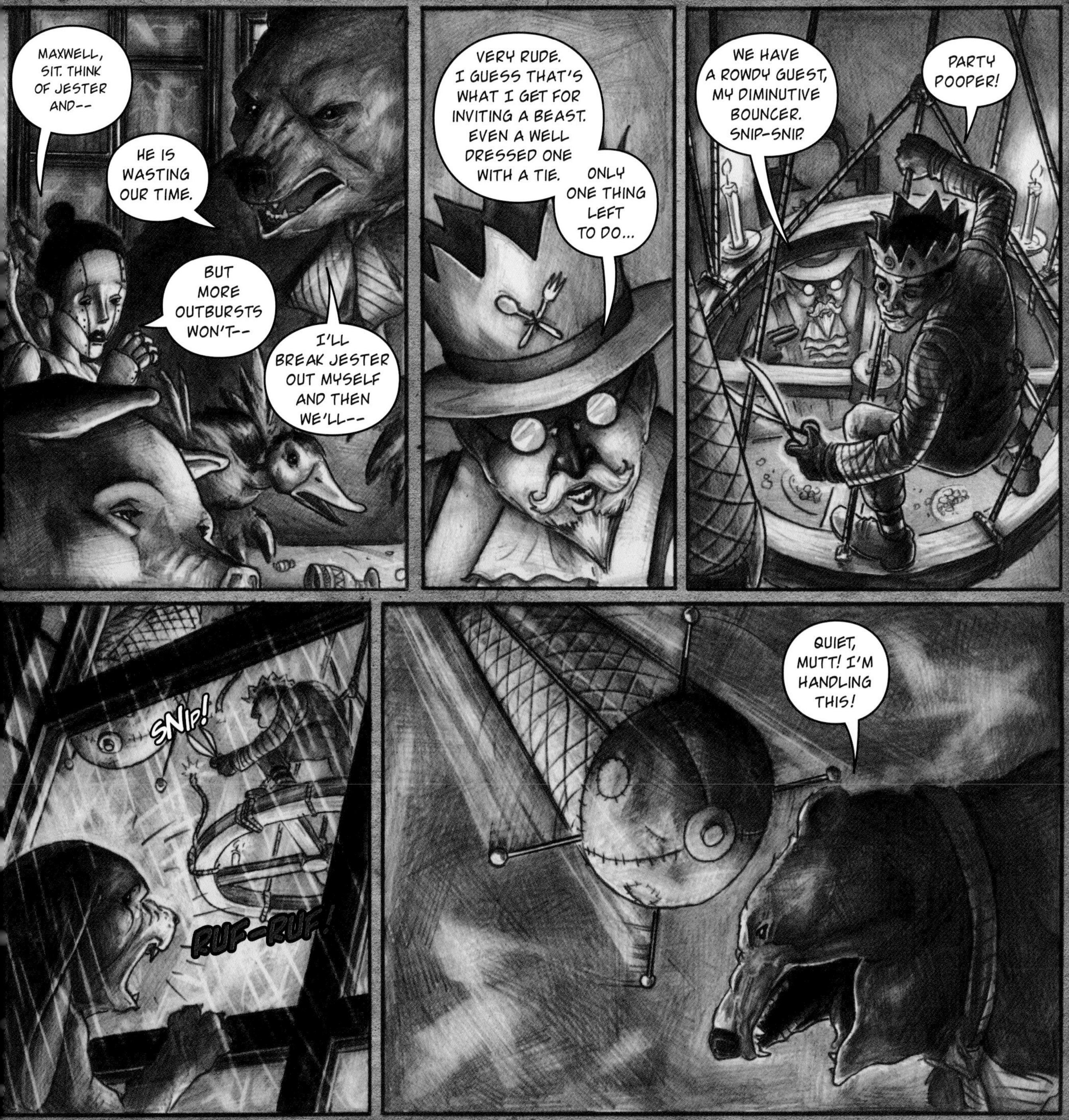
MAXWELL, SIT. THINK OF JESTER AND--
HE IS WASTING OUR TIME.
BUT MORE OUTBURSTS WON'T--
I'LL BREAK JESTER OUT MYSELF AND THEN WE'LL--
VERY RUDE. I GUESS THAT'S WHAT I GET FOR INVITING A BEAST. EVEN A WELL DRESSED ONE WITH A TIE.
ONLY ONE THING LEFT TO DO...
WE HAVE A ROWDY GUEST, MY DIMINUTIVE BOUNCER. SNIP-SNIP.
PARTY POOPER!
SNIP!
RUF-RUF!
QUIET, MUTT! I'M HANDLING THIS!

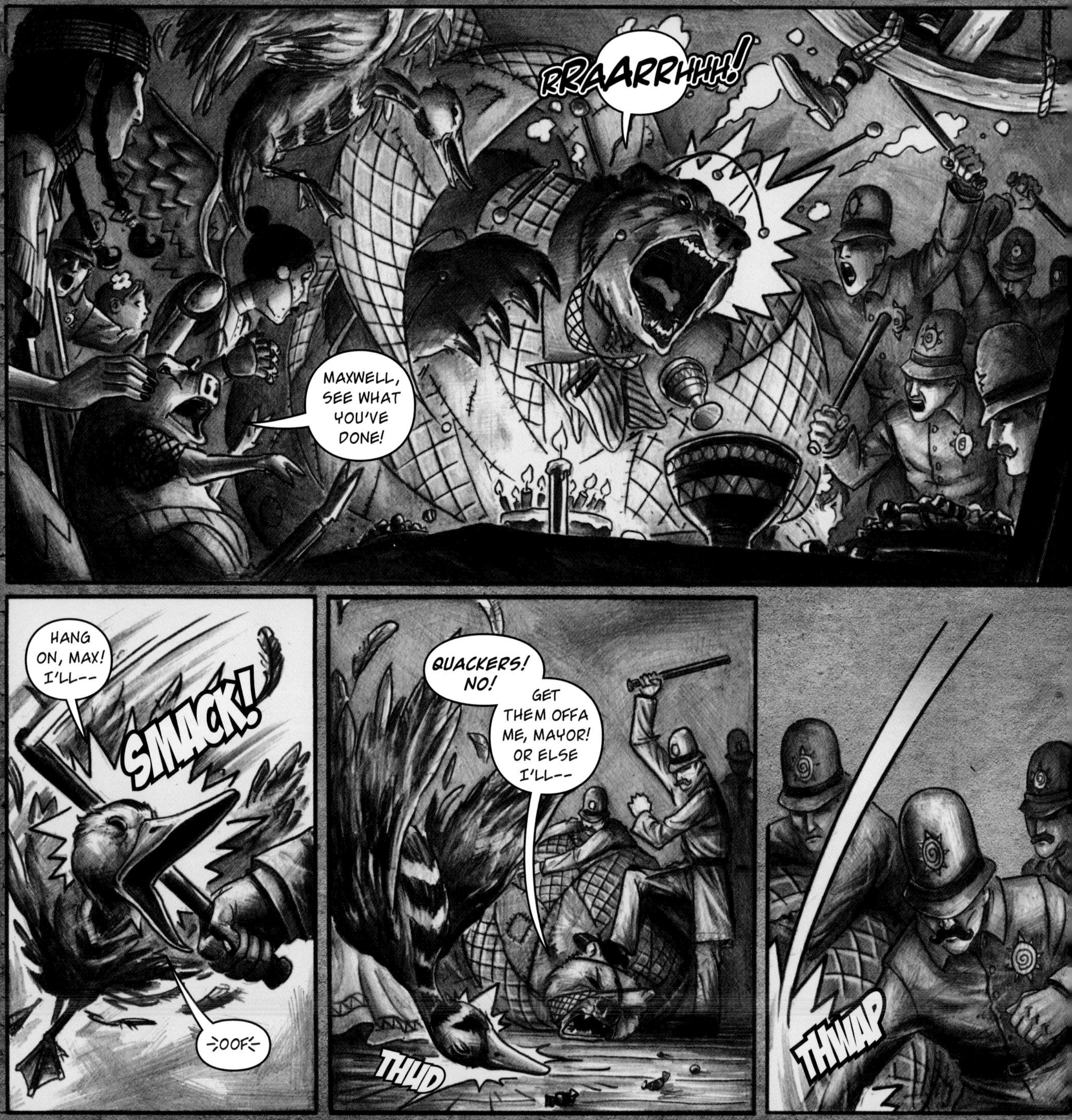
RRAARRHHH!
MAXWELL, SEE WHAT YOU'VE DONE!
HANG ON, MAX! I'LL--
SMACK!
OOF
QUACKERS! NO!
GET THEM OFFA ME, MAYOR! OR ELSE I'LL--
THUD
THWAP

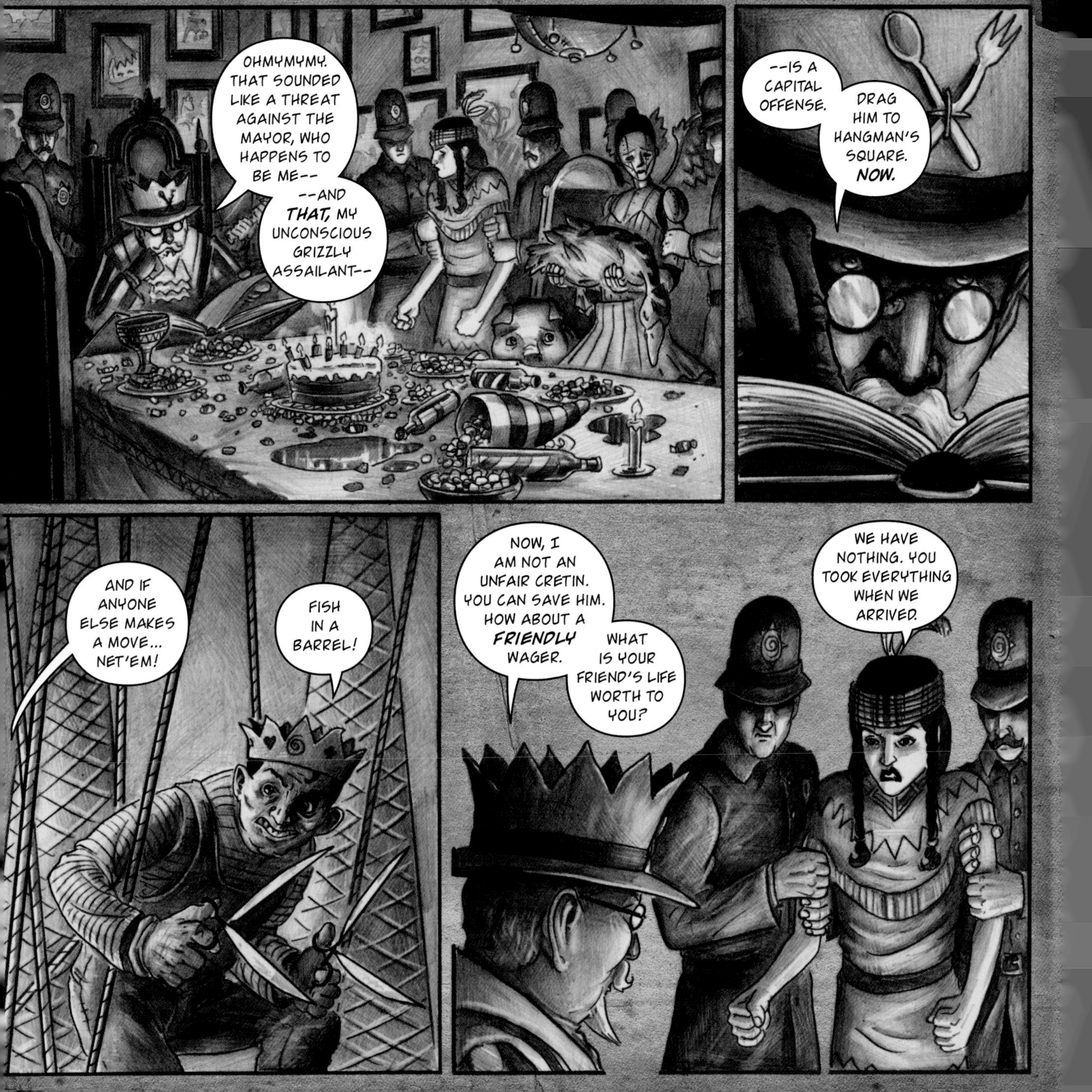
OHMYMYMY. THAT SOUNDED LIKE A THREAT AGAINST THE MAYOR, WHO HAPPENS TO BE ME--
--AND *THAT,* MY UNCONSCIOUS GRIZZLY ASSAILANT--
--IS A CAPITAL OFFENSE.
DRAG HIM TO HANGMAN'S SQUARE. ***NOW.***
AND IF ANYONE ELSE MAKES A MOVE... NET'EM!
FISH IN A BARREL!
NOW, I AM NOT AN UNFAIR CRETIN. YOU CAN SAVE HIM. HOW ABOUT A ***FRIENDLY*** WAGER.
WHAT IS YOUR FRIEND'S LIFE WORTH TO YOU?
WE HAVE NOTHING. YOU TOOK EVERYTHING WHEN WE ARRIVED.

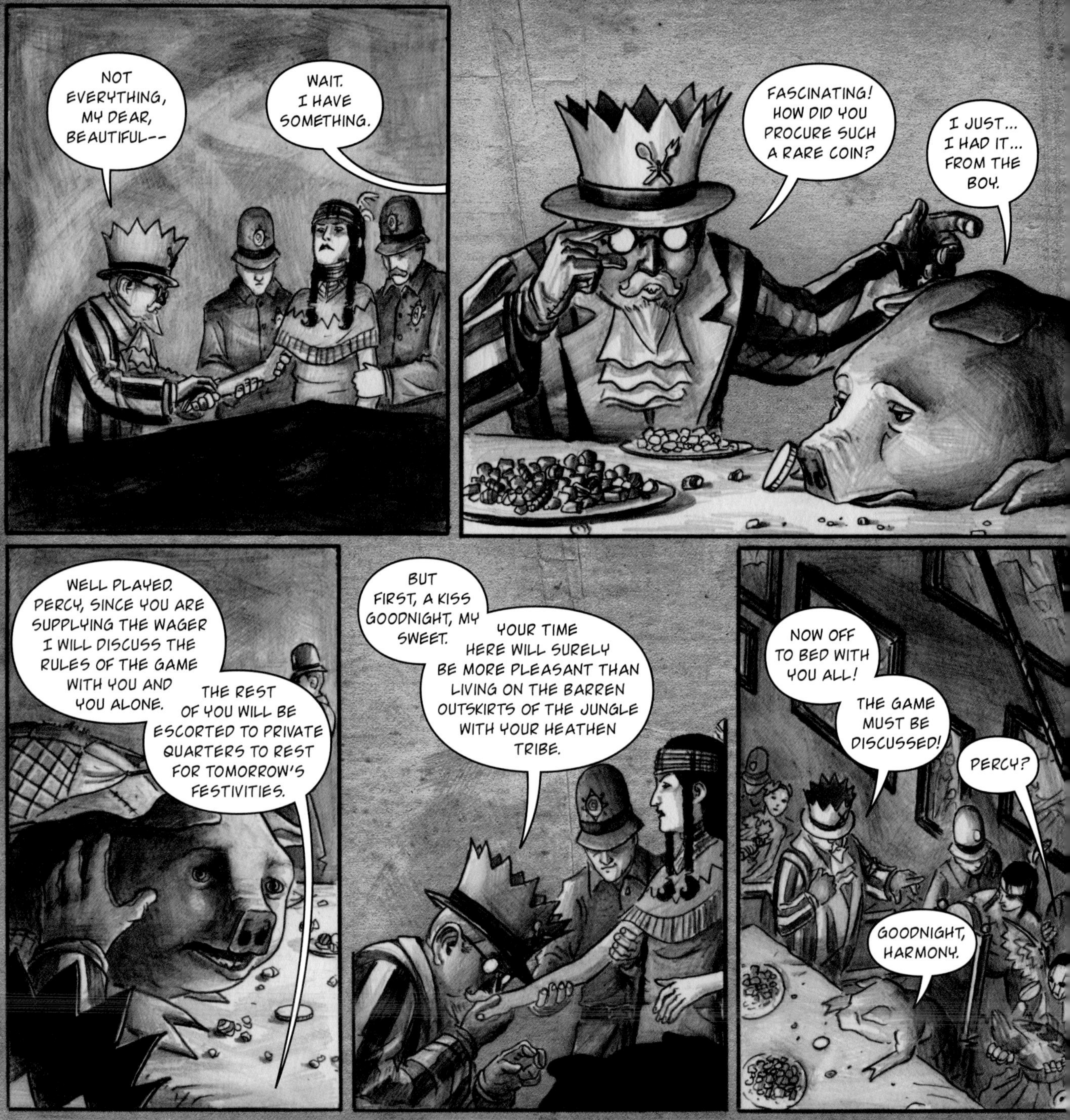
NOT EVERYTHING, MY DEAR, BEAUTIFUL--
WAIT. I HAVE SOMETHING.
FASCINATING! HOW DID YOU PROCURE SUCH A RARE COIN?
I JUST... I HAD IT... FROM THE BOY.
WELL PLAYED. PERCY, SINCE YOU ARE SUPPLYING THE WAGER I WILL DISCUSS THE RULES OF THE GAME WITH YOU AND YOU ALONE.
THE REST OF YOU WILL BE ESCORTED TO PRIVATE QUARTERS TO REST FOR TOMORROW'S FESTIVITIES.
BUT FIRST, A KISS GOODNIGHT, MY SWEET.
YOUR TIME HERE WILL SURELY BE MORE PLEASANT THAN LIVING ON THE BARREN OUTSKIRTS OF THE JUNGLE WITH YOUR HEATHEN TRIBE.
NOW OFF TO BED WITH YOU ALL!
THE GAME MUST BE DISCUSSED!
PERCY?
GOODNIGHT, HARMONY.

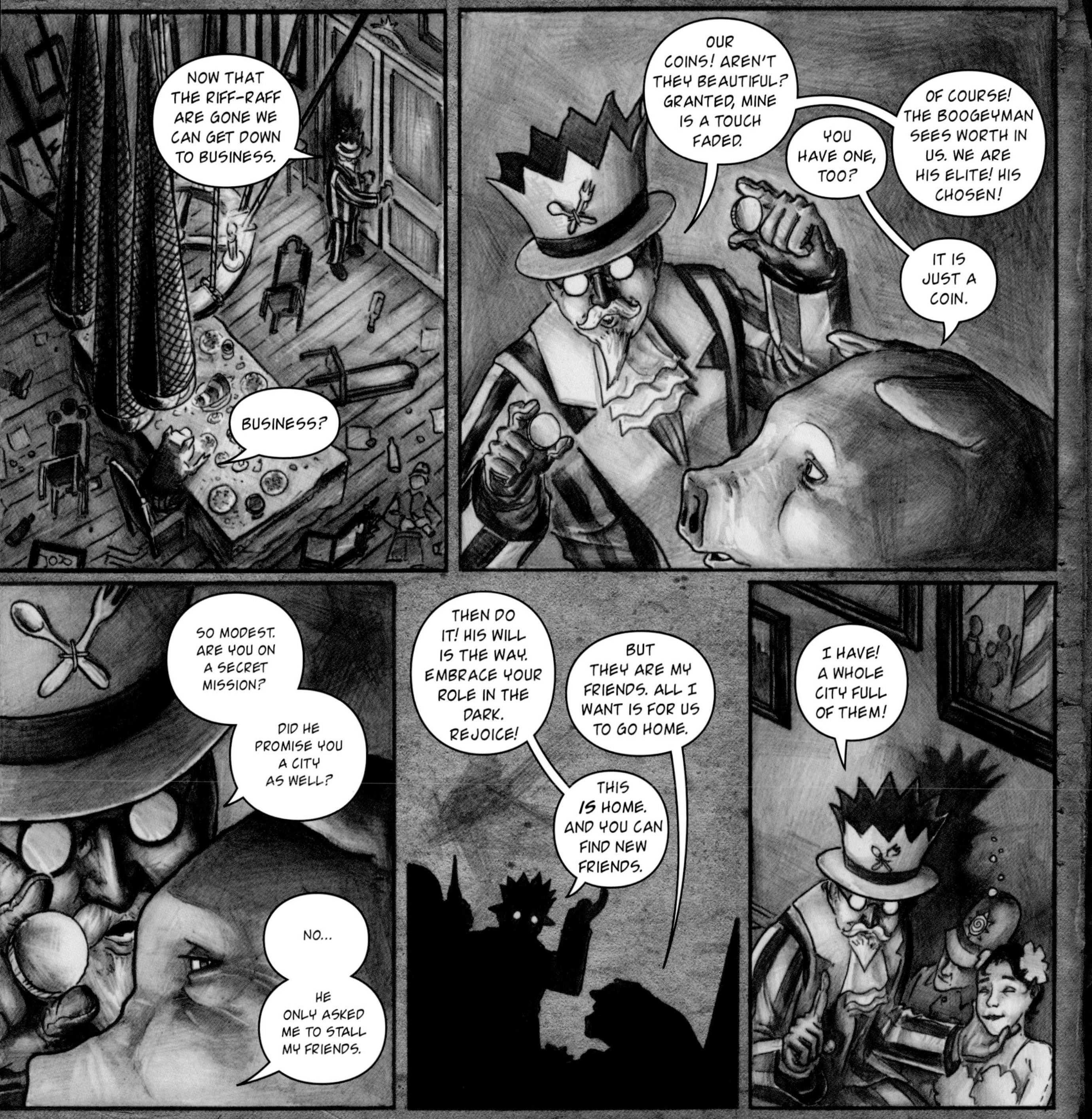
NOW THAT THE RIFF-RAFF ARE GONE WE CAN GET DOWN TO BUSINESS.
BUSINESS?
OUR COINS! AREN'T THEY BEAUTIFUL? GRANTED, MINE IS A TOUCH FADED.
YOU HAVE ONE, TOO?
IT IS JUST A COIN.
OF COURSE! THE BOOGEYMAN SEES WORTH IN US. WE ARE HIS ELITE! HIS CHOSEN!
SO MODEST. ARE YOU ON A SECRET MISSION?
DID HE PROMISE YOU A CITY AS WELL?
NO...
HE ONLY ASKED ME TO STALL MY FRIENDS.
THEN DO IT! HIS WILL IS THE WAY. EMBRACE YOUR ROLE IN THE DARK. REJOICE!
BUT THEY ARE MY FRIENDS. ALL I WANT IS FOR US TO GO HOME.
THIS *IS* HOME. AND YOU CAN FIND NEW FRIENDS.
I HAVE! A WHOLE CITY FULL OF THEM!

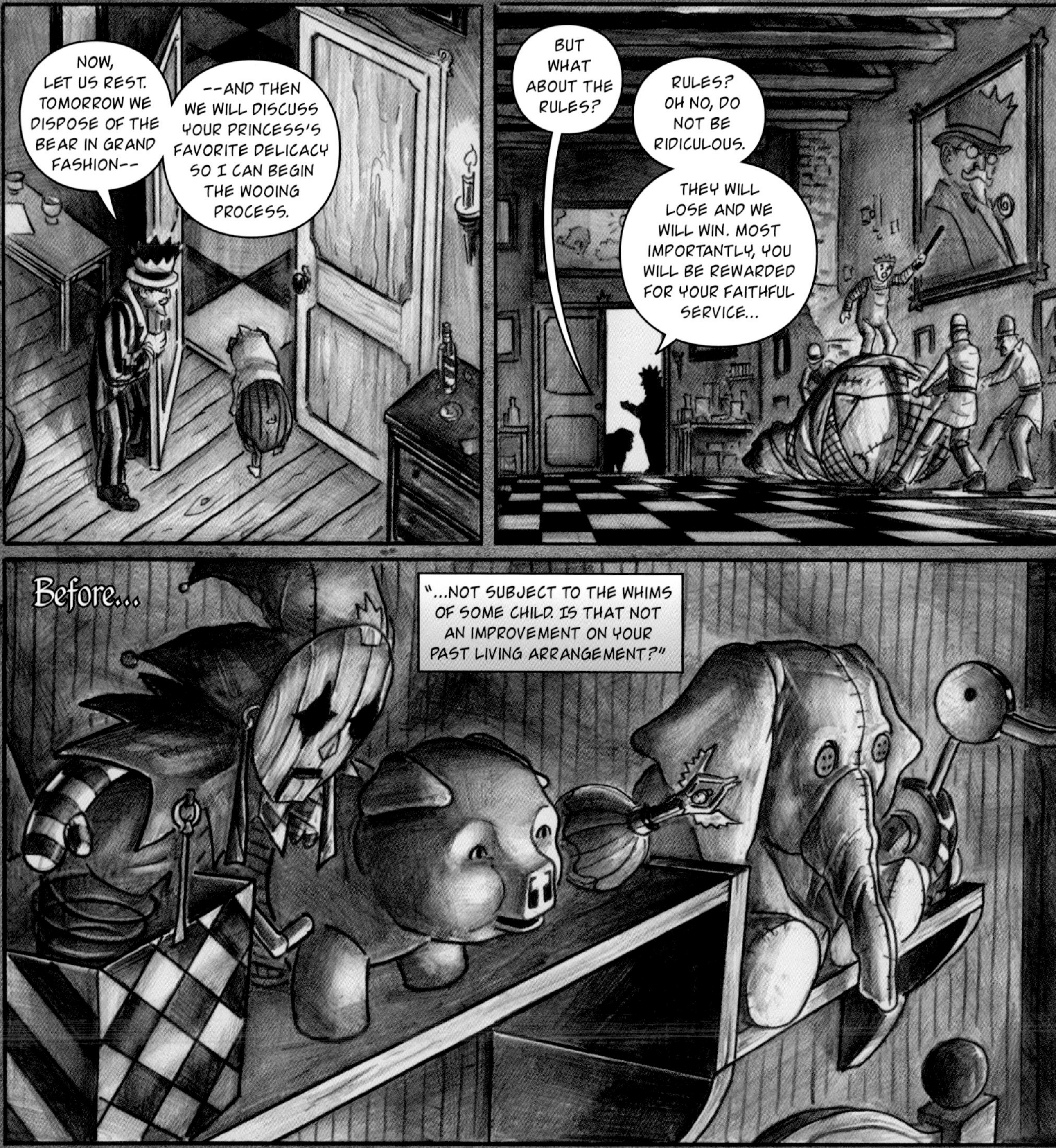
NOW, LET US REST. TOMORROW WE DISPOSE OF THE BEAR IN GRAND FASHION--
--AND THEN WE WILL DISCUSS YOUR PRINCESS'S FAVORITE DELICACY SO I CAN BEGIN THE WOOING PROCESS.
BUT WHAT ABOUT THE RULES?
RULES? OH NO, DO NOT BE RIDICULOUS.
THEY WILL LOSE AND WE WILL WIN. MOST IMPORTANTLY, YOU WILL BE REWARDED FOR YOUR FAITHFUL SERVICE...
Before...
"...NOT SUBJECT TO THE WHIMS OF SOME CHILD. IS THAT NOT AN IMPROVEMENT ON YOUR PAST LIVING ARRANGEMENT?"

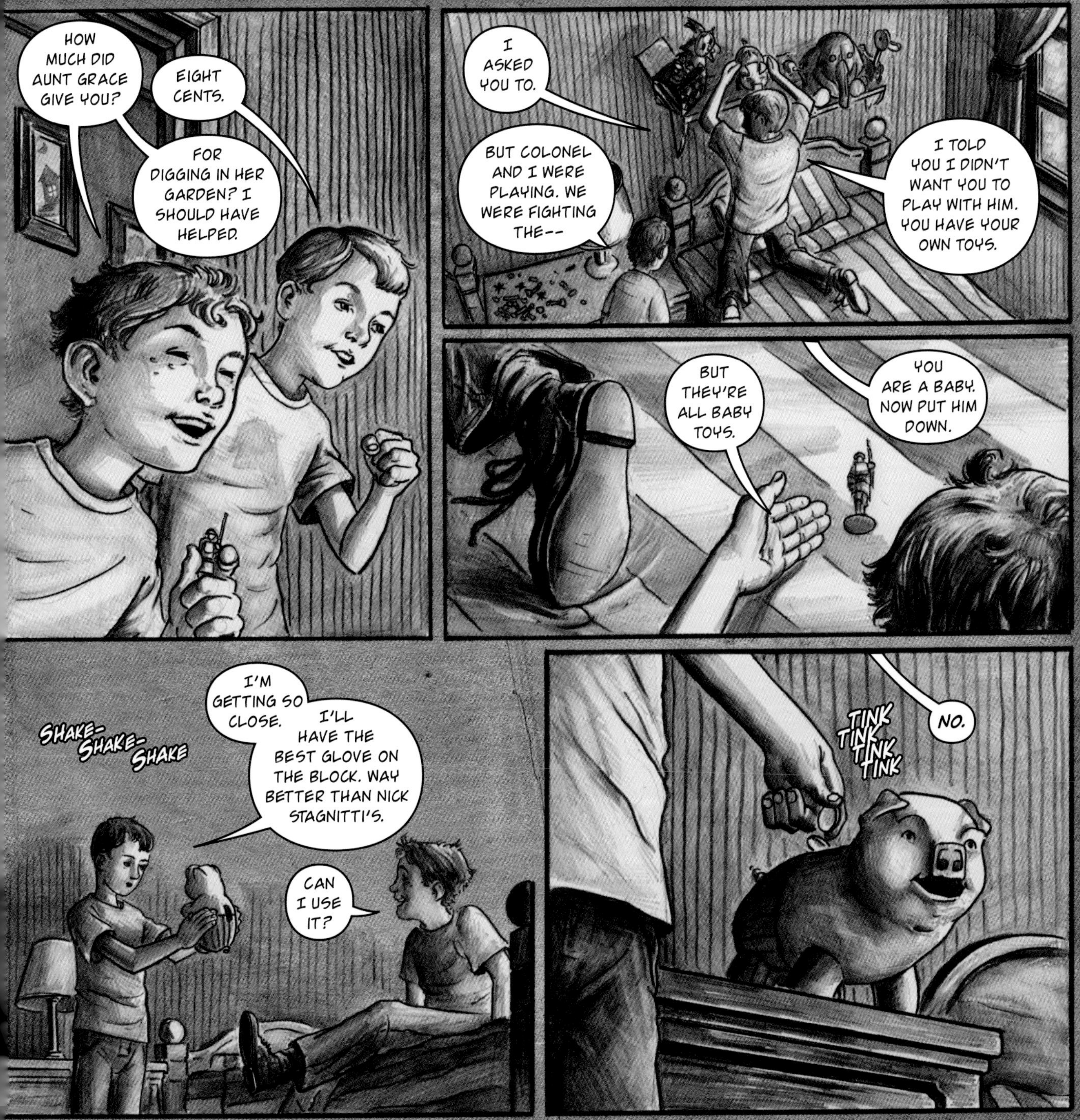
HOW MUCH DID AUNT GRACE GIVE YOU?
EIGHT CENTS.
FOR DIGGING IN HER GARDEN? I SHOULD HAVE HELPED.
I ASKED YOU TO.
BUT COLONEL AND I WERE PLAYING. WE WERE FIGHTING THE--
I TOLD YOU I DIDN'T WANT YOU TO PLAY WITH HIM. YOU HAVE YOUR OWN TOYS.
BUT THEY'RE ALL BABY TOYS.
YOU ARE A BABY. NOW PUT HIM DOWN.
SHAKE-SHAKE-SHAKE
I'M GETTING SO CLOSE.
I'LL HAVE THE BEST GLOVE ON THE BLOCK. WAY BETTER THAN NICK STAGNITTI'S.
CAN I USE IT?
NO.
TINK TINK TINK TINK

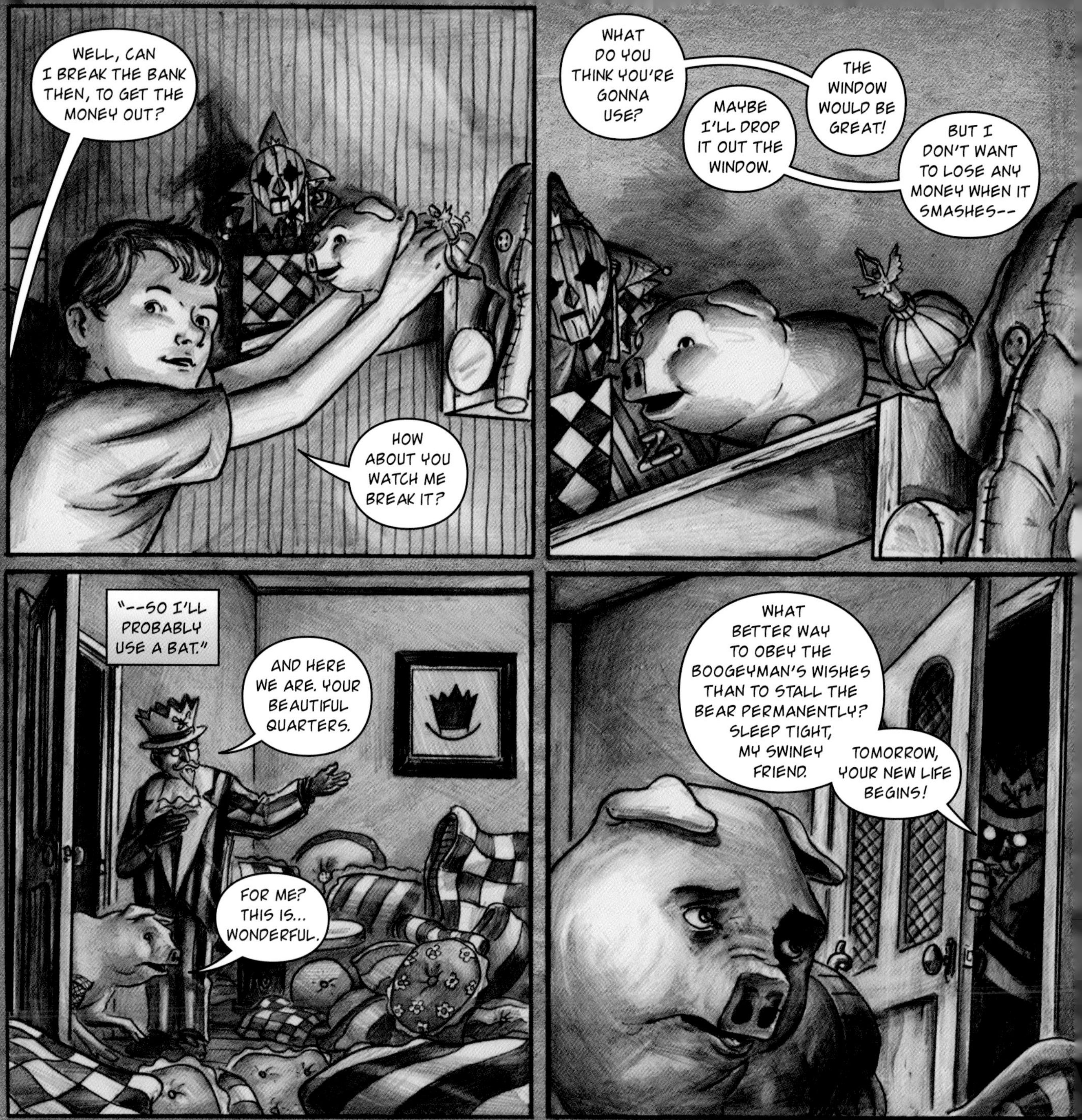
WELL, CAN I BREAK THE BANK THEN, TO GET THE MONEY OUT?
HOW ABOUT YOU WATCH ME BREAK IT?
WHAT DO YOU THINK YOU'RE GONNA USE?
THE WINDOW WOULD BE GREAT!
MAYBE I'LL DROP IT OUT THE WINDOW.
BUT I DON'T WANT TO LOSE ANY MONEY WHEN IT SMASHES--
"--SO I'LL PROBABLY USE A BAT."
AND HERE WE ARE. YOUR BEAUTIFUL QUARTERS.
FOR ME? THIS IS... WONDERFUL.
WHAT BETTER WAY TO OBEY THE BOOGEYMAN'S WISHES THAN TO STALL THE BEAR PERMANENTLY? SLEEP TIGHT, MY SWINEY FRIEND.
TOMORROW, YOUR NEW LIFE BEGINS!

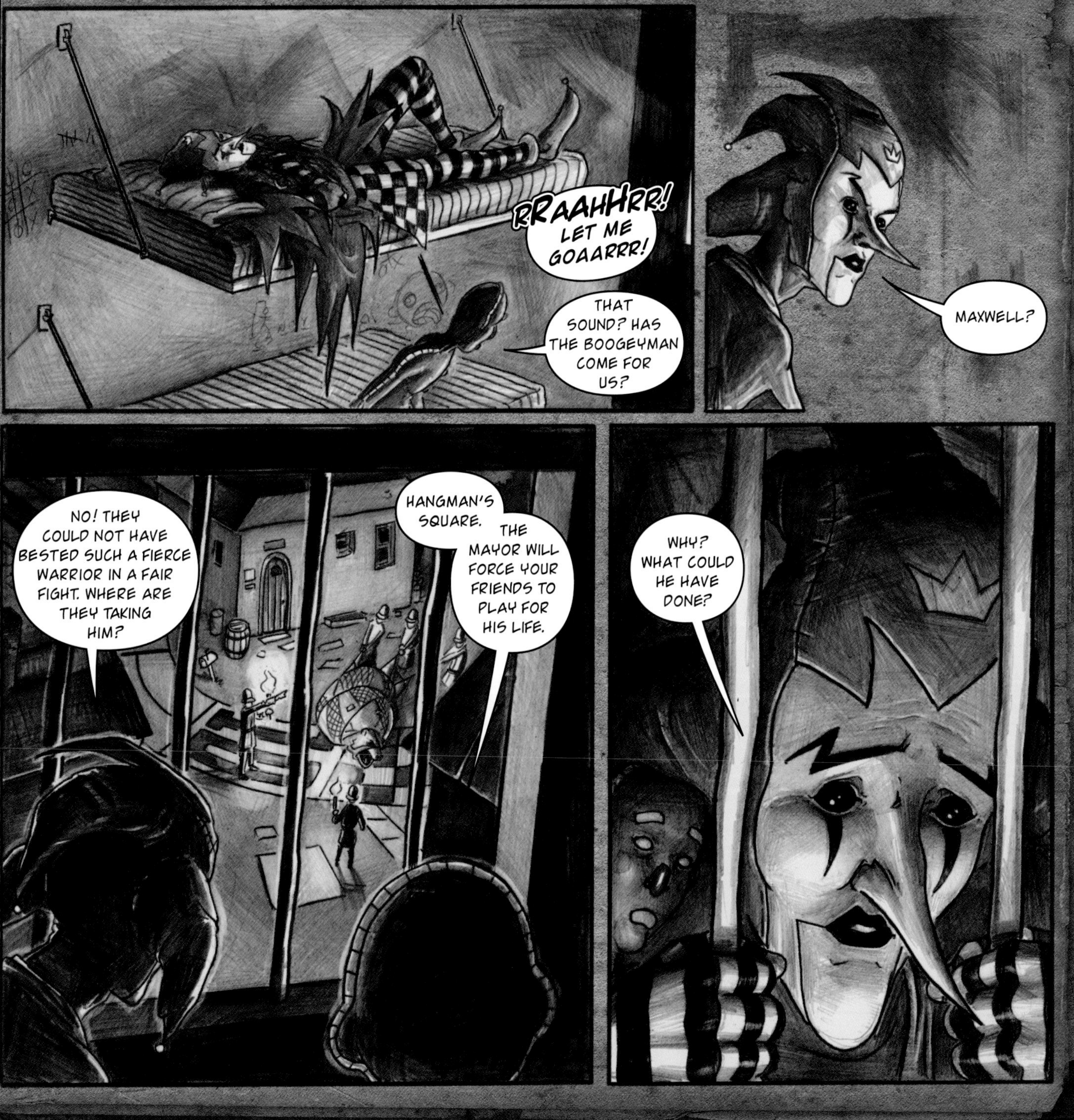
RRAAHHRR! LET ME GOAARRR!
THAT SOUND? HAS THE BOOGEYMAN COME FOR US?
MAXWELL?
NO! THEY COULD NOT HAVE BESTED SUCH A FIERCE WARRIOR IN A FAIR FIGHT. WHERE ARE THEY TAKING HIM?
HANGMAN'S SQUARE.
THE MAYOR WILL FORCE YOUR FRIENDS TO PLAY FOR HIS LIFE.
WHY? WHAT COULD HE HAVE DONE?

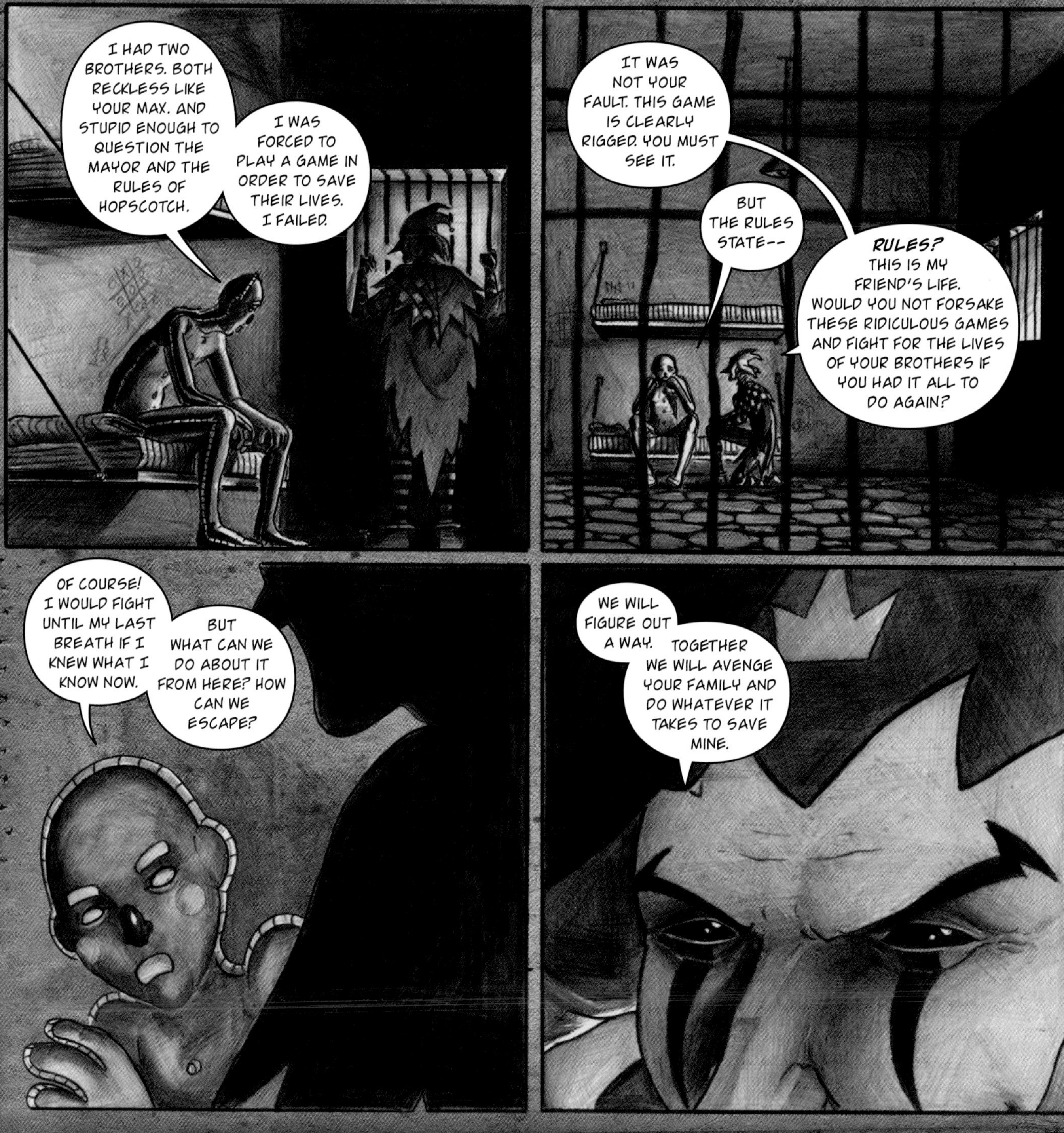
I HAD TWO BROTHERS. BOTH RECKLESS LIKE YOUR MAX. AND STUPID ENOUGH TO QUESTION THE MAYOR AND THE RULES OF HOPSCOTCH.
I WAS FORCED TO PLAY A GAME IN ORDER TO SAVE THEIR LIVES. I FAILED.
IT WAS NOT YOUR FAULT. THIS GAME IS CLEARLY RIGGED. YOU MUST SEE IT.
BUT THE RULES STATE--
RULES? THIS IS MY FRIEND'S LIFE. WOULD YOU NOT FORSAKE THESE RIDICULOUS GAMES AND FIGHT FOR THE LIVES OF YOUR BROTHERS IF YOU HAD IT ALL TO DO AGAIN?
OF COURSE! I WOULD FIGHT UNTIL MY LAST BREATH IF I KNEW WHAT I KNOW NOW.
BUT WHAT CAN WE DO ABOUT IT FROM HERE? HOW CAN WE ESCAPE?
WE WILL FIGURE OUT A WAY.
TOGETHER WE WILL AVENGE YOUR FAMILY AND DO WHATEVER IT TAKES TO SAVE MINE.

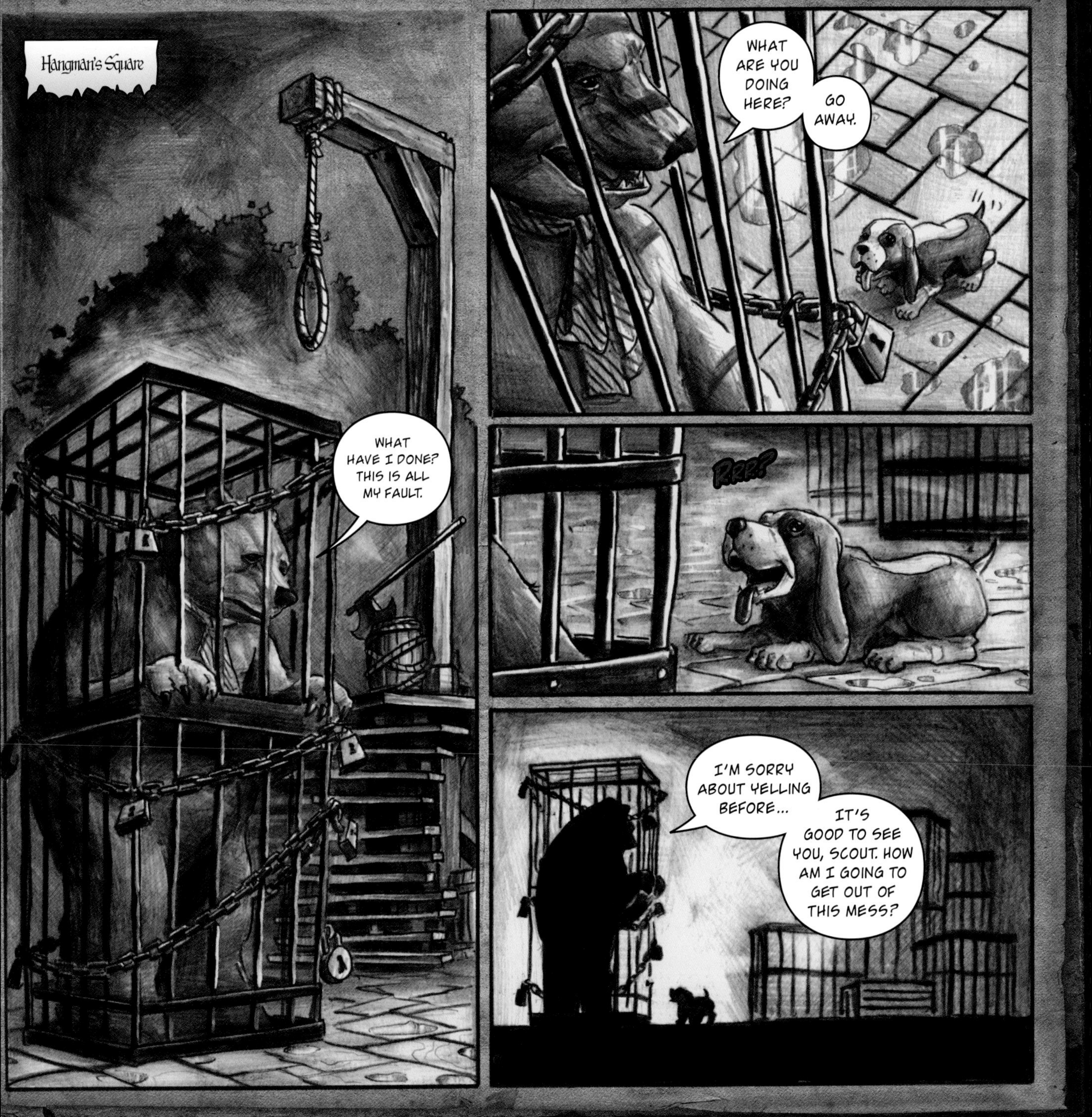
Hangman's Square
WHAT HAVE I DONE? THIS IS ALL MY FAULT.
WHAT ARE YOU DOING HERE?
GO AWAY.
RRR?
I'M SORRY ABOUT YELLING BEFORE...
IT'S GOOD TO SEE YOU, SCOUT. HOW AM I GOING TO GET OUT OF THIS MESS?

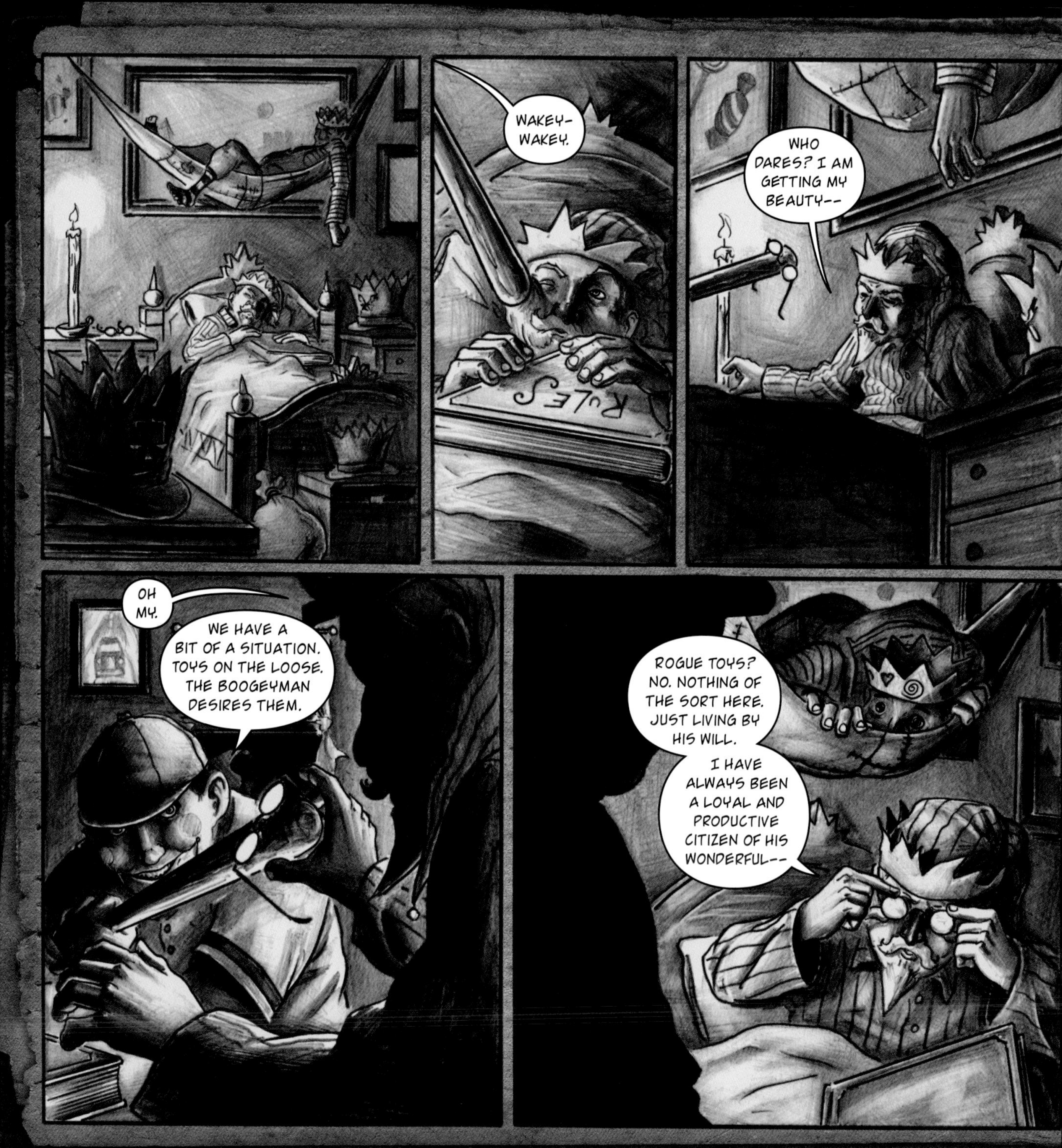
WAKEY-WAKEY.
RULES
WHO DARES? I AM GETTING MY BEAUTY--
OH MY.
WE HAVE A BIT OF A SITUATION. TOYS ON THE LOOSE. THE BOOGEYMAN DESIRES THEM.
ROGUE TOYS? NO. NOTHING OF THE SORT HERE. JUST LIVING BY HIS WILL.
I HAVE ALWAYS BEEN A LOYAL AND PRODUCTIVE CITIZEN OF HIS WONDERFUL--

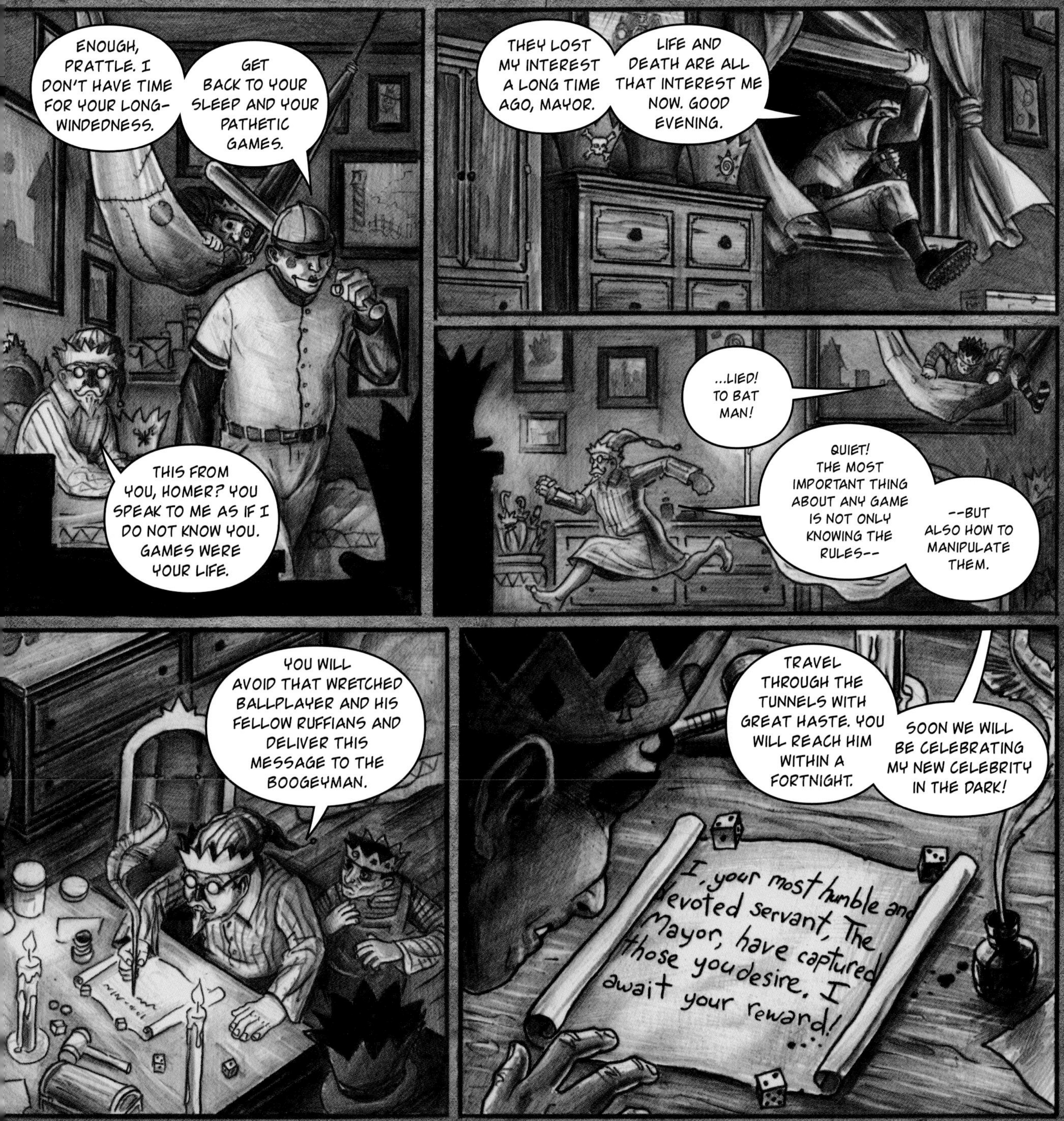
ENOUGH, PRATTLE. I DON'T HAVE TIME FOR YOUR LONG-WINDEDNESS.
GET BACK TO YOUR SLEEP AND YOUR PATHETIC GAMES.
THIS FROM YOU, HOMER? YOU SPEAK TO ME AS IF I DO NOT KNOW YOU. GAMES WERE YOUR LIFE.
THEY LOST MY INTEREST A LONG TIME AGO, MAYOR.
LIFE AND DEATH ARE ALL THAT INTEREST ME NOW. GOOD EVENING.
...LIED! TO BAT MAN!
QUIET! THE MOST IMPORTANT THING ABOUT ANY GAME IS NOT ONLY KNOWING THE RULES--
--BUT ALSO HOW TO MANIPULATE THEM.
YOU WILL AVOID THAT WRETCHED BALLPLAYER AND HIS FELLOW RUFFIANS AND DELIVER THIS MESSAGE TO THE BOOGEYMAN.
TRAVEL THROUGH THE TUNNELS WITH GREAT HASTE. YOU WILL REACH HIM WITHIN A FORTNIGHT.
SOON WE WILL BE CELEBRATING MY NEW CELEBRITY IN THE DARK!
I, your most humble and devoted servant, The Mayor, have captured those youdesire. I await your reward!

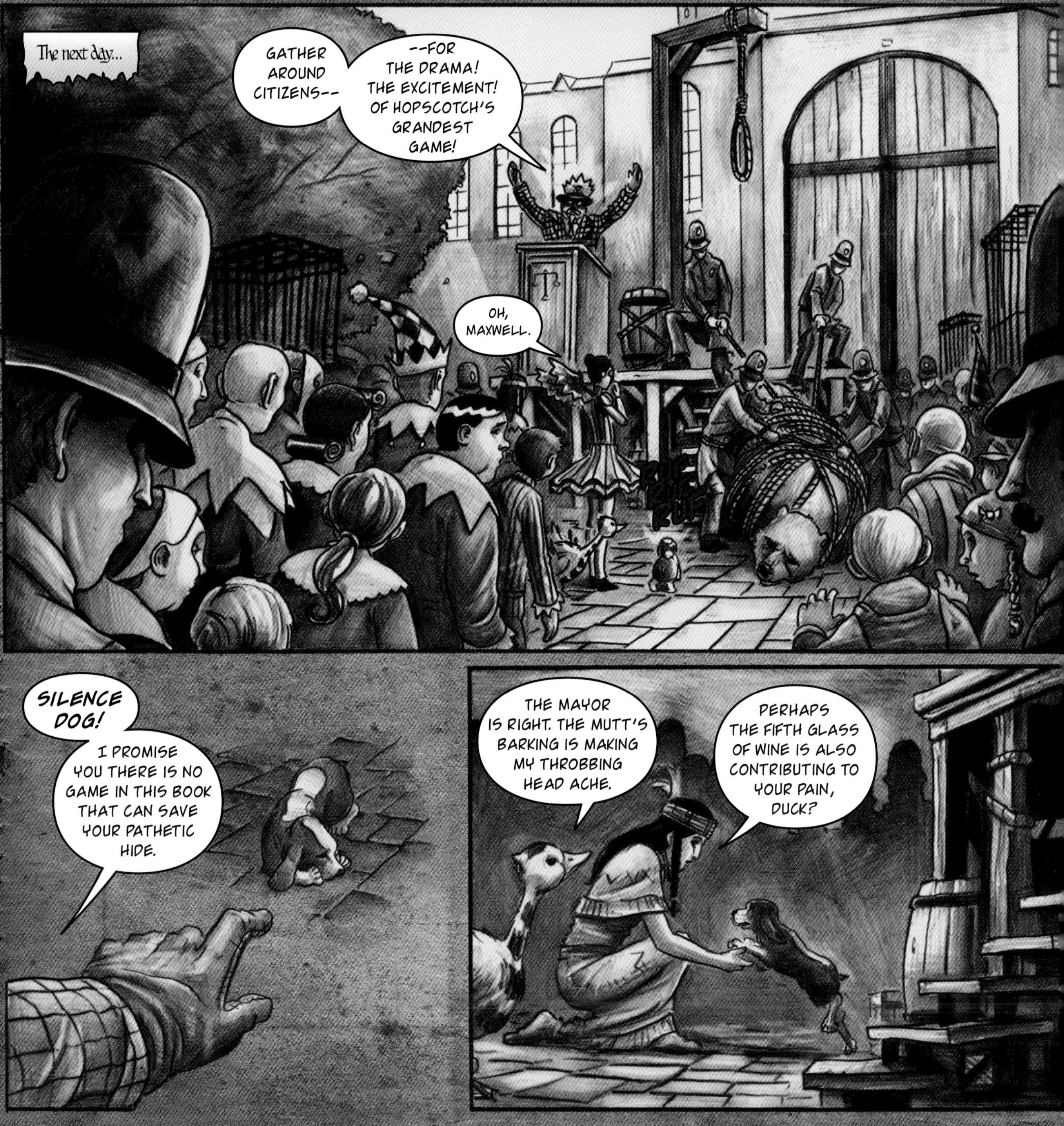
The next day...
GATHER AROUND CITIZENS--
--FOR THE DRAMA! THE EXCITEMENT! OF HOPSCOTCH'S GRANDEST GAME!
OH, MAXWELL.
SILENCE DOG!
I PROMISE YOU THERE IS NO GAME IN THIS BOOK THAT CAN SAVE YOUR PATHETIC HIDE.
THE MAYOR IS RIGHT. THE MUTT'S BARKING IS MAKING MY THROBBING HEAD ACHE.
PERHAPS THE FIFTH GLASS OF WINE IS ALSO CONTRIBUTING TO YOUR PAIN, DUCK?

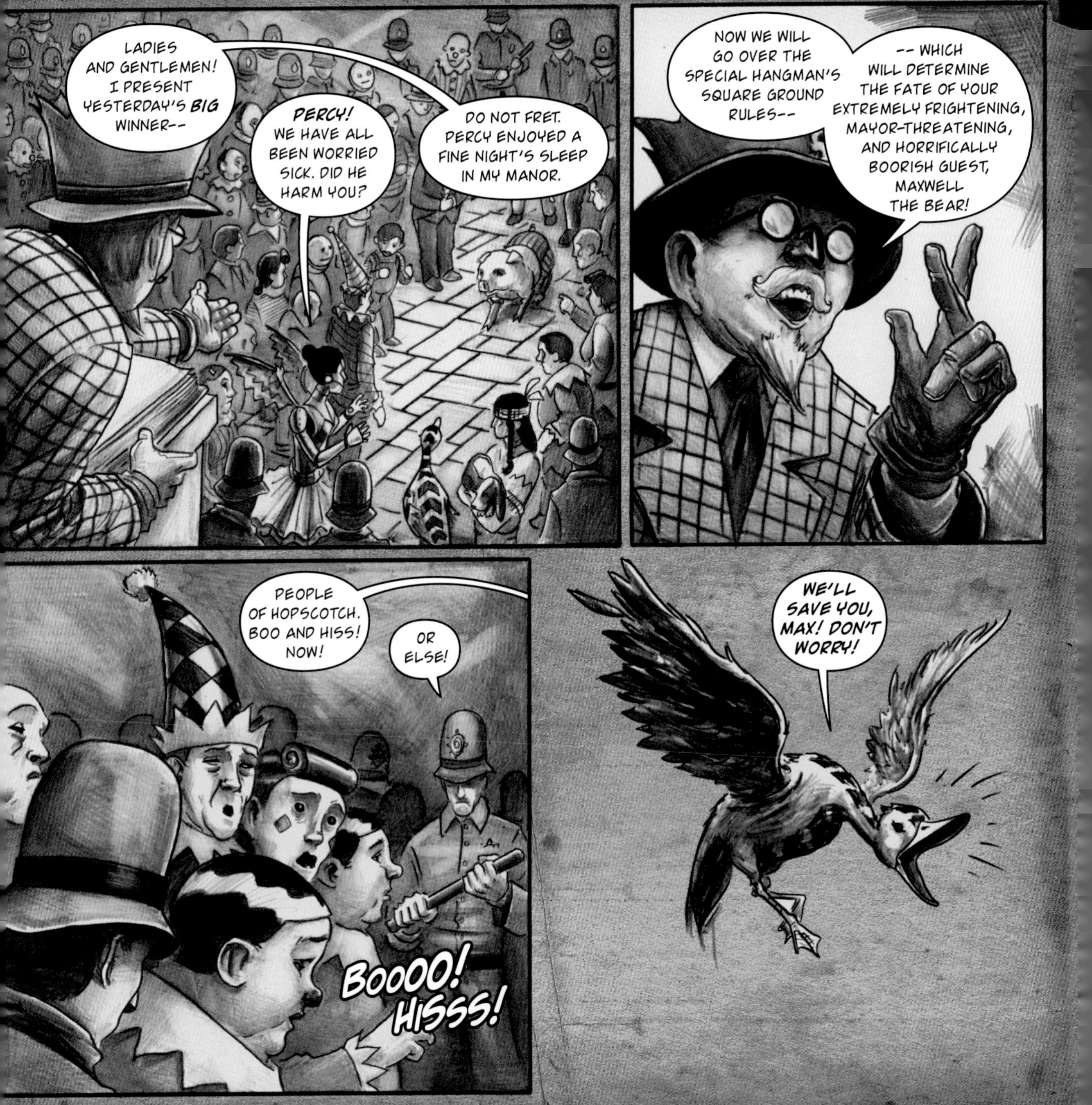
LADIES AND GENTLEMEN! I PRESENT YESTERDAY'S **BIG** WINNER--
PERCY! WE HAVE ALL BEEN WORRIED SICK. DID HE HARM YOU?
DO NOT FRET. PERCY ENJOYED A FINE NIGHT'S SLEEP IN MY MANOR.
NOW WE WILL GO OVER THE SPECIAL HANGMAN'S SQUARE GROUND RULES--
-- WHICH WILL DETERMINE THE FATE OF YOUR EXTREMELY FRIGHTENING, MAYOR-THREATENING, AND HORRIFICALLY BOORISH GUEST, MAXWELL THE BEAR!
PEOPLE OF HOPSCOTCH. BOO AND HISS! NOW!
OR ELSE!
BOOOO! HISSS!
WE'LL SAVE YOU, MAX! DON'T WORRY!

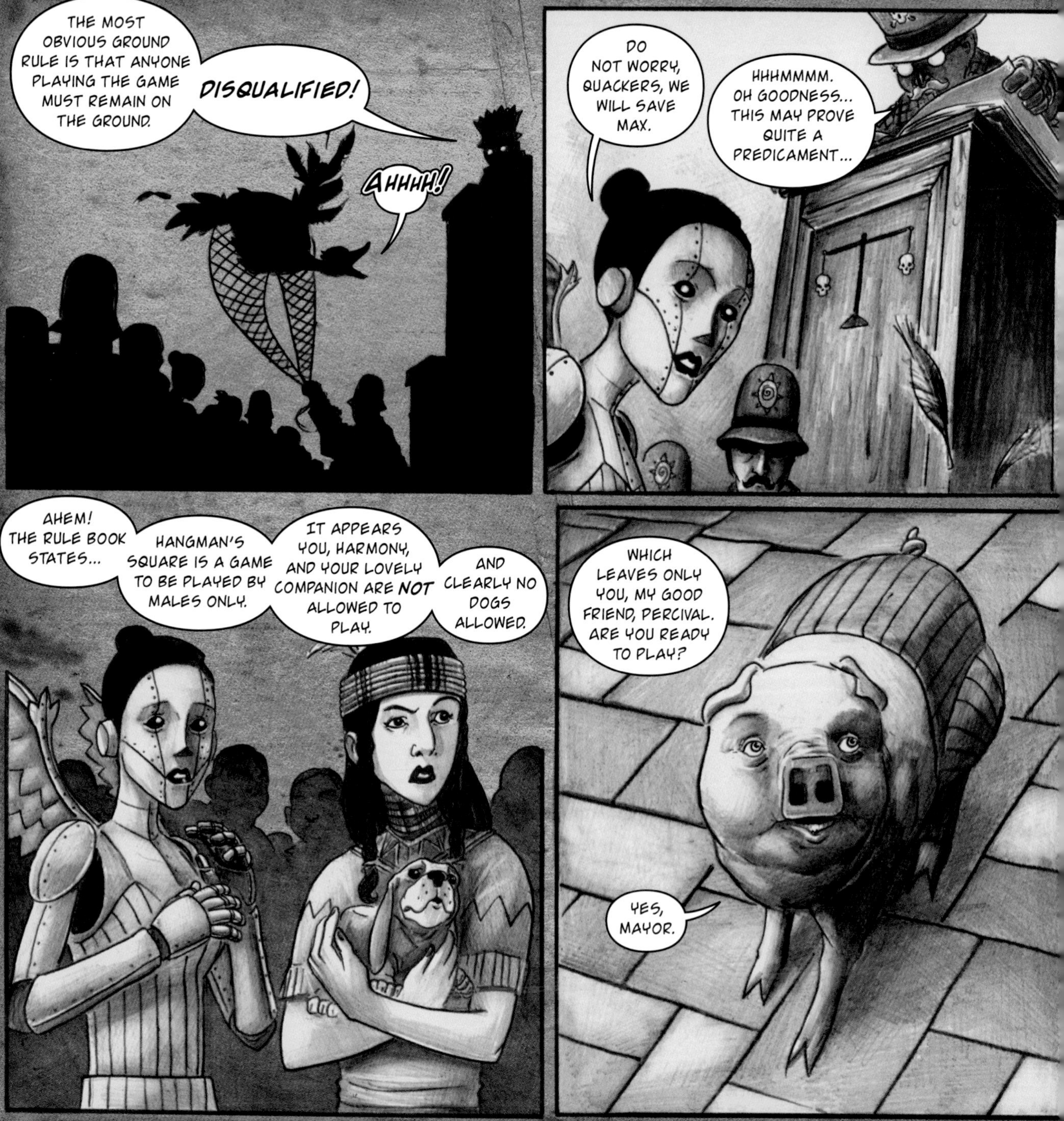
THE MOST OBVIOUS GROUND RULE IS THAT ANYONE PLAYING THE GAME MUST REMAIN ON THE GROUND.
DISQUALIFIED!
AHHHH!
DO NOT WORRY, QUACKERS, WE WILL SAVE MAX.
HHHMMMM. OH GOODNESS... THIS MAY PROVE QUITE A PREDICAMENT...
AHEM! THE RULE BOOK STATES...
HANGMAN'S SQUARE IS A GAME TO BE PLAYED BY MALES ONLY.
IT APPEARS YOU, HARMONY, AND YOUR LOVELY COMPANION ARE **NOT** ALLOWED TO PLAY.
AND CLEARLY NO DOGS ALLOWED.
WHICH LEAVES ONLY YOU, MY GOOD FRIEND, PERCIVAL. ARE YOU READY TO PLAY?
YES, MAYOR.

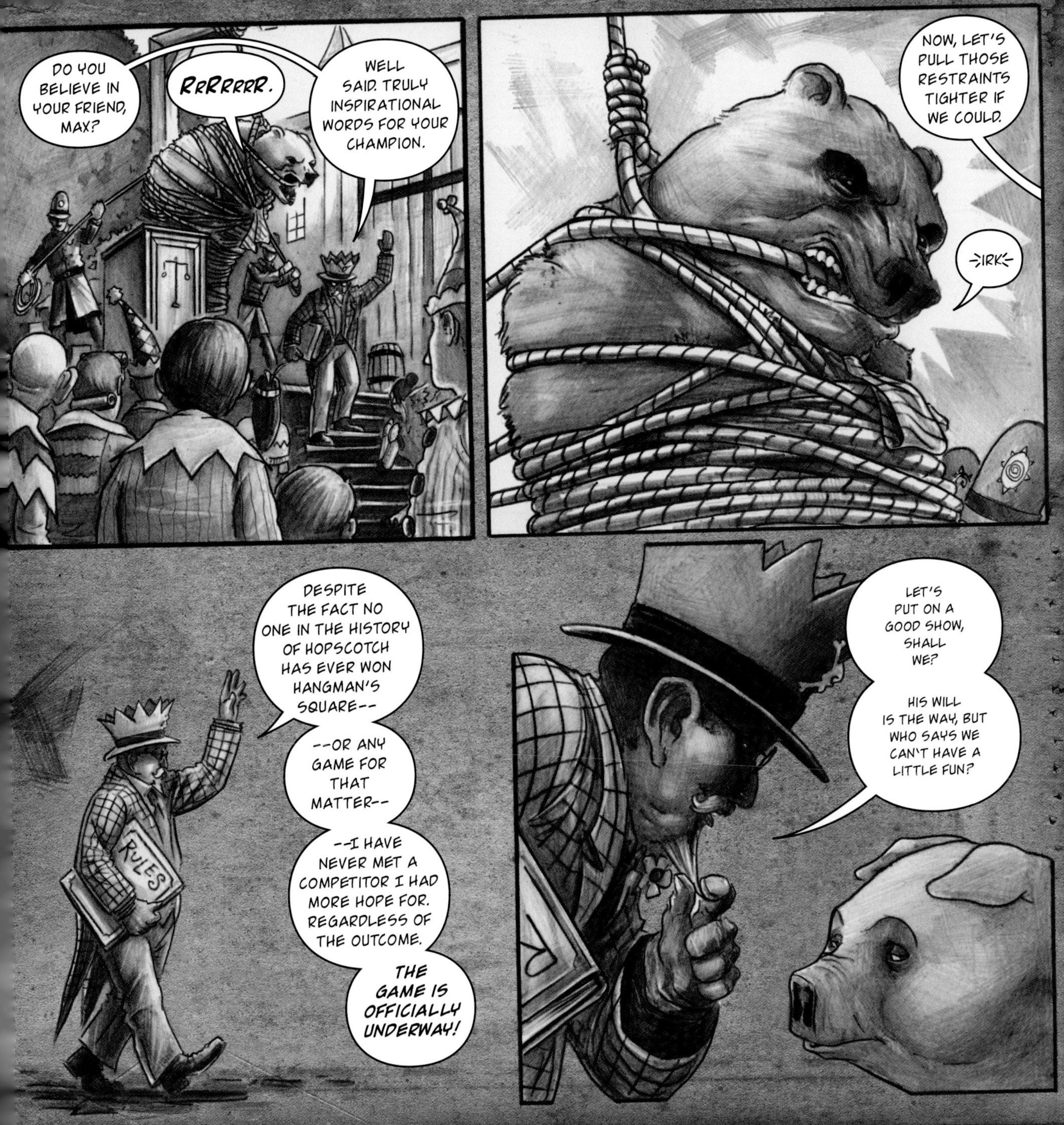

DO YOU BELIEVE IN YOUR FRIEND, MAX?
RRRRRRR.
WELL SAID. TRULY INSPIRATIONAL WORDS FOR YOUR CHAMPION.
NOW, LET'S PULL THOSE RESTRAINTS TIGHTER IF WE COULD.
IRK
DESPITE THE FACT NO ONE IN THE HISTORY OF HOPSCOTCH HAS EVER WON HANGMAN'S SQUARE--
--OR ANY GAME FOR THAT MATTER--
--I HAVE NEVER MET A COMPETITOR I HAD MORE HOPE FOR. REGARDLESS OF THE OUTCOME.
THE GAME IS OFFICIALLY UNDERWAY!
RULES
LET'S PUT ON A GOOD SHOW, SHALL WE?
HIS WILL IS THE WAY, BUT WHO SAYS WE CAN'T HAVE A LITTLE FUN?

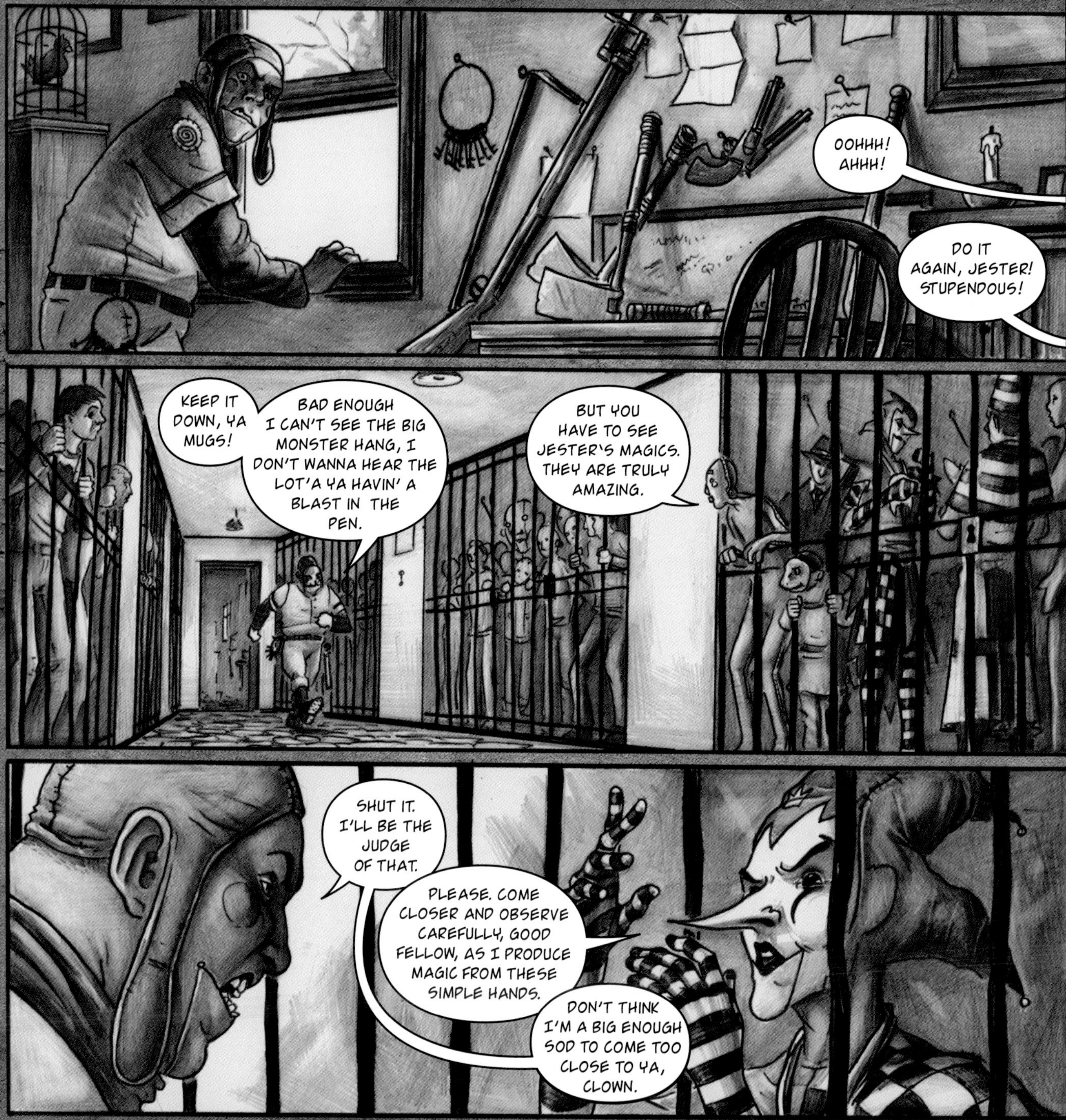
OOHHH! AHHH!
DO IT AGAIN, JESTER! STUPENDOUS!
KEEP IT DOWN, YA MUGS!
BAD ENOUGH I CAN'T SEE THE BIG MONSTER HANG, I DON'T WANNA HEAR THE LOT'A YA HAVIN' A BLAST IN THE PEN.
BUT YOU HAVE TO SEE JESTER'S MAGICS. THEY ARE TRULY AMAZING.
SHUT IT. I'LL BE THE JUDGE OF THAT.
PLEASE. COME CLOSER AND OBSERVE CAREFULLY, GOOD FELLOW, AS I PRODUCE MAGIC FROM THESE SIMPLE HANDS.
DON'T THINK I'M A BIG ENOUGH SOD TO COME TOO CLOSE TO YA, CLOWN.

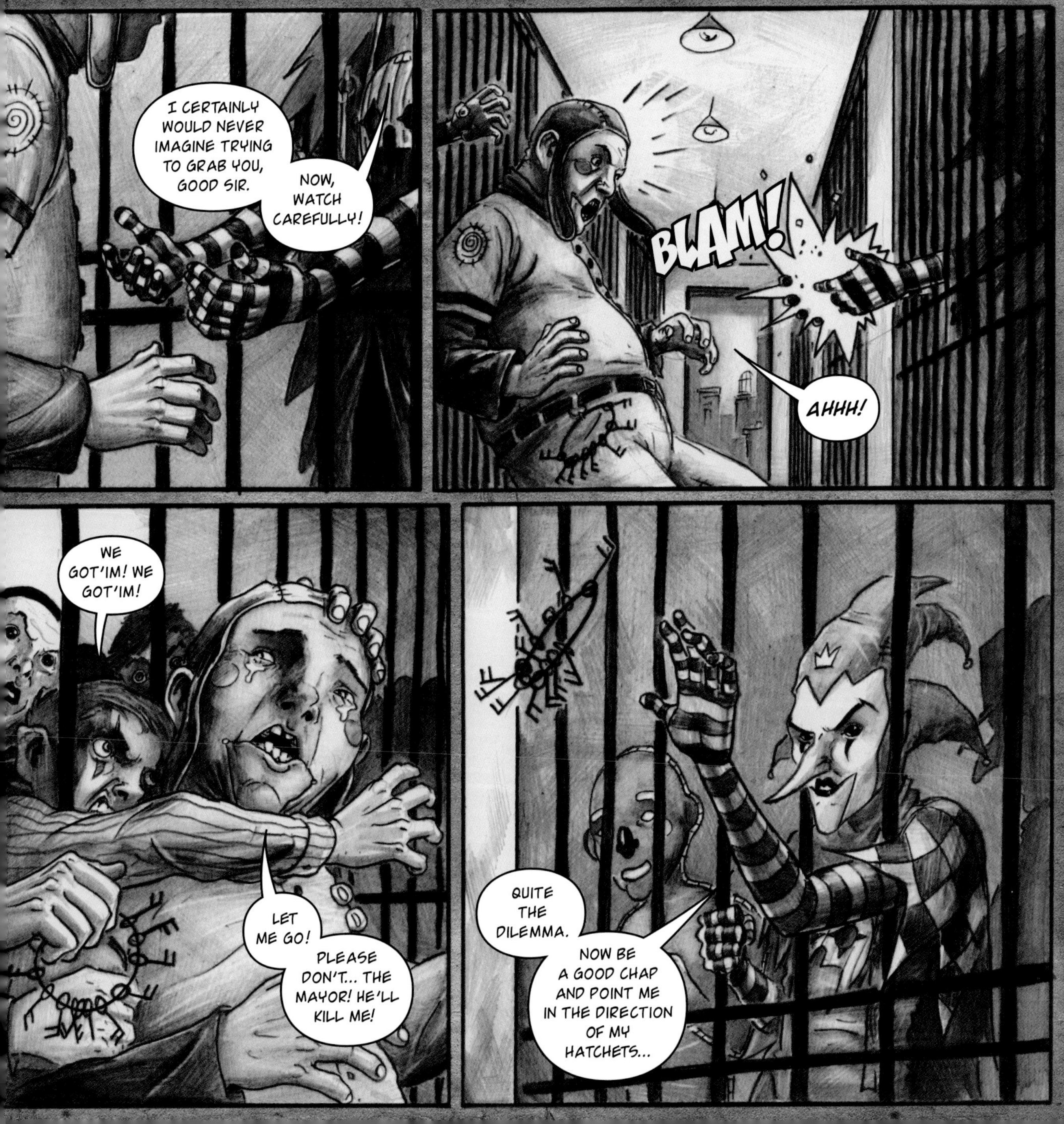
I CERTAINLY WOULD NEVER IMAGINE TRYING TO GRAB YOU, GOOD SIR.
NOW, WATCH CAREFULLY!
BLAM!
AHHH!
WE GOT'IM! WE GOT'IM!
LET ME GO!
PLEASE DON'T... THE MAYOR! HE'LL KILL ME!
QUITE THE DILEMMA.
NOW BE A GOOD CHAP AND POINT ME IN THE DIRECTION OF MY HATCHETS...

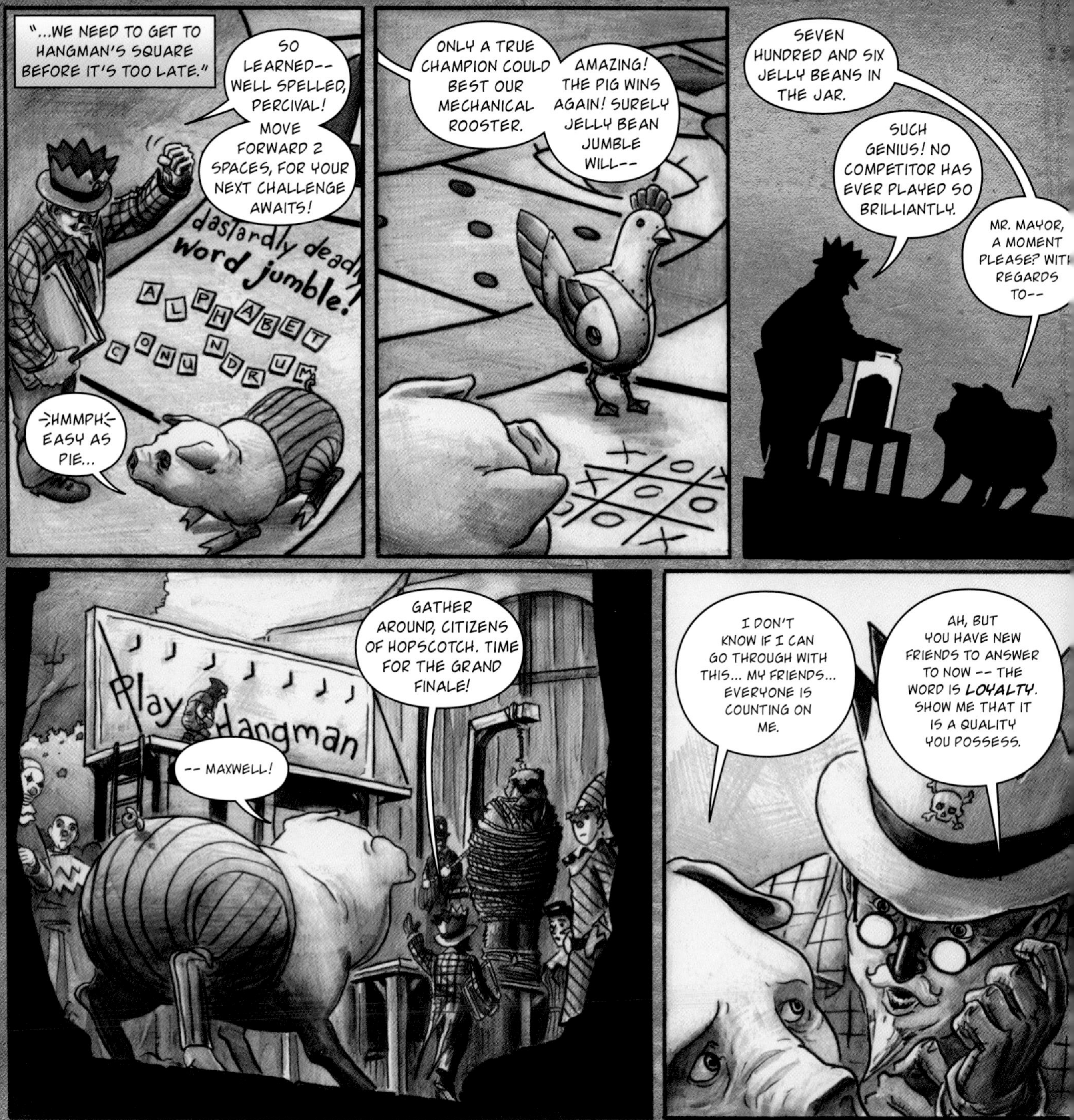
"...WE NEED TO GET TO HANGMAN'S SQUARE BEFORE IT'S TOO LATE."
SO LEARNED-- WELL SPELLED, PERCIVAL!
MOVE FORWARD 2 SPACES, FOR YOUR NEXT CHALLENGE AWAITS!
dastardly deadly word jumble!
ALPHABET CONUNDRUM
HMMPH EASY AS PIE...
ONLY A TRUE CHAMPION COULD BEST OUR MECHANICAL ROOSTER.
AMAZING! THE PIG WINS AGAIN! SURELY JELLY BEAN JUMBLE WILL--
SEVEN HUNDRED AND SIX JELLY BEANS IN THE JAR.
SUCH GENIUS! NO COMPETITOR HAS EVER PLAYED SO BRILLIANTLY.
MR. MAYOR, A MOMENT PLEASE? WITH REGARDS TO--
GATHER AROUND, CITIZENS OF HOPSCOTCH. TIME FOR THE GRAND FINALE!
Play Hangman
-- MAXWELL!
I DON'T KNOW IF I CAN GO THROUGH WITH THIS... MY FRIENDS... EVERYONE IS COUNTING ON ME.
AH, BUT YOU HAVE NEW FRIENDS TO ANSWER TO NOW -- THE WORD IS LOYALTY. SHOW ME THAT IT IS A QUALITY YOU POSSESS.

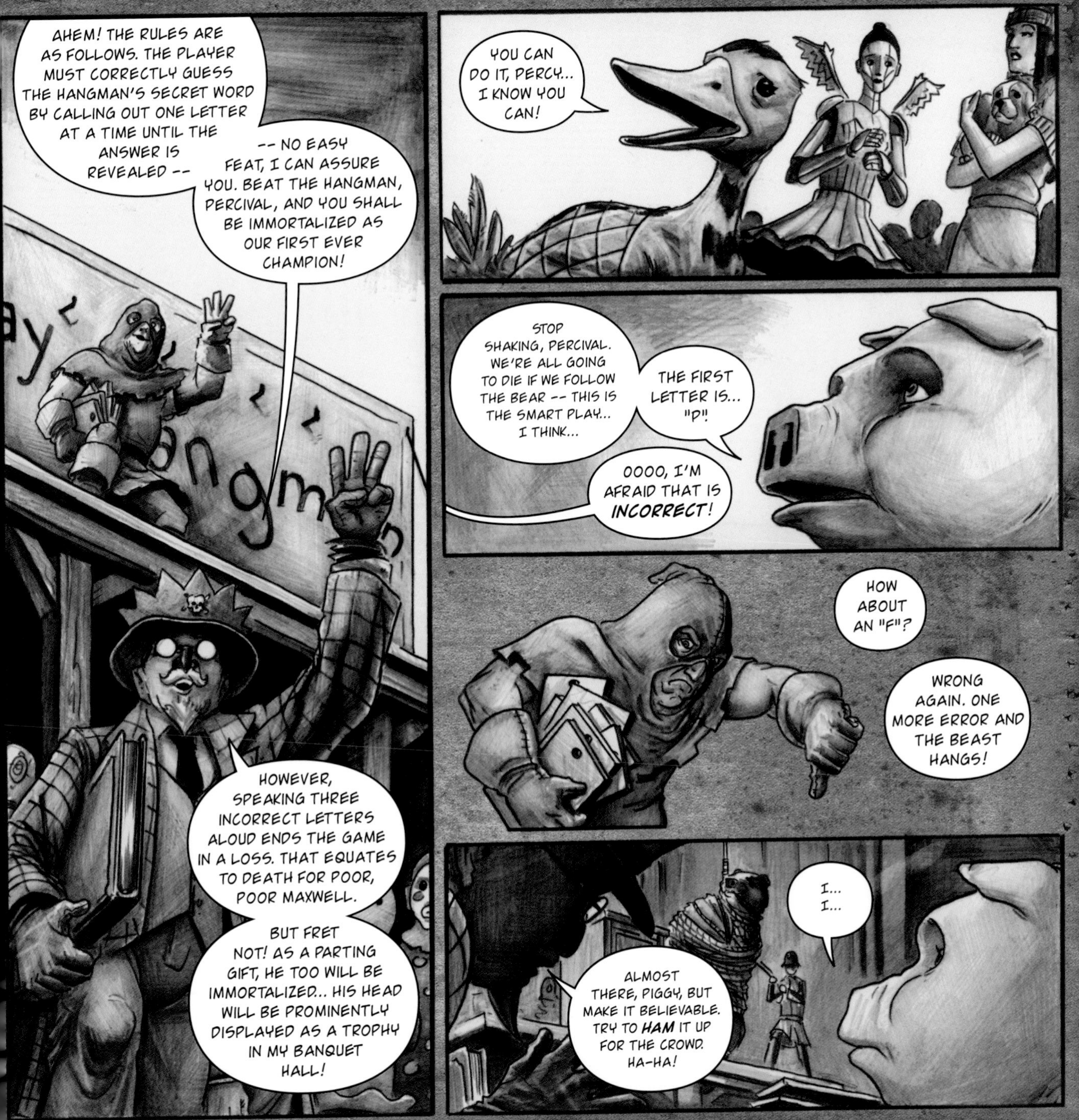
AHEM! THE RULES ARE AS FOLLOWS. THE PLAYER MUST CORRECTLY GUESS THE HANGMAN'S SECRET WORD BY CALLING OUT ONE LETTER AT A TIME UNTIL THE ANSWER IS REVEALED --
-- NO EASY FEAT, I CAN ASSURE YOU. BEAT THE HANGMAN, PERCIVAL, AND YOU SHALL BE IMMORTALIZED AS OUR FIRST EVER CHAMPION!
HOWEVER, SPEAKING THREE INCORRECT LETTERS ALOUD ENDS THE GAME IN A LOSS. THAT EQUATES TO DEATH FOR POOR, POOR MAXWELL.
BUT FRET NOT! AS A PARTING GIFT, HE TOO WILL BE IMMORTALIZED... HIS HEAD WILL BE PROMINENTLY DISPLAYED AS A TROPHY IN MY BANQUET HALL!
YOU CAN DO IT, PERCY... I KNOW YOU CAN!
STOP SHAKING, PERCIVAL. WE'RE ALL GOING TO DIE IF WE FOLLOW THE BEAR -- THIS IS THE SMART PLAY... I THINK...
THE FIRST LETTER IS... "P"!
OOOO, I'M AFRAID THAT IS **INCORRECT**!
HOW ABOUT AN "F"?
WRONG AGAIN. ONE MORE ERROR AND THE BEAST HANGS!
I... I...
ALMOST THERE, PIGGY, BUT MAKE IT BELIEVABLE. TRY TO **HAM** IT UP FOR THE CROWD. HA-HA!

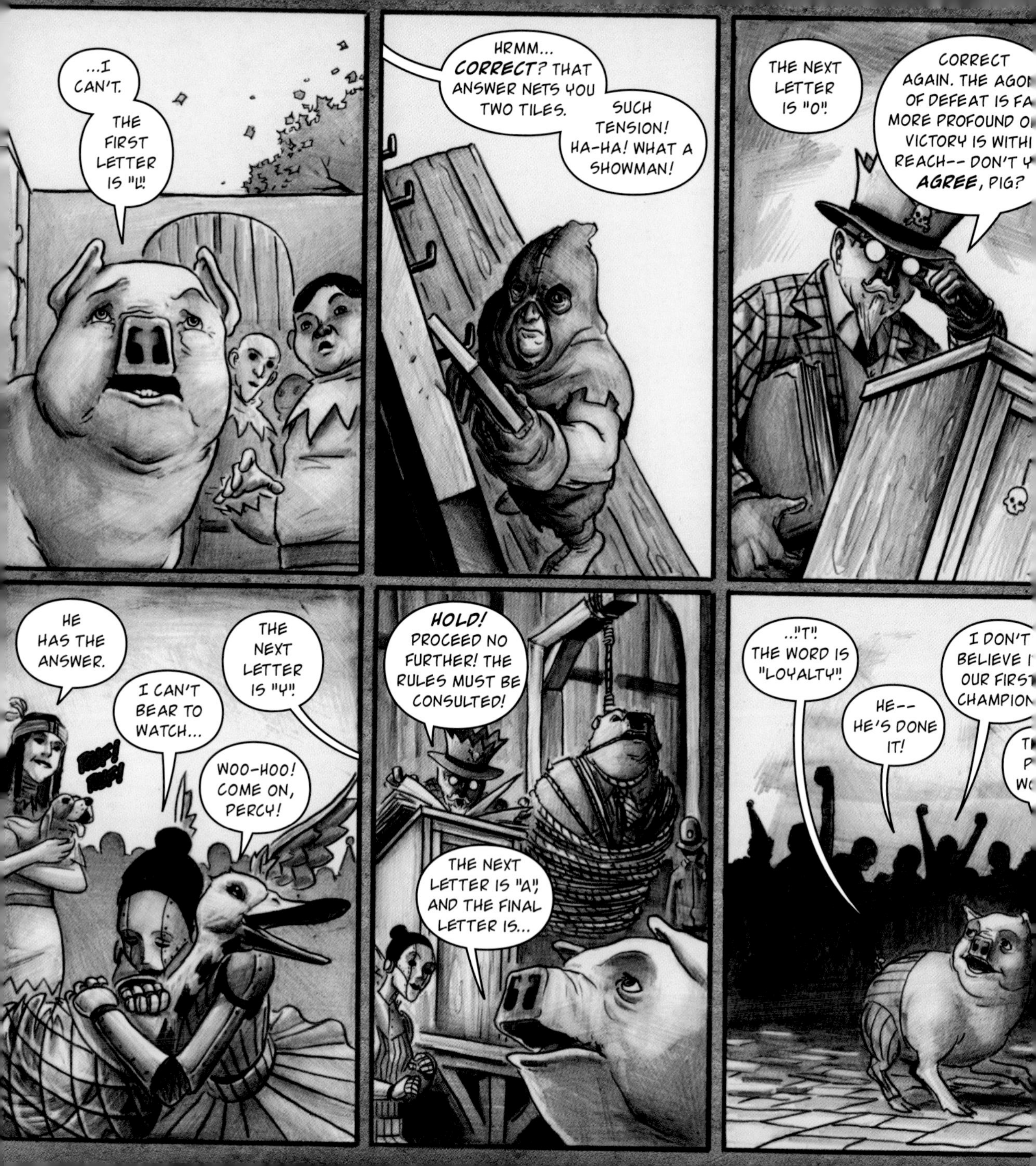
...I CAN'T.
THE FIRST LETTER IS "L".
HRMM... CORRECT? THAT ANSWER NETS YOU TWO TILES.
SUCH TENSION! HA-HA! WHAT A SHOWMAN!
THE NEXT LETTER IS "O".
CORRECT AGAIN. THE AGON OF DEFEAT IS FA MORE PROFOUND O VICTORY IS WITHI REACH-- DON'T Y AGREE, PIG?
HE HAS THE ANSWER.
I CAN'T BEAR TO WATCH...
THE NEXT LETTER IS "Y".
WOO-HOO! COME ON, PERCY!
HOLD! PROCEED NO FURTHER! THE RULES MUST BE CONSULTED!
THE NEXT LETTER IS "A", AND THE FINAL LETTER IS...
..."T". THE WORD IS "LOYALTY".
HE-- HE'S DONE IT!
I DON'T BELIEVE I OUR FIRST CHAMPION

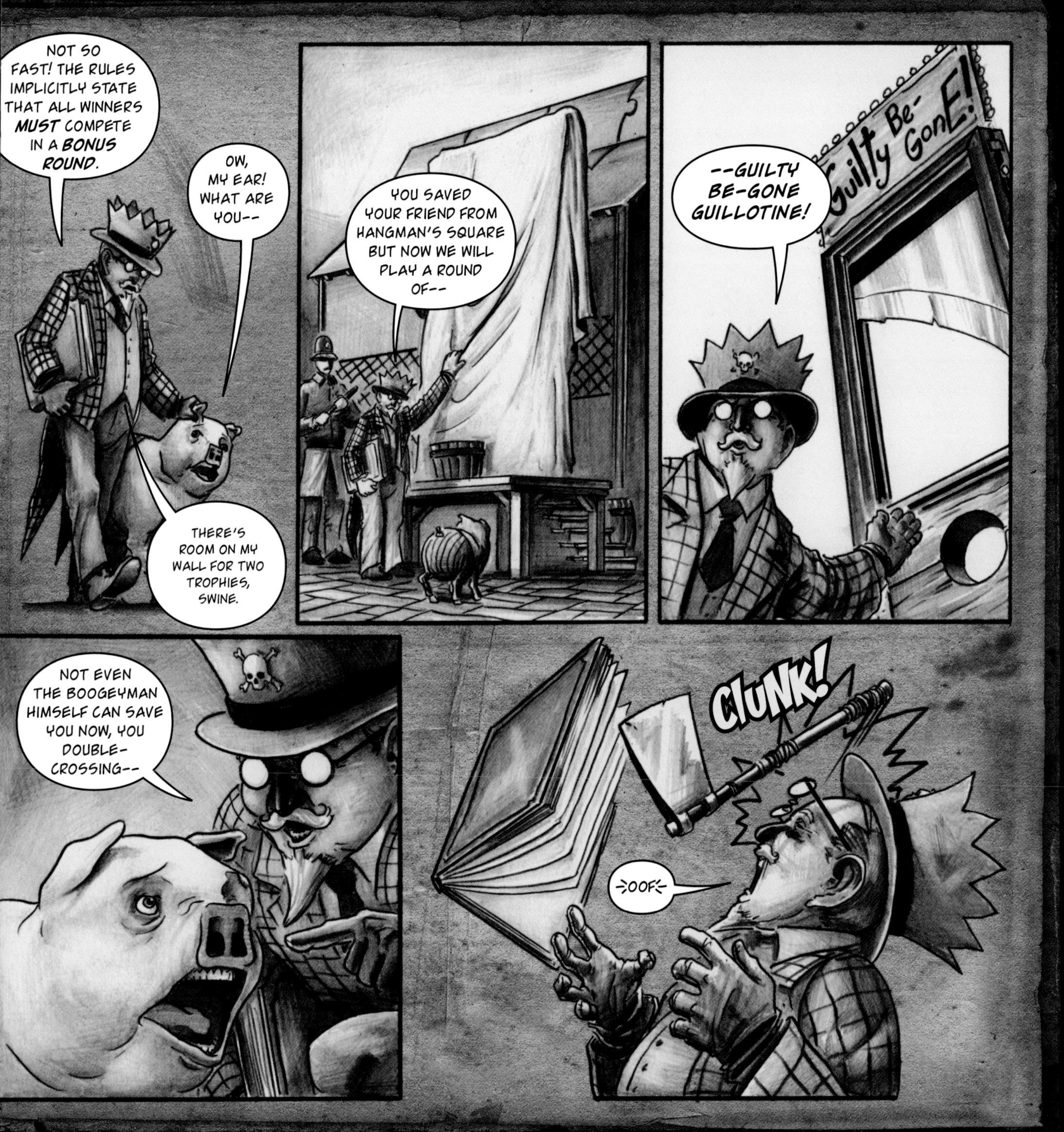
NOT SO FAST! THE RULES IMPLICITLY STATE THAT ALL WINNERS **MUST** COMPETE IN A **BONUS ROUND**.
OW, MY EAR! WHAT ARE YOU--
THERE'S ROOM ON MY WALL FOR TWO TROPHIES, SWINE.
YOU SAVED YOUR FRIEND FROM HANGMAN'S SQUARE BUT NOW WE WILL PLAY A ROUND OF--
--GUILTY BE-GONE GUILLOTINE!
Guilty Be-GonE!
NOT EVEN THE BOOGEYMAN HIMSELF CAN SAVE YOU NOW, YOU DOUBLE-CROSSING--
CLUNK!
OOF

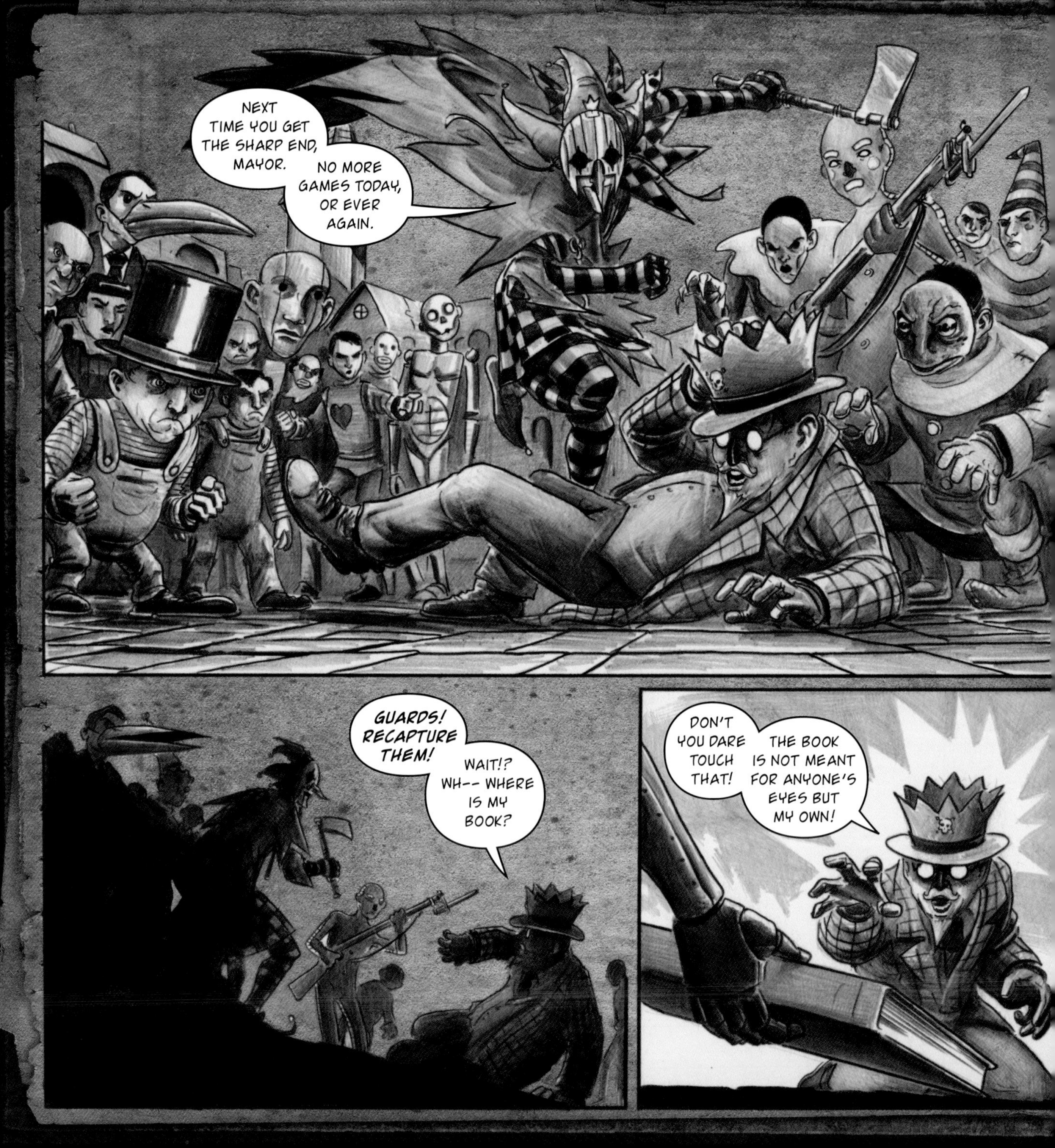
NEXT TIME YOU GET THE SHARP END, MAYOR.
NO MORE GAMES TODAY, OR EVER AGAIN.
GUARDS! RECAPTURE THEM!
WAIT!? WH-- WHERE IS MY BOOK?
DON'T YOU DARE TOUCH THAT!
THE BOOK IS NOT MEANT FOR ANYONE'S EYES BUT MY OWN!

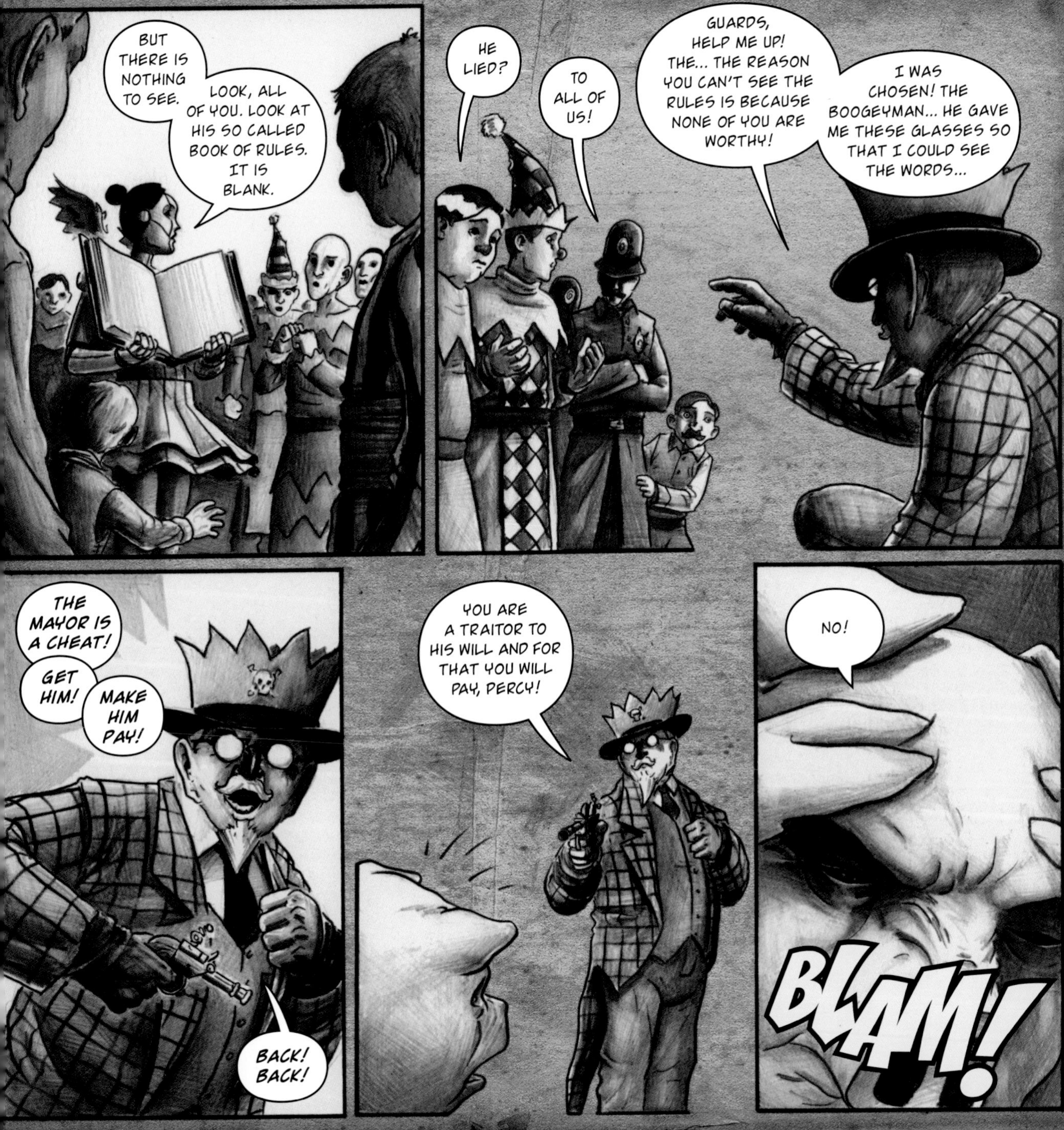
BUT THERE IS NOTHING TO SEE.
LOOK, ALL OF YOU. LOOK AT HIS SO CALLED BOOK OF RULES. IT IS BLANK.
HE LIED?
TO ALL OF US!
GUARDS, HELP ME UP! THE... THE REASON YOU CAN'T SEE THE RULES IS BECAUSE NONE OF YOU ARE WORTHY!
I WAS CHOSEN! THE BOOGEYMAN... HE GAVE ME THESE GLASSES SO THAT I COULD SEE THE WORDS...
THE MAYOR IS A CHEAT!
GET HIM!
MAKE HIM PAY!
BACK! BACK!
YOU ARE A TRAITOR TO HIS WILL AND FOR THAT YOU WILL PAY, PERCY!
NO!
BLAM!

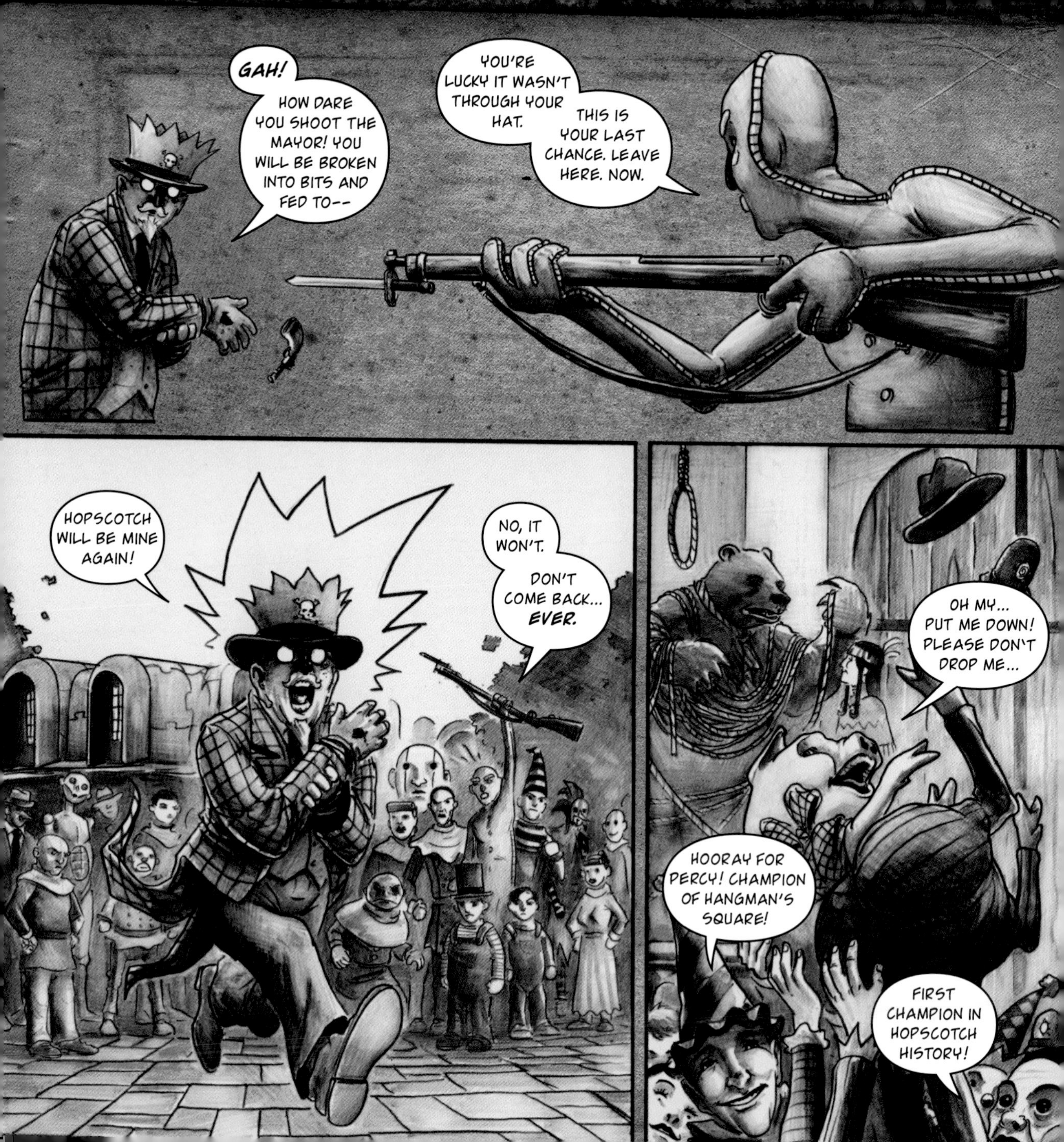
GAH!
HOW DARE YOU SHOOT THE MAYOR! YOU WILL BE BROKEN INTO BITS AND FED TO--
YOU'RE LUCKY IT WASN'T THROUGH YOUR HAT.
THIS IS YOUR LAST CHANCE. LEAVE HERE. NOW.
HOPSCOTCH WILL BE MINE AGAIN!
NO, IT WON'T.
DON'T COME BACK... EVER.
OH MY... PUT ME DOWN! PLEASE DON'T DROP ME...
HOORAY FOR PERCY! CHAMPION OF HANGMAN'S SQUARE!
FIRST CHAMPION IN HOPSCOTCH HISTORY!

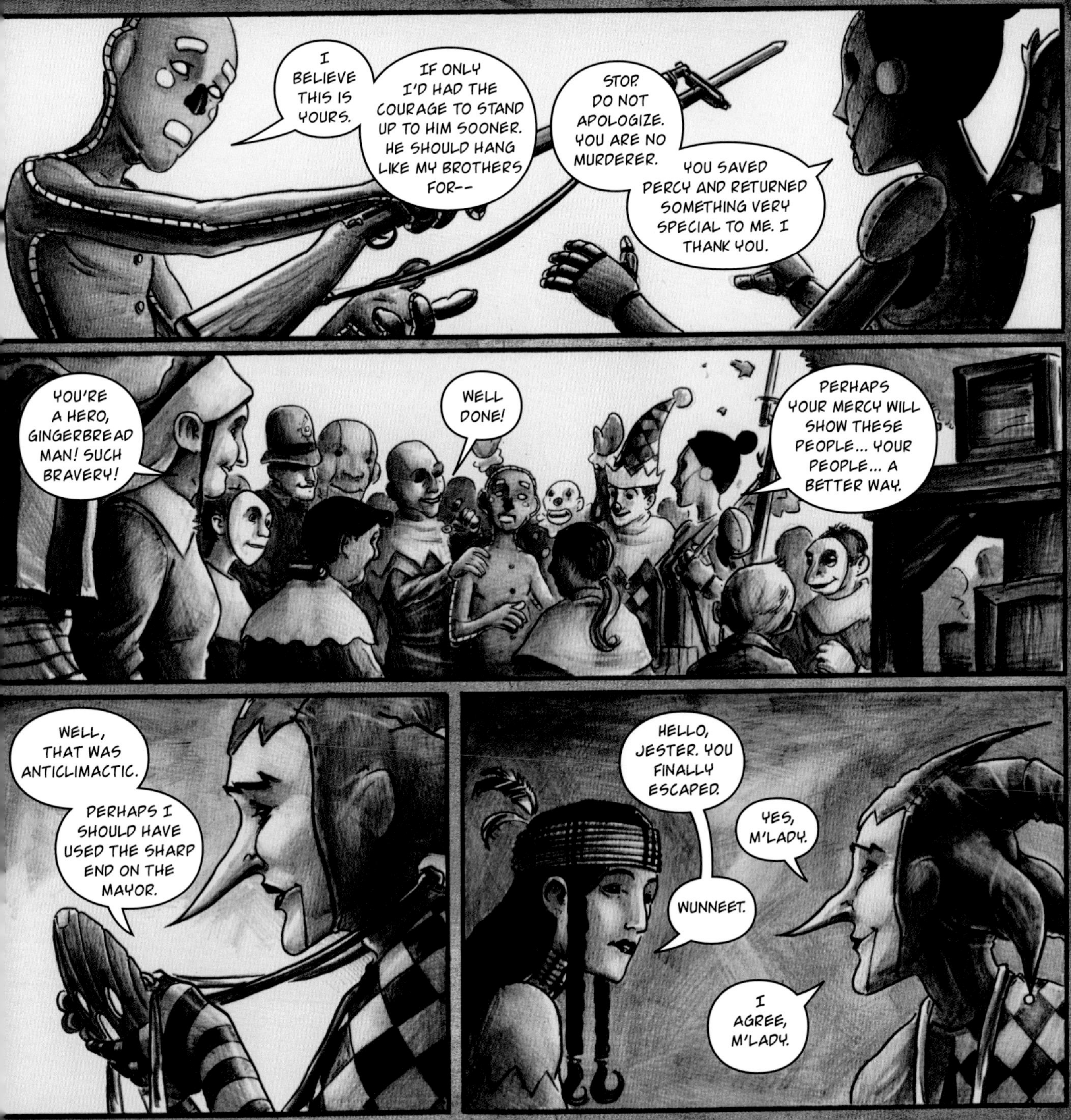
I BELIEVE THIS IS YOURS.
IF ONLY I'D HAD THE COURAGE TO STAND UP TO HIM SOONER. HE SHOULD HANG LIKE MY BROTHERS FOR--
STOP. DO NOT APOLOGIZE. YOU ARE NO MURDERER.
YOU SAVED PERCY AND RETURNED SOMETHING VERY SPECIAL TO ME. I THANK YOU.
YOU'RE A HERO, GINGERBREAD MAN! SUCH BRAVERY!
WELL DONE!
PERHAPS YOUR MERCY WILL SHOW THESE PEOPLE... YOUR PEOPLE... A BETTER WAY.
WELL, THAT WAS ANTICLIMACTIC.
PERHAPS I SHOULD HAVE USED THE SHARP END ON THE MAYOR.
HELLO, JESTER. YOU FINALLY ESCAPED.
YES, M'LADY.
WUNNEET.
I AGREE, M'LADY.

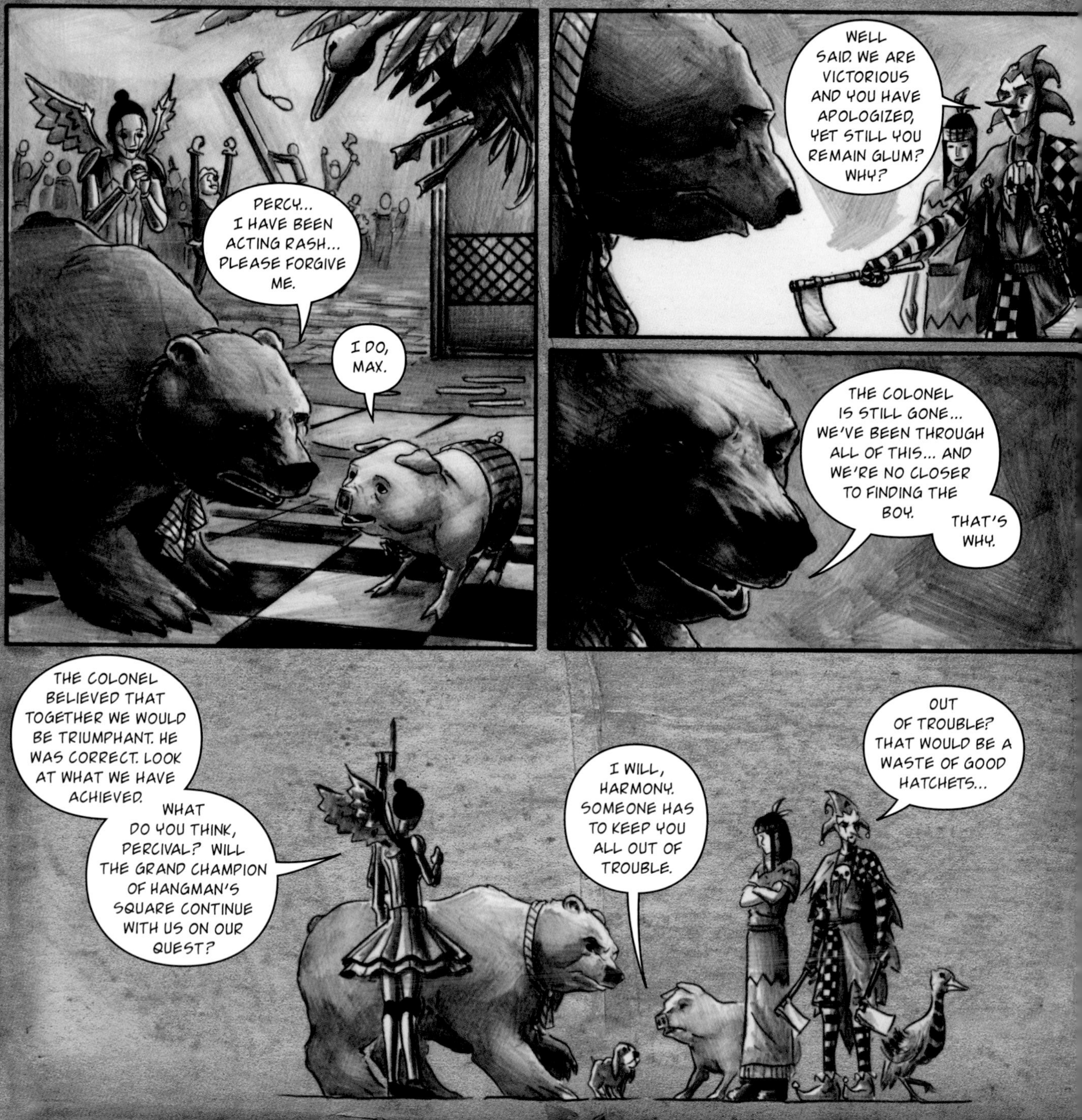
PERCY... I HAVE BEEN ACTING RASH... PLEASE FORGIVE ME.
I DO, MAX.
WELL SAID. WE ARE VICTORIOUS AND YOU HAVE APOLOGIZED, YET STILL YOU REMAIN GLUM? WHY?
THE COLONEL IS STILL GONE... WE'VE BEEN THROUGH ALL OF THIS... AND WE'RE NO CLOSER TO FINDING THE BOY.
THAT'S WHY.
THE COLONEL BELIEVED THAT TOGETHER WE WOULD BE TRIUMPHANT. HE WAS CORRECT. LOOK AT WHAT WE HAVE ACHIEVED.
WHAT DO YOU THINK, PERCIVAL? WILL THE GRAND CHAMPION OF HANGMAN'S SQUARE CONTINUE WITH US ON OUR QUEST?
I WILL, HARMONY. SOMEONE HAS TO KEEP YOU ALL OUT OF TROUBLE.
OUT OF TROUBLE? THAT WOULD BE A WASTE OF GOOD HATCHETS...

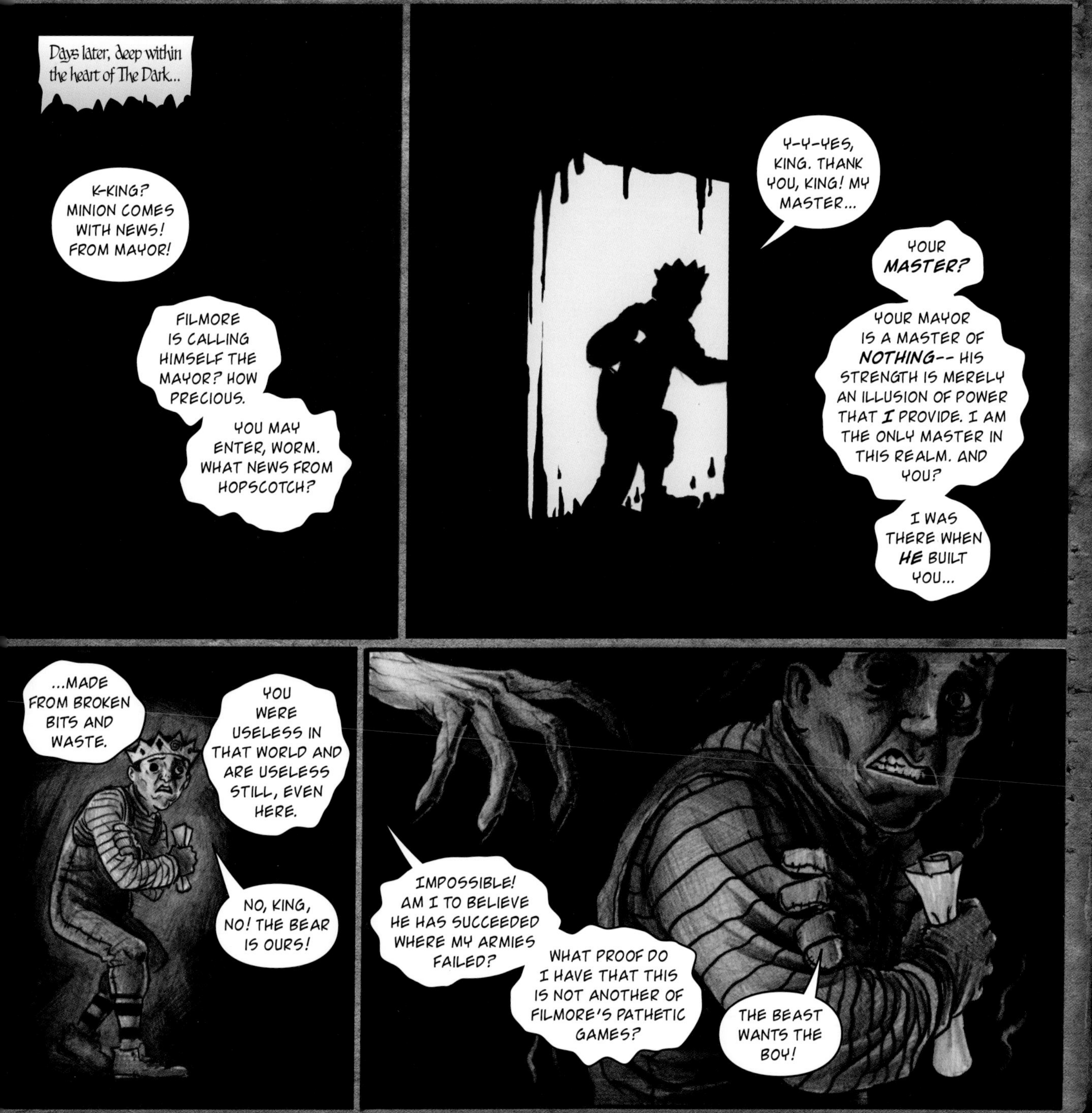

Days later, deep within the heart of The Dark...
K-KING? MINION COMES WITH NEWS! FROM MAYOR!
FILMORE IS CALLING HIMSELF THE MAYOR? HOW PRECIOUS.
YOU MAY ENTER, WORM. WHAT NEWS FROM HOPSCOTCH?
Y-Y-YES, KING. THANK YOU, KING! MY MASTER...
YOUR MASTER?
YOUR MAYOR IS A MASTER OF NOTHING-- HIS STRENGTH IS MERELY AN ILLUSION OF POWER THAT I PROVIDE. I AM THE ONLY MASTER IN THIS REALM. AND YOU?
I WAS THERE WHEN HE BUILT YOU...
...MADE FROM BROKEN BITS AND WASTE.
YOU WERE USELESS IN THAT WORLD AND ARE USELESS STILL, EVEN HERE.
NO, KING, NO! THE BEAR IS OURS!
IMPOSSIBLE! AM I TO BELIEVE HE HAS SUCCEEDED WHERE MY ARMIES FAILED?
WHAT PROOF DO I HAVE THAT THIS IS NOT ANOTHER OF FILMORE'S PATHETIC GAMES?
THE BEAST WANTS THE BOY!

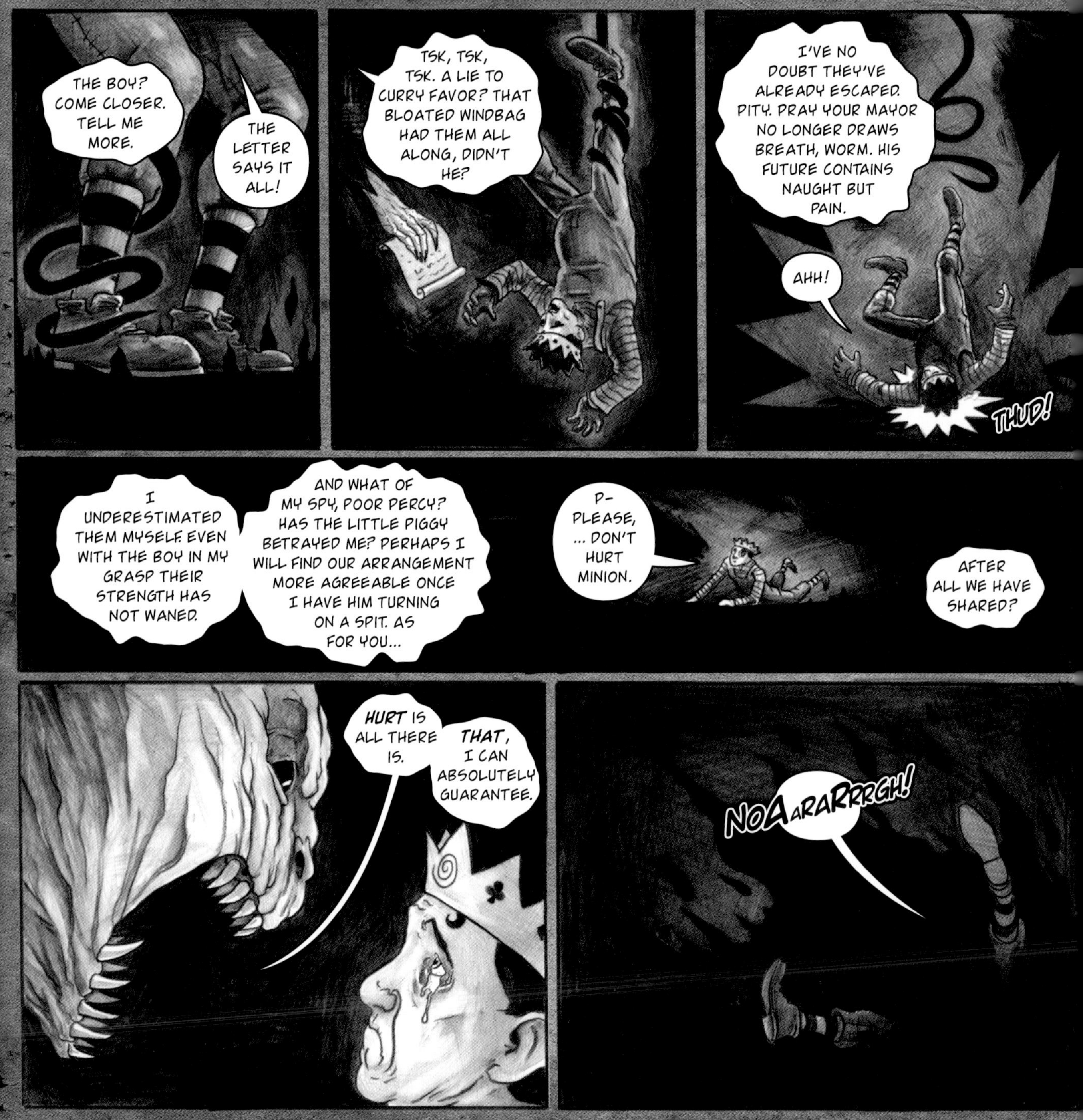
THE BOY? COME CLOSER. TELL ME MORE.
THE LETTER SAYS IT ALL!
TSK, TSK, TSK. A LIE TO CURRY FAVOR? THAT BLOATED WINDBAG HAD THEM ALL ALONG, DIDN'T HE?
I'VE NO DOUBT THEY'VE ALREADY ESCAPED. PITY. PRAY YOUR MAYOR NO LONGER DRAWS BREATH, WORM. HIS FUTURE CONTAINS NAUGHT BUT PAIN.
AHH!
THUD!
I UNDERESTIMATED THEM MYSELF. EVEN WITH THE BOY IN MY GRASP THEIR STRENGTH HAS NOT WANED.
AND WHAT OF MY SPY, POOR PERCY? HAS THE LITTLE PIGGY BETRAYED ME? PERHAPS I WILL FIND OUR ARRANGEMENT MORE AGREEABLE ONCE I HAVE HIM TURNING ON A SPIT. AS FOR YOU...
P-PLEASE, ... DON'T HURT MINION.
AFTER ALL WE HAVE SHARED?
HURT IS ALL THERE IS.
THAT, I CAN ABSOLUTELY GUARANTEE.
NOAARARRRGH!

The Colonel's War Journal

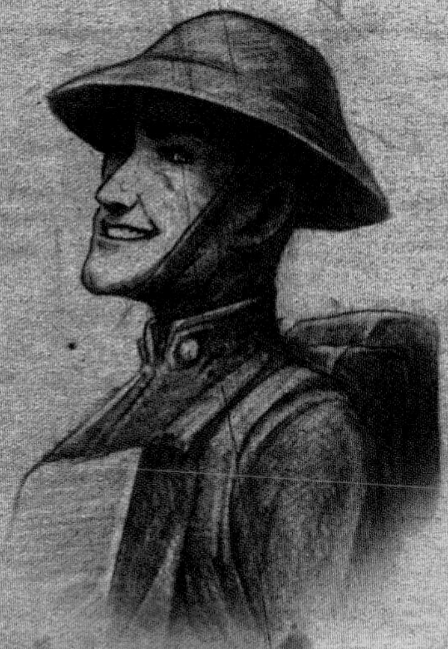

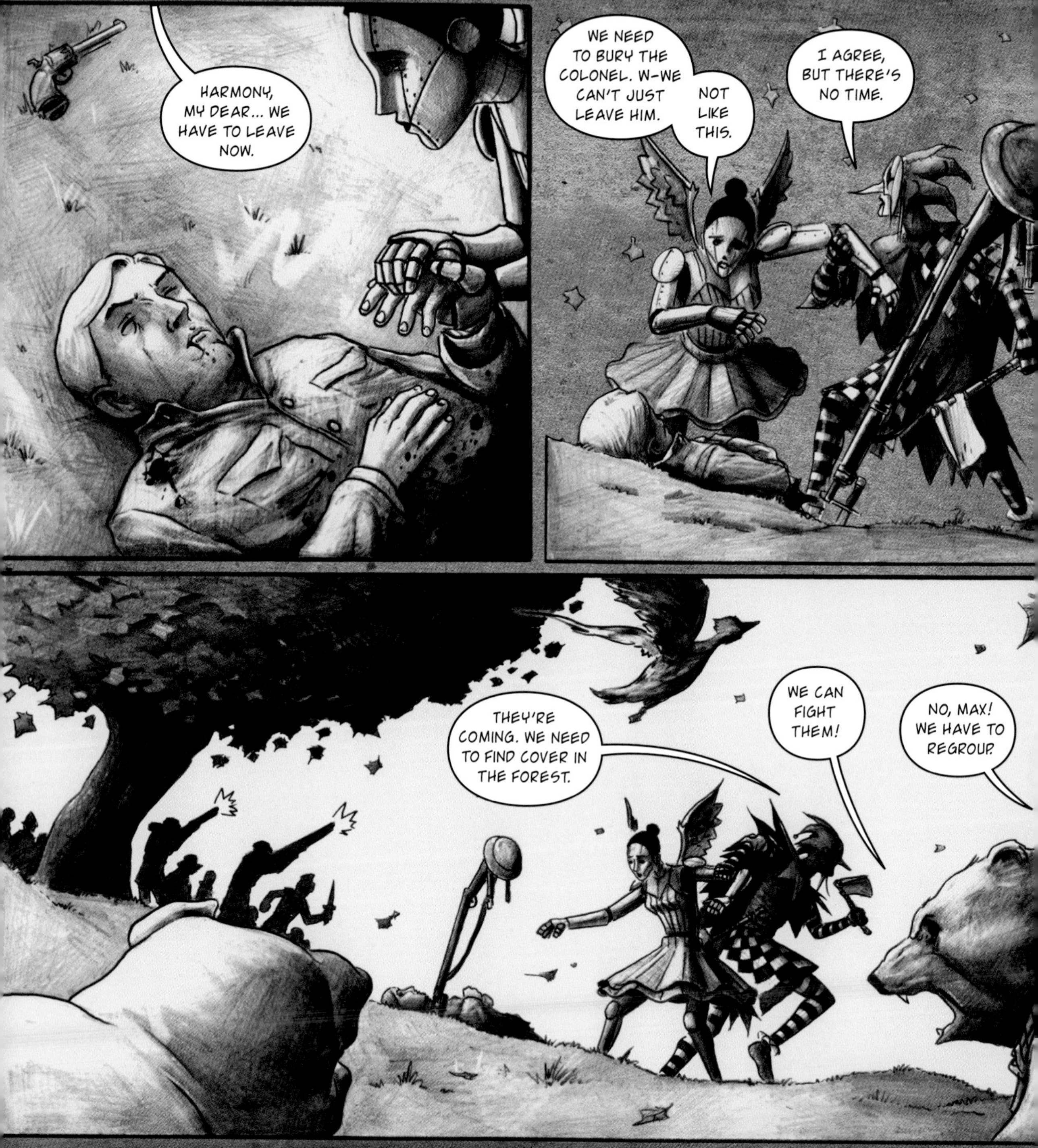
HARMONY, MY DEAR... WE HAVE TO LEAVE NOW.
WE NEED TO BURY THE COLONEL. W-WE CAN'T JUST LEAVE HIM.
NOT LIKE THIS.
I AGREE, BUT THERE'S NO TIME.
THEY'RE COMING. WE NEED TO FIND COVER IN THE FOREST.
WE CAN FIGHT THEM!
NO, MAX! WE HAVE TO REGROUP.

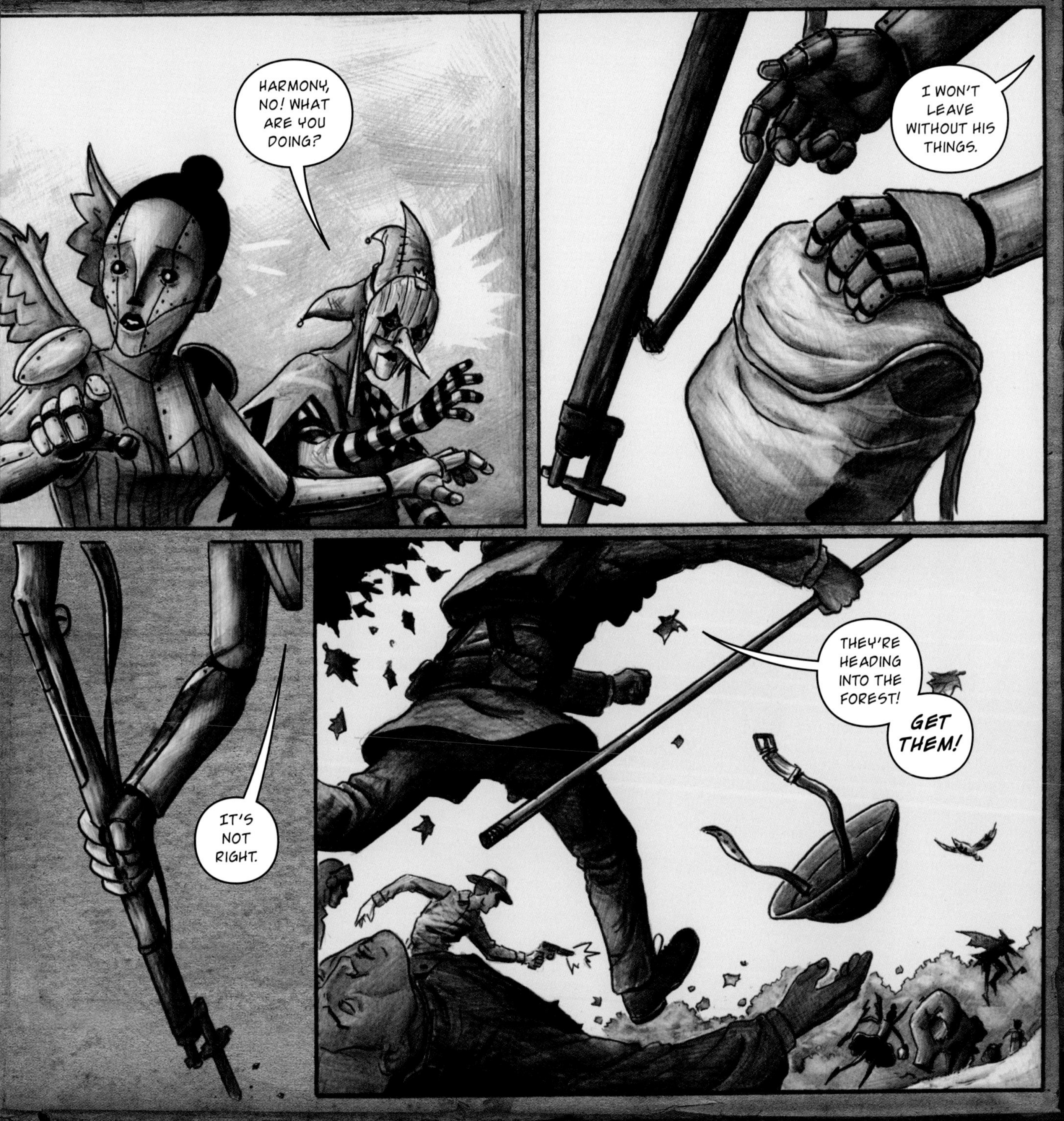
HARMONY, NO! WHAT ARE YOU DOING?
I WON'T LEAVE WITHOUT HIS THINGS.
IT'S NOT RIGHT.
THEY'RE HEADING INTO THE FOREST!
GET THEM!

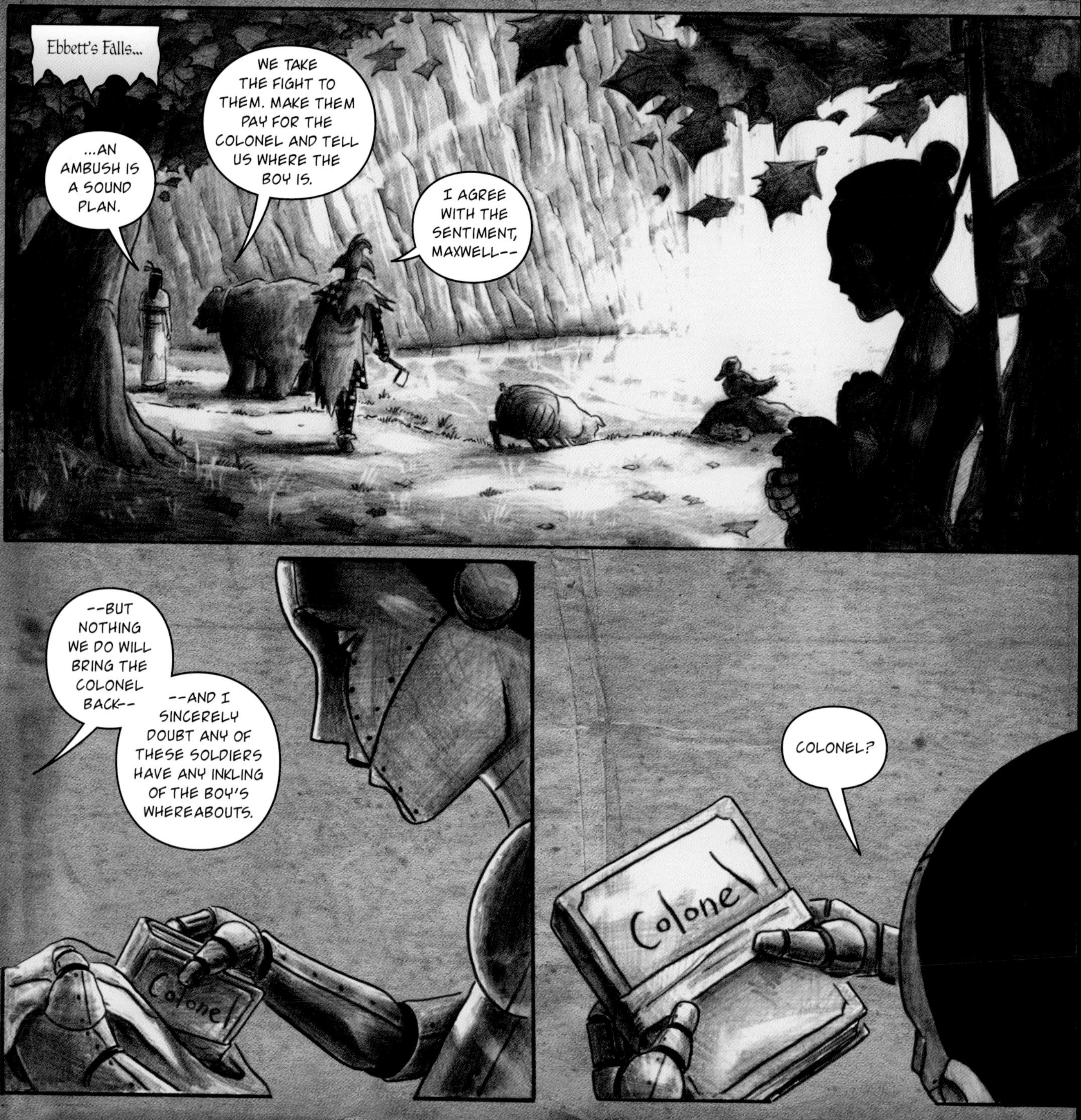
Ebbett's Falls...
...AN AMBUSH IS A SOUND PLAN.
WE TAKE THE FIGHT TO THEM. MAKE THEM PAY FOR THE COLONEL AND TELL US WHERE THE BOY IS.
I AGREE WITH THE SENTIMENT, MAXWELL--
--BUT NOTHING WE DO WILL BRING THE COLONEL BACK--
--AND I SINCERELY DOUBT ANY OF THESE SOLDIERS HAVE ANY INKLING OF THE BOY'S WHEREABOUTS.
Colonel
COLONEL?
Colonel

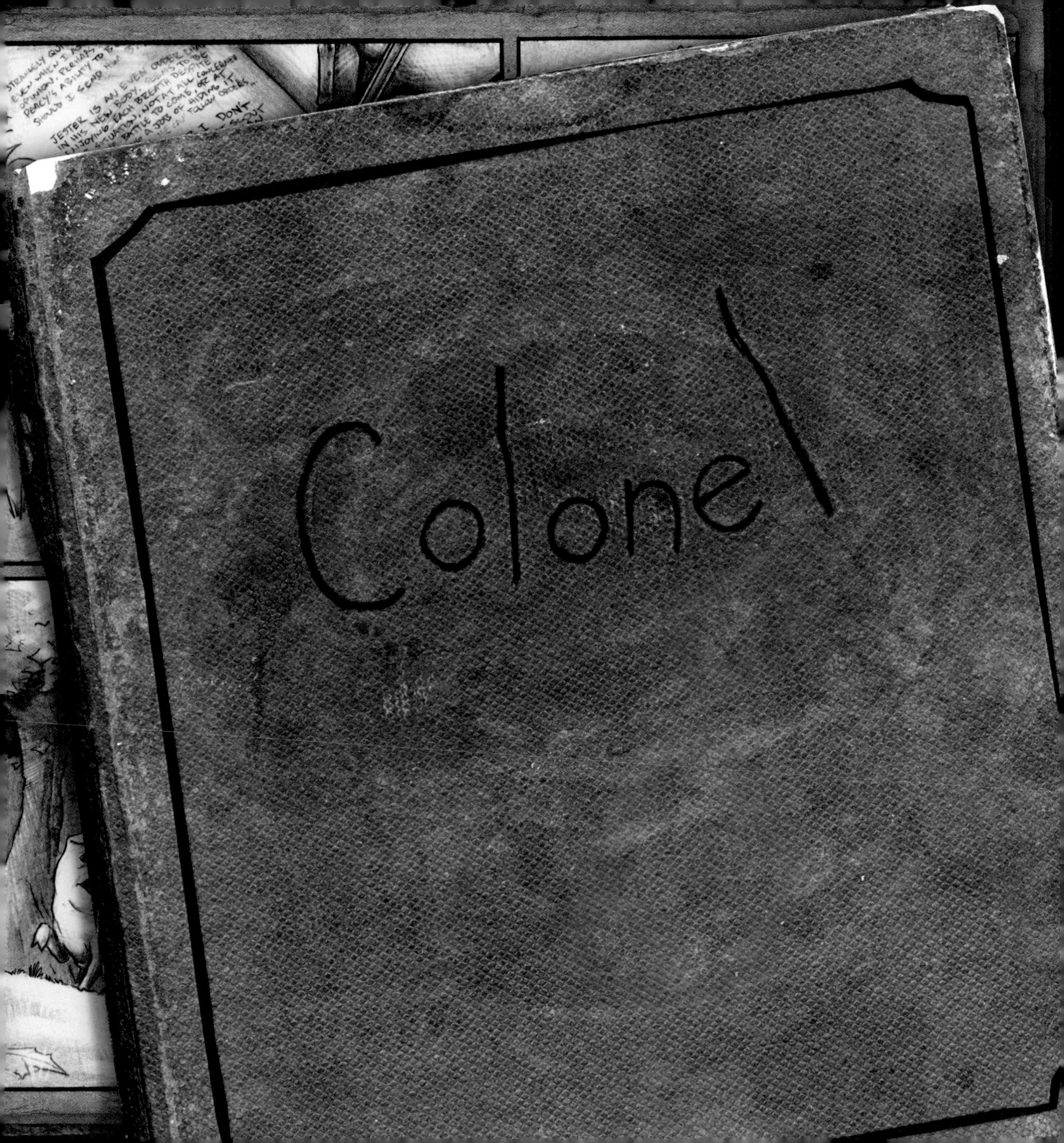
Colonel

THE BOY HAS BEEN TAKEN BY THE BOOGEYMAN. OUR LIVES HAVE CHANGED FOREVER. MY COMRADES AND I HAVE DONE THE UNTHINKABLE, BUT UNDER THE CIRCUMSTANCES IT WAS THE ONLY CHOICE. WE HAVE VENTURED INTO THE DARK, DESPERATE TO RECOVER THAT WHICH WAS STOLEN.

I DISCOVERED THIS JOURNAL IN MY BACKPACK. ODDLY ENOUGH, I'D NEVER BEEN ABLE TO OPEN THE SACK BEFORE COMING HERE. WHO WOULD HAVE GUESSED ENTERING THIS FRIGHTENING PLACE WOULD HAVE BROUGHT SO MANY... SURPRISES.

I WANT TO CHRONICLE OUR QUEST WITH A MAP AND JOURNAL ENTRIES. I DON'T KNOW IF THIS WILL JUST TURN BACK INTO LEAD, MAKING IT UNREADABLE, UPON OUR RETURN FROM THE DARK, BUT I DO THINK IT IS IMPORTANT TO KEEP A RECORD OF OUR JOURNEY. IT MAY HELP OTHER TOYS THAT ARE FORCED TO FOLLOW IN OUR FOOTSTEPS IN THE FUTURE... ESPECIALLY IF WE FACE INSURMOUNTABLE ODDS AND HAVE TO SEND FOR REINFORCEMENTS.

THE MOST AMAZING AND UNEXPECTED THING TO OCCUR SINCE OUR ARRIVAL IN THE DARK IS THE SUDDEN CHANGE TO OUR APPEARANCE. WE HAVE BECOME REAL, ALL OF US NOW TOWERING ABOVE SCOUT. QUACKERS AND MAX HAVE BEEN EYEING THE PUPPY, TALKING ABOUT REVENGE. THEY SEEM TO BE JOKING, BUT PRINCESS HAS REMINDED THEM THAT THE DOG WILL RETURN TO HIS NORMAL SIZE ONCE WE LEAVE. THAT QUIETED THEM.

REGARDLESS, SEEING EVERYONE LIKE THIS WAS SOMETHING I HAD NEVER EVEN DREAMT COULD BE POSSIBLE.

I HAVE FOUND GREAT JOY IN SEEING THE ONCE STIFF EXPRESSIONS OF MY FRIENDS FILLED WITH AS MUCH LIFE AND WONDER AS THE BOY'S IN HIS HAPPIEST MOMENTS. YET IT SADDENS ME TO SEE SOME OF THOSE SAME FACES FILLED WITH DREAD AT WHAT IS TO COME. TO THINK I ASKED THEM TO JOIN ME... THEIR LIVES ARE IN MY HANDS. I WILL NOT LET THEM DOWN.

I HOPE, ONCE THIS IS OVER, TO CARRY THEIR NEW FACES WITH ME. ALWAYS.

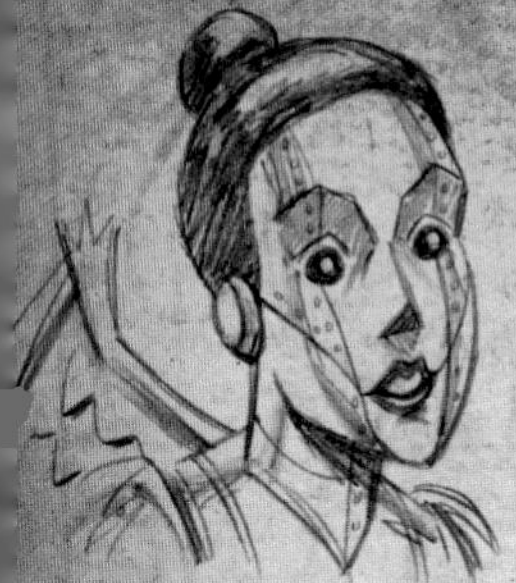

DISARMINGLY BEAUTIFUL IN THE DARK. I FIND MYSELF REGRETTING ALLOWING HARMONY TO COME ALONG. HER GENTLE NATURE IS NOT MEANT FOR WAR.

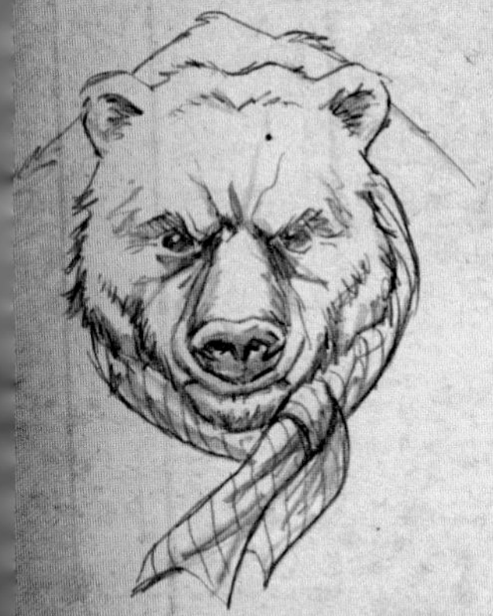

THE BOY'S DISAPPEARANCE HAS HIT HIM HARD. NO SURPRISE AS HE AND THE BOY SHARED SO MUCH TOGETHER. HE HAS BEEN BY THE BOY'S SIDE LONGER THAN THE BOY HAS OWNED ME. I CAN'T IMAGINE HIS RAGE AT LOSING HIM-- MAX WILL BE A FORCE OF NATURE ON THE BATTLEFIELD.

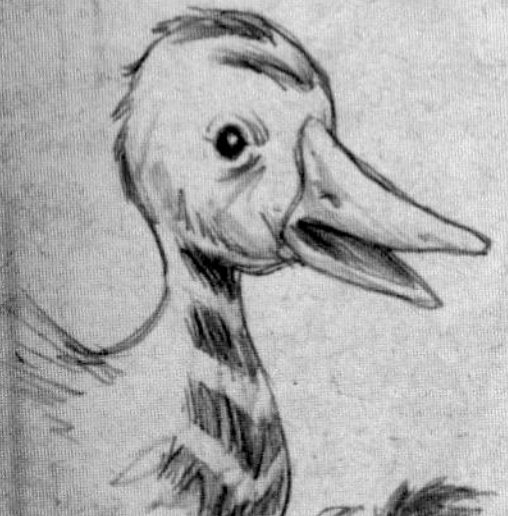

OVERJOYED AT HAVING REAL WINGS. HAS FLOWN HALF A DOZEN RECONNAISSANCE MISSIONS ALREADY. QUACKERS WILL BE INVALUABLE TO US HERE. WHAT WILL WAR DO TO HIS JOVIAL NATURE?

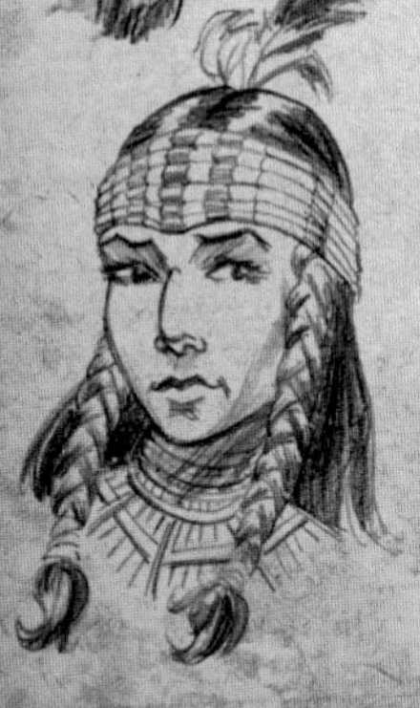

PRINCESS IS THE LEAST NERVOUS OF US ALL... SHE'S CONSTANTLY SUGGESTING STRATEGIES! VERY BOLD. PERHAPS HER ROLE AS THE DAMSEL DURING THE BOY'S GAMES FOR ALL OF THESE YEARS WAS IN ERROR.

WAR JOURNAL ILLUSTRATIONS BY ADAM WALMSLEY

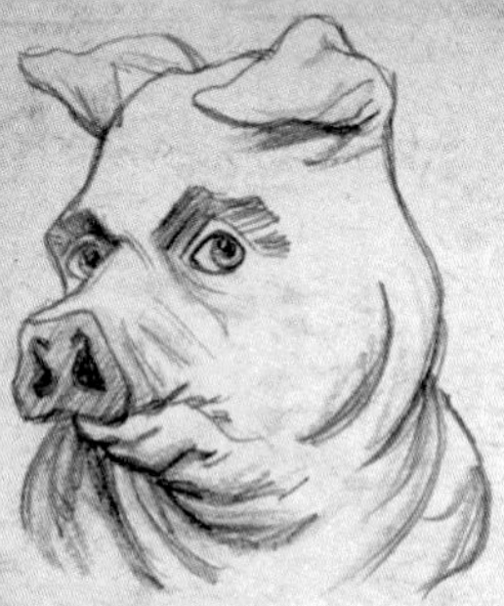

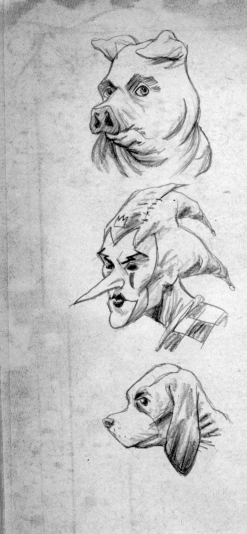

STRANGELY QUIET ON OUR JOURNEY, EVEN WHEN I ASK HIM FOR HIS OPINION. PERHAPS I OVERESTIMATED PERCY'S ABILITY TO BLOSSOM HERE. SHOULD I SEND HIM BACK?

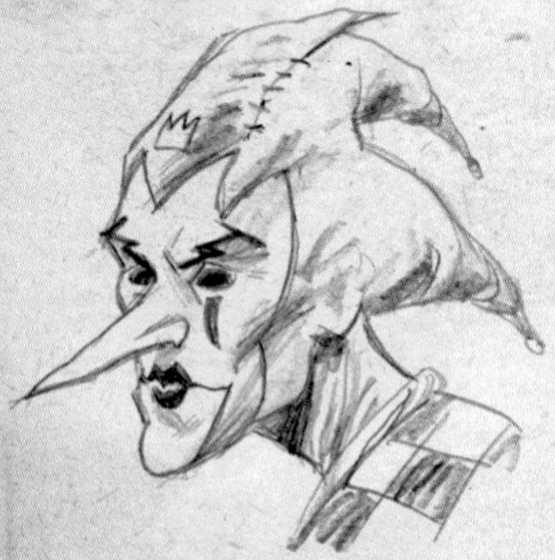

JESTER IS AN EVEN ODDER CHAP IN HIS NEW BODY. SEEMS TO BE ENJOYING EACH BREATH DESPITE OUR SITUATION. NOT AT ALL CONCERNED WITH THE BATTLE TO COME, OR AT LEAST DOING A GOOD JOB OF HIDING IT. HERE'S HOPING HE CAN FOLLOW ORDERS...

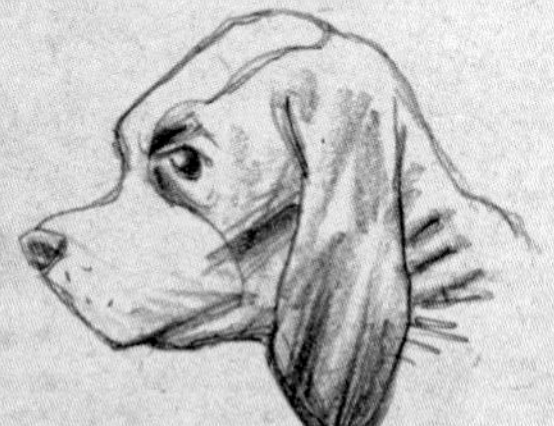

A GOOD, LOYAL PUP. I DON'T LIKE TO SHOW IT, BUT SCOUT HAS CHEERED ME MORE THAN ONCE DURING OUR JOURNEY ALREADY.

DAYS ON THE WATER HAVE LEFT US ALL A BIT EXHAUSTED, BUT TODAY WE FINALLY SEE LAND.
I AM FILLED WITH EXCITEMENT, AND SOMETHING I HAVE NEVER FELT BEFORE ENTERING A BATTLE... DREAD. A SENSE OF UNCERTAINTY. IT IS INVIGORATING AND FRIGHTENING ALL AT THE SAME TIME, AND I WORRY THAT I SHOULD HAVE TAKEN ON THIS MISSION ALONE. THE BOY AND I HAVE WON COUNTLESS BATTLES AGAINST HUNDREDS OF FOES. MY WHOLE LIFE HAS PREPARED ME FOR THE HARSHNESS OF WAR, BUT WHAT WILL BECOME OF MY FRIENDS? THEY HAVE NOT TRAINED LIKE I HAVE. HOW WILL THEY RESPOND? I WILL DO ALL I CAN TO MAKE SURE THEY ALL SURVIVE.
IT IS MY RESPONSIBILITY.
AS WE FLOAT ACROSS BROOKLYN CREEK TOWARD OUR FIRST ENCOUNTER IN THE DARK, I PRAY I CAN KEEP US TOGETHER LONG ENOUGH TO SAVE THE BOY. INSPIRING YOUR MEN IN BATTLE IS JUST AS IMPORTANT AS KILLING A THOUSAND ENEMY TROOPS, AND IT IS MY DUTY TO LEAD AND INSPIRE MY FAMILY ON OUR QUEST. WE WILL FIND THE BOY AND BRING HIM HOME. THAT I KNOW FOR SURE.

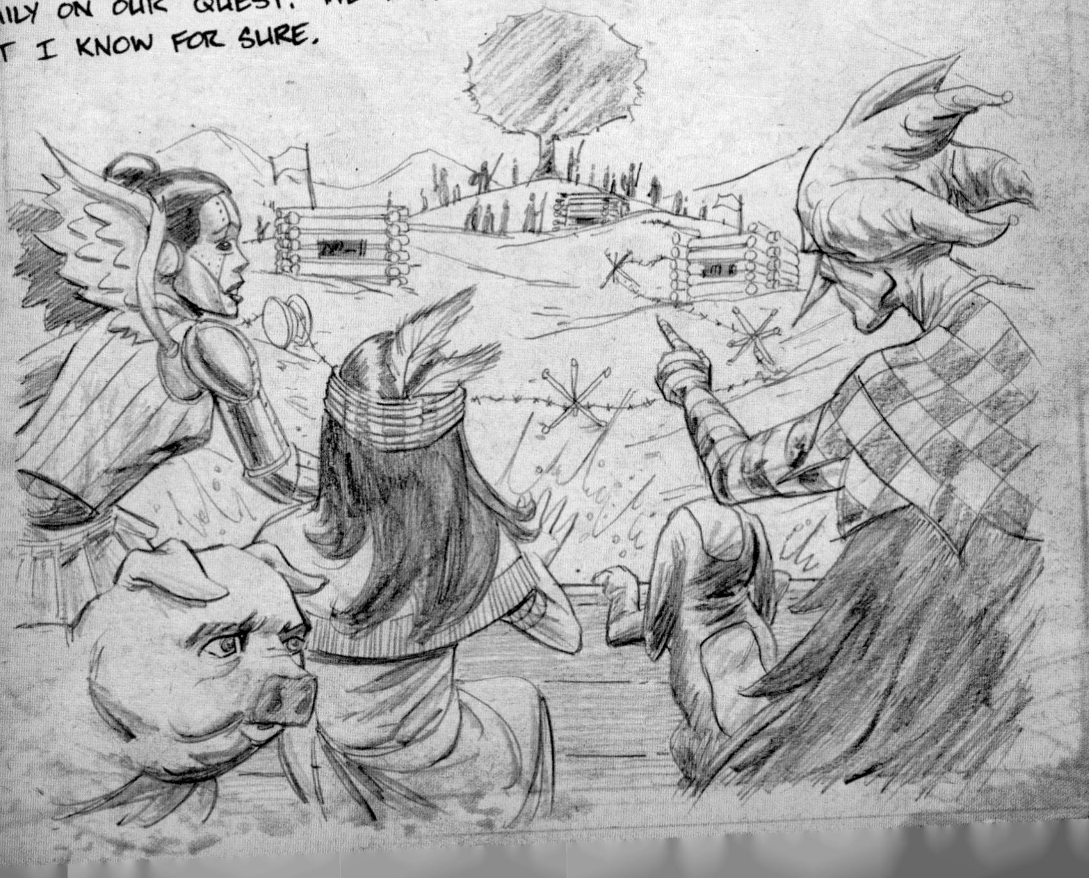

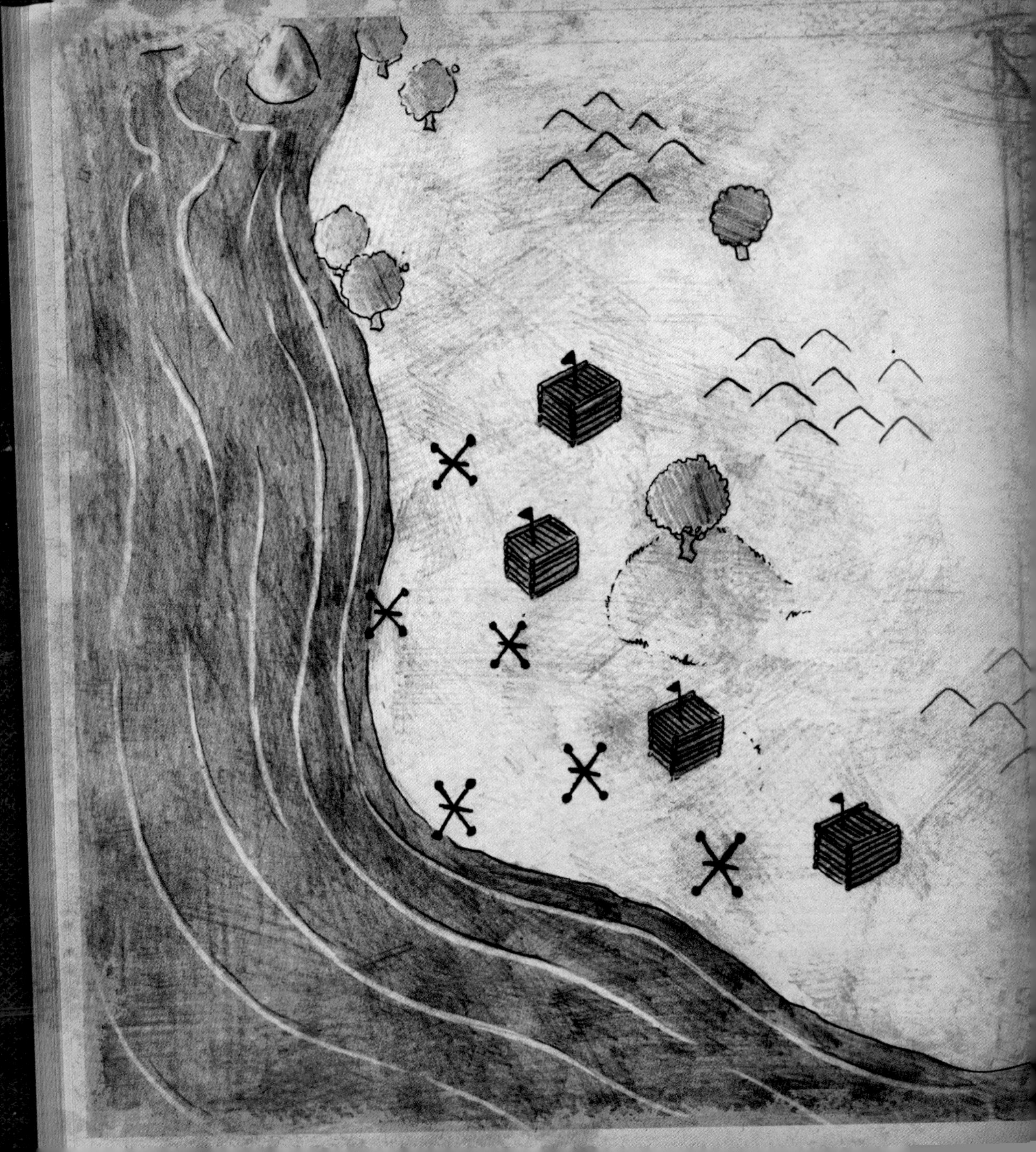

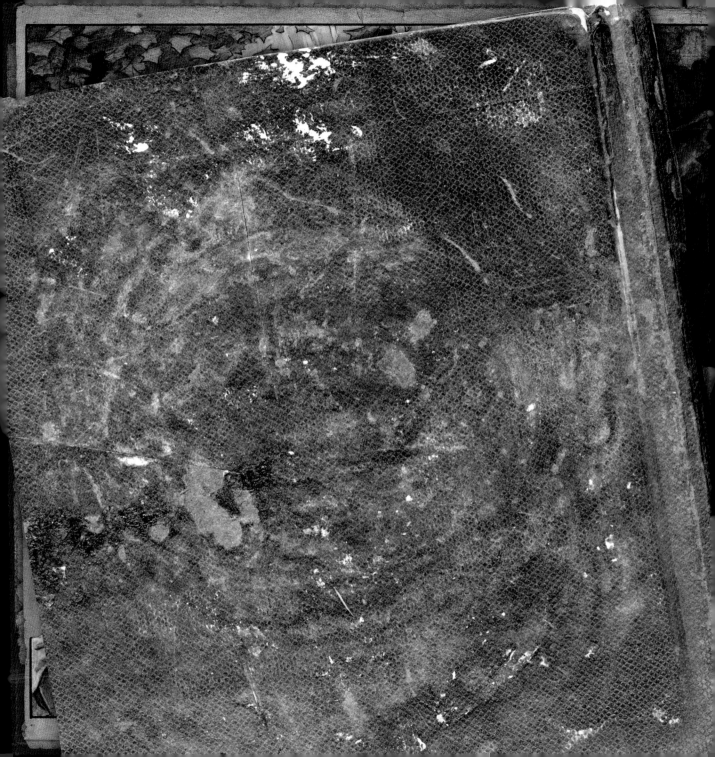

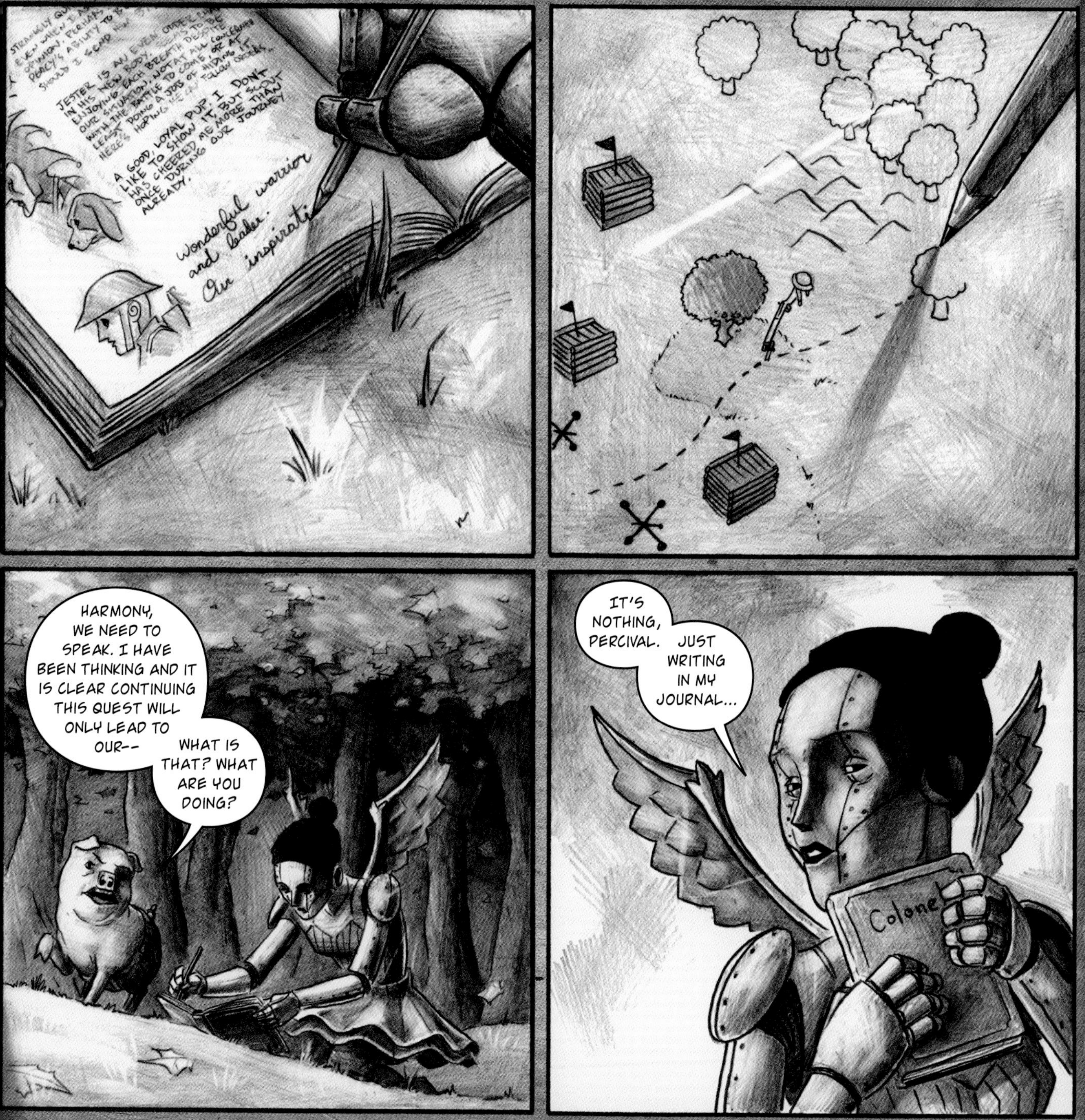
A GOOD, LOYAL PUP. I DON'T LIKE TO SHOW IT, BUT SCOUT HAS CHEERED ME MORE THAN ONCE DURING OUR JOURNEY ALREADY.
Wonderful warrior and leader. Our inspirati
HARMONY, WE NEED TO SPEAK. I HAVE BEEN THINKING AND IT IS CLEAR CONTINUING THIS QUEST WILL ONLY LEAD TO OUR--
WHAT IS THAT? WHAT ARE YOU DOING?
IT'S NOTHING, PERCIVAL.
JUST WRITING IN MY JOURNAL...
Colone

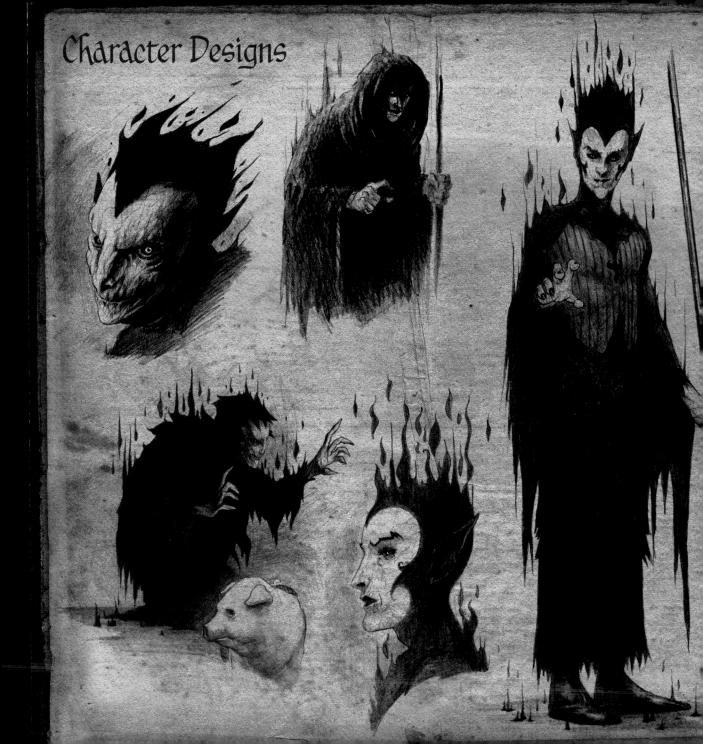

Character Designs

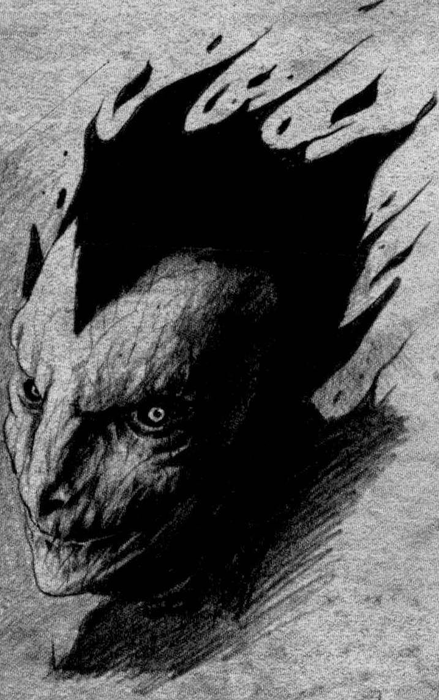

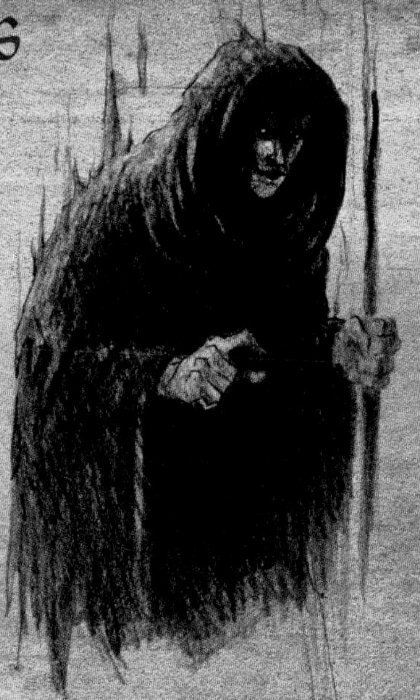

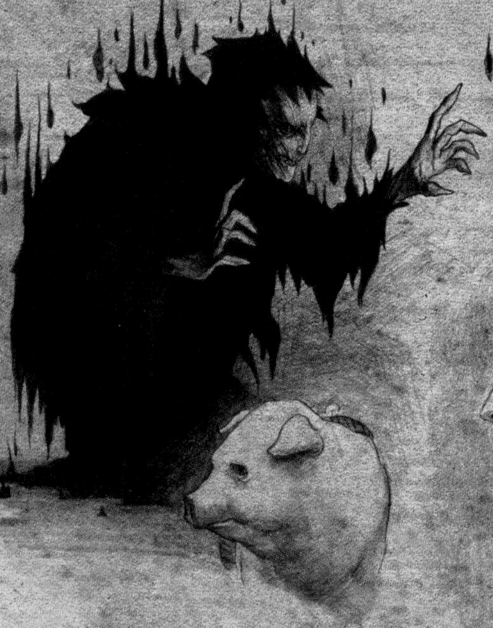

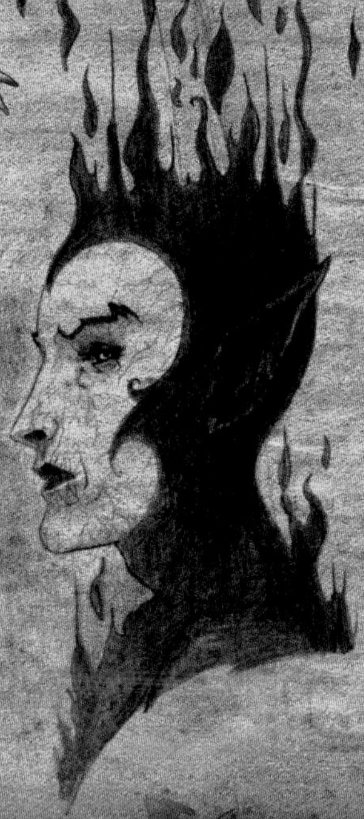

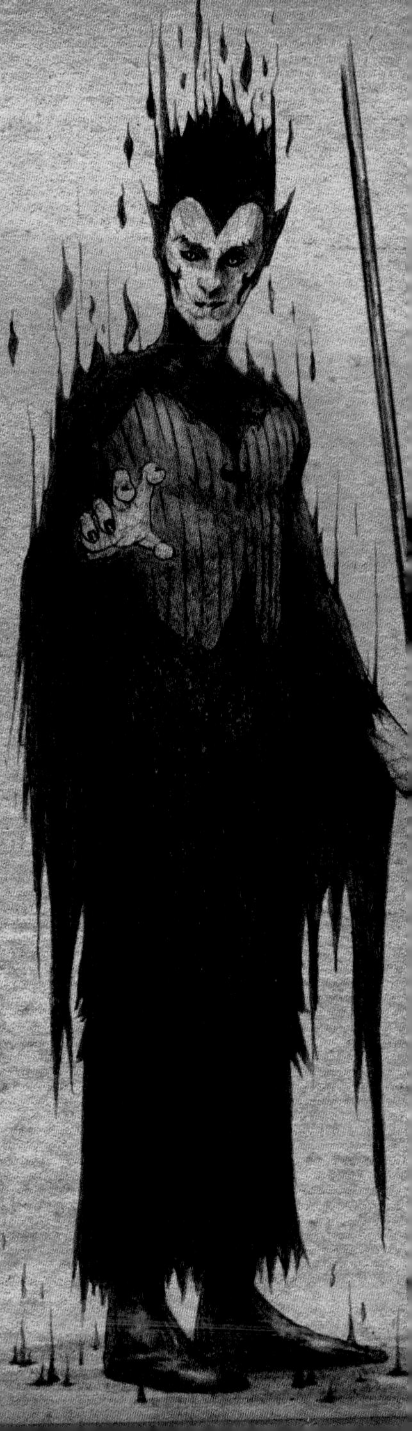

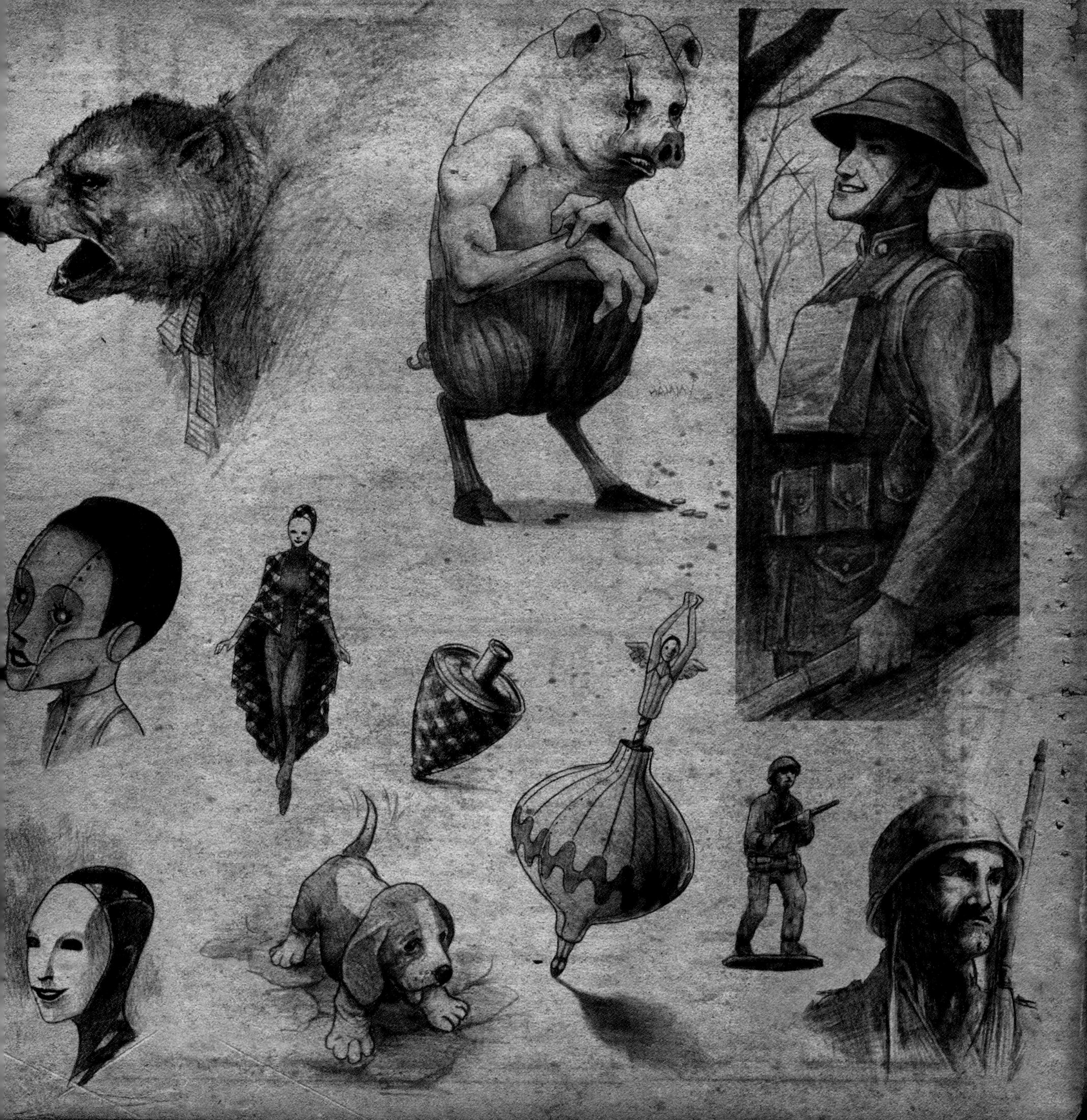

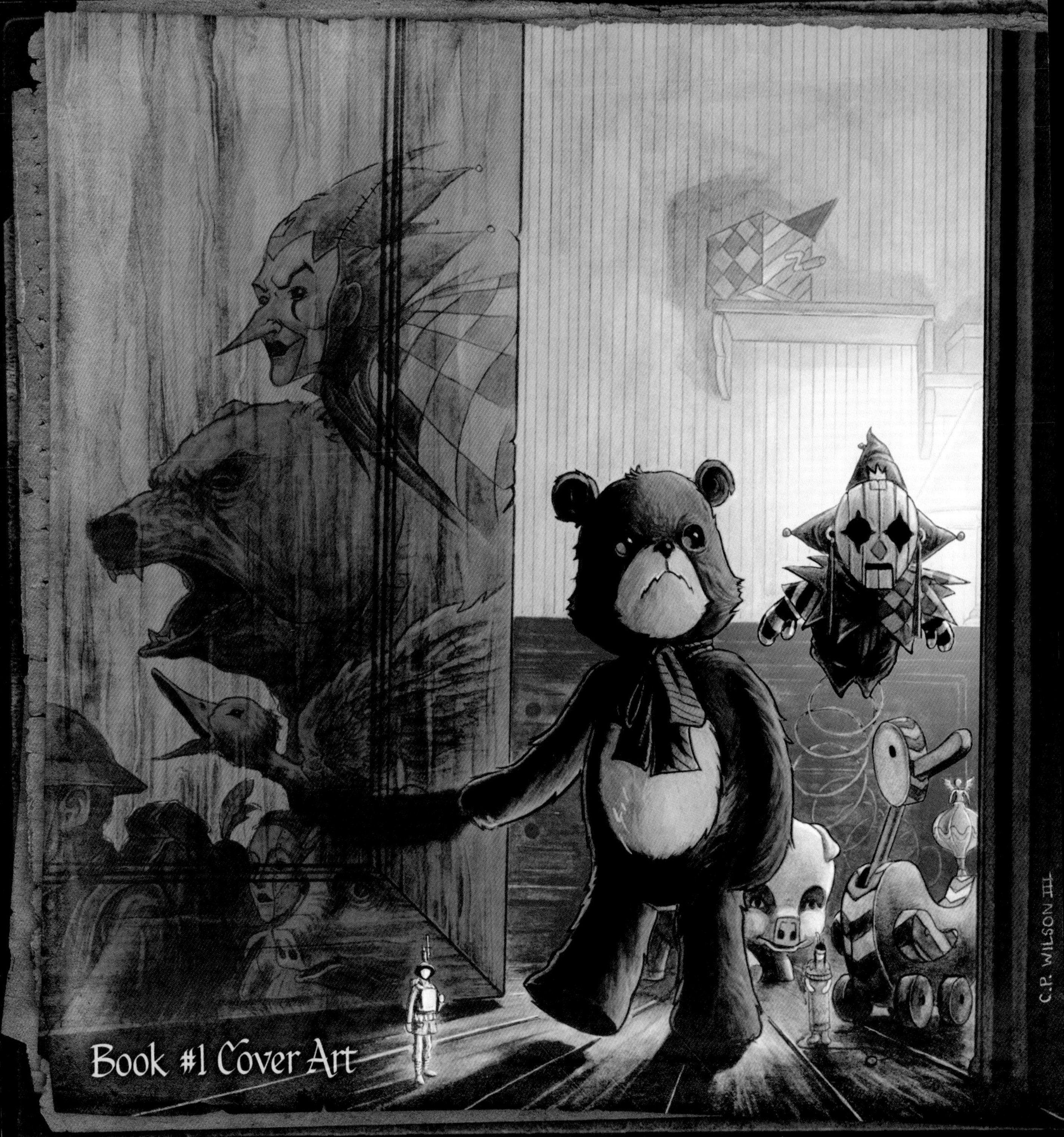
C.P. WILSON III
Book #1 Cover Art

Book #2 Cover Art

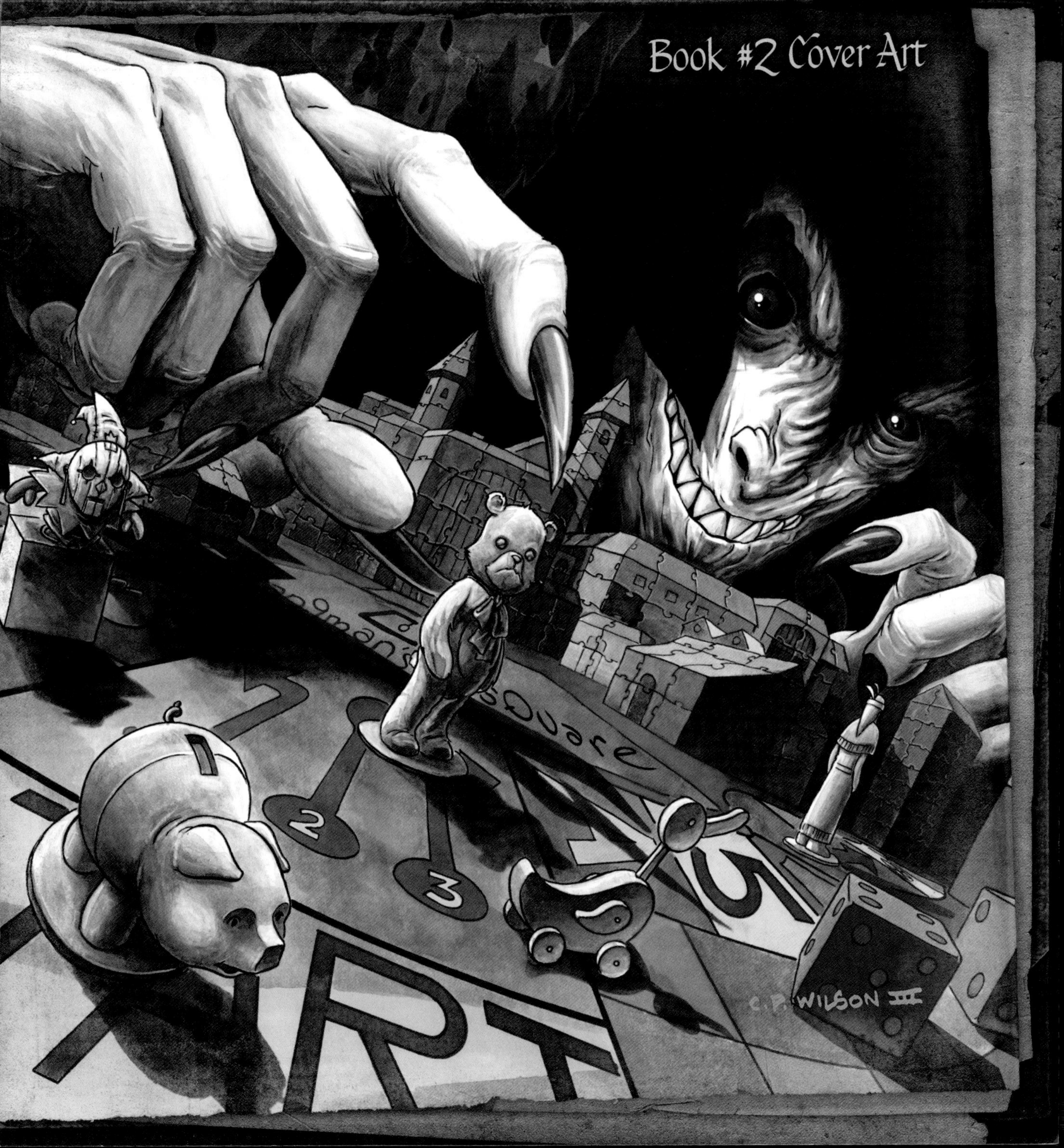
Square
2
3
C.P. WILSON III

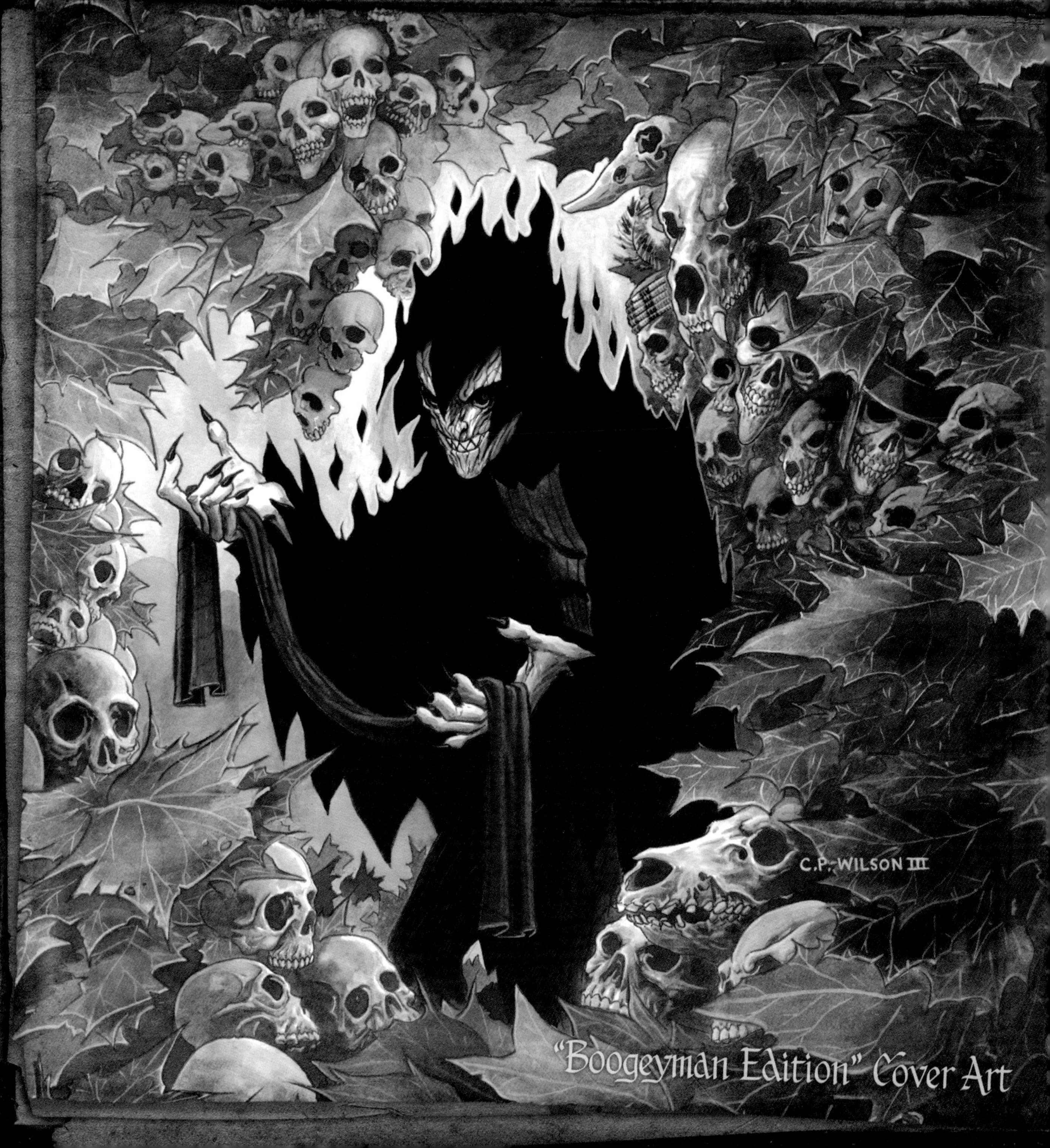
C.P. WILSON III

"Boogeyman Edition" Cover Art